MODERN MONETARY THEORY

T0295797

This book offers a rigorous, detailed, and balanced analysis of the various contributions to the Modern Monetary Theory (MMT) debate, incorporating both the arguments of proponents and those who point to its limitations and obstacles. Modern Monetary Theory has soared in popularity, particularly in response to the Covid-19 pandemic and subsequent impacts on the economy which have led to deeper discussions about monetary and financial systems, fiscal and monetary policies, inflation, and employment. The main characteristic of Modern Monetary Theory is that it offers a revolutionary way of thinking about all these issues, allowing us to abandon many of the myths that conventional economic theory installed in the collective imagination. Breaking down these false beliefs is an essential requirement for thinking and devising economic policy proposals that allow full employment to be achieved without suffering worrying inflation rates. However, this approach has also attracted many criticisms and it is also instructive to consider these in more detail to reach a fully rounded conclusion about the potential or merits of MMT. Written to be accessible to the non-economist, this book will be of great interest to readers from across the social sciences, and outside of academia who want to gain a fuller understanding of the Modern Monetary Theory phenomenon.

Eduardo Garzón Espinosa, PhD in Economics, Lecturer in the Department of Economy and Public Finance, the Autonomous University of Madrid (Spain).

MODERN MONETARY THEORY

A Comprehensive and Constructive Criticism

Eduardo Garzón Espinosa

Routledge
Taylor & Francis Group

LONDON AND NEW YORK

Designed cover image: © Getty Images

First published 2024
by Routledge
4 Park Square, Milton Park, Abingdon, Oxon OX14 4RN

and by Routledge
605 Third Avenue, New York, NY 10158

Routledge is an imprint of the Taylor & Francis Group, an informa business

British Library Cataloguing-in-Publication Data
A catalogue record for this book is available from the British Library

ISBN: 9781032443669 (hbk)
ISBN: 9781032443652 (pbk)
ISBN: 9781003371809 (ebk)

DOI: 10.4324/9781003371809

Typeset in Times New Roman
by Deanta Global Publishing Services, Chennai, India

CONTENTS

INTRODUCTION

Modern Monetary Theory (MMT) is the name coined in the 1990s by a group of economists to refer to a specific approach to economic theory (Mosler, 1995; Wray, 1998). The main topics addressed by MMT relate to the nature and origin of money, monetary sovereignty of states, fiscal policy space, and the limits they face, as well as the pursuit of full employment with price stability.

Among the key points of MMT, it emphasises that any state with monetary sovereignty can spend without the need to have collected or borrowed money beforehand, as any spending would essentially be money creation. However, MMT recognises and acknowledges the need for taxes, not because they are necessary to finance spending, but for other reasons related to attributing value to the created currency, addressing inequality, and establishing incentives and disincentives for certain economic behaviours. Public deficits are thus understood differently from the conventional view: they result from creating and injecting more money into the economy (through public spending) than the money withdrawn from it (through taxes). Nonetheless, the fact that a sovereign state has no financial constraints on its fiscal policy does not mean it should increase the public deficit without limits; rather, it should do so up to the level that allows achieving full employment with price stability. Maintaining the public deficit below this level would lead to unemployment and deflation, while exceeding it would lead to inflation. However, MMT posits that the only way to achieve the goal of full employment with price stability is through a Job Guarantee programme, in which the state guarantees a job to all those willing and able to work at a wage equivalent to the minimum wage.

As a theoretical framework, MMT draws primarily, according to its most prominent pioneers, from Keynes' analysis of monetary economies of production, Abba Lerner's Functional Finance theory, Hyman Minsky's hypothesis of financial instability, Wynne Godley's macroeconomic sectoral balance approach, and the money theories of Georg Friedrich Knapp and Mitchell Innes (Fullwiller et al., 2012, p. 24; Juniper et al., 2014, p. 1). As evident, the authors of MMT recognise that their approach aligns fundamentally with post-Keynesian and chartalist theoretical perspectives.

DOI: 10.4324/9781003371809-1

This has led some post-Keynesian economists to criticise the fact that MMT proponents have given it a distinct name and portrayed it as a novel set of economic approaches (Palley, 2018). In fact, MMT has often been referred to as "neochartalism" since it is seen as a simple revision or recovery of Knapp's chartalist ideas (Parguez and Secareccia, 2000; Febrero, 2009; Fiebiger, 2012; Lavoie, 2013). Some post-Keynesian economists, however, have acknowledged certain contributions from MMT to economic theory, particularly in analysing the relationship between the state, the central bank, and banks within the payment system (Van Lear, 2002; Lavoie, 2013, 2019), although some argue that the analytical framework used may not be the most appropriate for the institutional reality of most economies (Lavoie, 2013, 2019).

Although its origins date back to the 1990s, it was not until 2008, following the outbreak of the Great Financial Crisis, that MMT began to gain some popularity beyond academic circles, as many sought alternative economic policy responses to the crisis. However, its popularity soared in 2019 when it was incorporated into the electoral campaign of U.S. Congressman Bernie Sanders, championed by MMT economist Stephanie Kelton. This led Nobel laureate economists, central bank presidents, and other prominent figures to publicly position themselves on this economic current (Krugman, 2019; Mankiw, 2020; Blanchard, 2019; Rogoff, 2019; Summers, 2019). According to Google Trends, searches for "Modern Monetary Theory" increased from around 10% popularity between 2008 and 2018 to 100% in March 2019, dropping to 30%, and then rising again to 89% with the outbreak of the COVID-19 pandemic in March 2020. During this period, many economic policies implemented by most governments worldwide resembled MMT prescriptions (particularly significant and unrestricted increases in public deficits and the state's support for many labour incomes). Since then, interest has stabilised at around 15% (as of mid-2023), which remains substantially higher than pre-2019 levels.

This noteworthy popularity is striking because it had been many decades since a relatively delimited heterodox economic approach had gained such prominence in public discourse. This is largely due to two characteristics that make MMT special: first, it presents a clear narrative that criticises the ideas used to implement austerity policies in recent years, making it attractive to certain political actors. Second, its messages can sometimes appear simple or counter-intuitive, leading to caricature and ridicule by influential figures (Bloomberg, 2019; Krugman, 2019; The Verge, 2019; Rajan, 2020). However, some authors consider that MMT faces many difficulties in becoming hegemonic due to an incomplete understanding of key macroeconomic terms among economic commentators, especially journalists, and the wider community and the deployment of key macroeconomic terms (incorrectly) in the context of pervasive cultural metaphors to support policy interventions that effectively benefit a privileged few at the expense of the majority (Connors & Mitchell, 2017).

MMT has also had a significant impact on academia. Many critical analyses have been published seeking to question or qualify the theoretical tenets of this school of thought, while other works aim to add new contributions to the debate, including applying this analytical approach to economic development (Liang, 2021) and to other areas of study such as ecology (William & Taylor, 2022; Olk et al., 2022), political communication, the healthcare sector (Hensher et al., 2021; Ehnts & Paetz, 2021; Pandit, 2022), the education sector (Backer, 2022), international law (Haskell, 2021), or sport and recreation (Hammond, 2022). Therefore, it is expected that publications on MMT will continue to increase in the future.

The purpose of this work is to provide an exhaustive and detailed review of all that has been published about MMT, offering a broad overview that includes original works that inspired its approach, publications that have developed and consolidated it, recent contributions that expand and strengthen this school of thought, and, above all, the various criticisms it has received from both heterodox and orthodox perspectives. Given the vast bibliography on MMT, I have prioritised indexed journal publications and books from reputable publishers. However, when necessary, I have referred to working papers and even articles from the blogosphere, as MMT originated in that internet realm and some MMTers almost exclusively publish there. In addition, I have quoted verbatim wherever possible in order to avoid possible misinterpretation. I believe this approach covers the vast majority of the most important publications on the subject, although it is inevitable that some may have been omitted. Regarding criticisms of MMT, I have given priority to constructive heterodox critiques, but I have also included several critiques from orthodox perspectives, which I think are important to consider.

I must acknowledge that I personally sympathise with MMT's propositions, although I am not a fanatic defender of it, and I pay close attention to all constructive criticisms that have been raised, many of which I believe are very pertinent and improve the theoretical framework presented here. Despite my personal stance, I will strive to honestly and faithfully reflect both MMT's postulates and the detected criticisms, and only in the final section of each chapter will I present my conclusions after a thorough analysis of all the preceding material. I sincerely believe that many elements of MMT have been enhanced and enriched by criticism, and the added value of this book lies in identifying and discussing them. There are many books that present this framework uncritically, and many others that attempt to incorporate a large portion of the criticisms it receives, but as far as I know, none extract conclusions from the debates that such criticisms have triggered. This book aims to fill that gap by not only explaining in detail what MMT entails and how it has evolved to the present day but also how it can be improved based on constructive criticisms.

To achieve this, the work is structured into seven chapters, each dedicated to one of the central themes of MMT. It is important to note that this division by themes is purely subjective and aims to provide a logical and illustrative exposition, maintaining a cohesive thread that connects the topics from the most basic and general concepts to specific policy proposals. Although the chapters should not be regarded as isolated compartments (as the content of each is strongly interrelated with the others), I consider that each chosen theme is susceptible to receiving its own analysis, relatively differentiated from the others. Taking all this into account, the order of the chapters is as follows: the origin of money, chartalism, monetary sovereignty, public deficit and debt, endogenous money, functional finance, and job guarantee.

References

Backer, D. (2022). *Modern monetary theory and education (February 11).* https://ssrn.com/abstract=4032757 or http://dx.doi.org/10.2139/ssrn.4032757

Blanchard, O. (2019). Public debt and low interest rates. *American Economic Review, 109*(4), 1197–1229.

Bloomberg. (2019, March 15). *Buffett no fan of modern monetary theory with its danger zones.* https://www.bloomberg.com/news/articles/2019-03-15/buffett-no-fan-of-modern-monetary-theory-with-its-danger-zones

Connors, L., & Mitchell, W. (2017). Framing modern monetary theory. *Journal of Post Keynesian Economics, 40*(2), 239–259. https://doi.org/10.1080/01603477.2016.1262746

Ehnst, D., & Paetz, M. (2021). Wie finanzieren wir die Corona-Schulden?: Versuch einer richtigen "Antwort auf eine falsche" Frage aus Sicht der modern monetary theory [How do we finance the

Corona debt? Attempting a "right" answer to the "wrong" question from the perspective of modern monetary theory]. *Wirtschaftsdienst, 101*(3), 200–206. German. https://doi.org/10.1007/s10273-021 -2874-9. Epub 2021 Mar 17. PMID: 33746304; PMCID: PMC7964462

Febrero, E. (2009). Three difficulties with neo-chartalism. *Journal of Post Keynesian Economics, 31*(3), 523–541. https://doi.org/10.2753/PKE0160-3477310308

Fiebiger, B. (2012, January 17–26). *Modern money theory and the 'real-world' accounting of 1–1<0: The U.S. treasury does not spend as per a bank.* Political Economy Research Institute. www.peri.umass .edu/fileadmin/pdf/working_papers/working_papers_251-300/WP279.pdf

Fullwiler, S., Bell, S., & Wray, L. (2012). Modern money theory: A response to critics. *SSRN Electronic Journal.* https://doi.org/10.2139/ssrn.2008542

Hammond, A. M. (2022). Financing sport post-COVID-19: Using modern monetary theory (MMT) to help make a case for economic recovery through spending on sport and recreation. *Managing Sport and Leisure, 27*(1–2), 40–44. https://doi.org/10.1080/23750472.2020.1850326

Haskell, J. (2021). Modern money theory and international law. *Journal of Law and Political Economy, 2*(1). http://dx.doi.org/10.5070/LP62155390

Hensher, M., Robson, S., Kelton, S., Hail, S., & McCall, L. (2021). *Modern monetary theory and healthcare in Australia* (Position Paper). Institute for Health Transformation, Deakin University.

Juniper, J., Sharpe, T. P., & Watts, M. J. (2014). Modern monetary theory: Contributions and critics. *Journal of Post Keynesian Economics, 37*(2), 281–307. https://doi.org/10.2753/PKE0160-3477370205 .2015.11082991

Krugman, P. (2019). *What's wrong with functional finance?* https://nam-students.blogspot.com/2019/03/ whats-wrong-with-functional-finance.html

Lavoie, M. (2013). The monetary and fiscal nexus of neo-chartalism: A friendly critique. *Journal of Economic Issues, 47*(1), 1–32. https://doi.org/10.2753/JEI0021-3624470101

Lavoie, M. (2019). Modern monetary theory and post-Keynesian economics. *Real-World Economics Review, 89,* 97–108.

Liang, Y. (2021). Implications of modern money theory on development finance. In B. Bonizzi, A. Kaltenbrunner, & R. A. Ramos (Eds.), *Emerging economies and the global financial system: Post-Keynesian analysis* (pp. 217–229). Routledge.

Mankiw, N. G. (2020). A skeptic's guide to modern monetary theory. *AEA Papers and Proceedings, 110,* 141–144.

Mosler, W. (1995). *Soft currency economics* (3rd ed.). Adams, Viner and Mosler.

Olk, C., Schneider, C., & Hickel, J. (2022). *How to pay for saving the world: Modern monetary theory for a degrowth transition.* https://ssrn.com/abstract=4172005 or http://dx.doi.org/10.2139/ssrn.4172005

Palley, T. (2018, April 6). *Modern Money Theory (MMT) vs. structural Keynesianism. Thomas Palley – Economics for democratic and open societies.* https://thomaspalley.com/?p=1145

Pandit, J. J. (2022). Modern monetary theory for the post-pandemic NHS: Why budget deficits do not matter. *British Journal of Healthcare Management, 28*(1), 37–46.

Parguez, A., & Seccareccia, M. (2000). The credit theory of money: The monetary circuit approach. In J. Smithin (Ed.), *What is money?* (pp. 101–123). Routledge.

Rajan, R. G. (2020, November 30). How much debt is too much? *Project Syndicate.* https://www.project -syndicate.org/commentary/borrowing-and-spending-limits-in-ultra-low-interest-rate-environment -by-raghuram-rajan-2020-11

Rogoff, K. (2019, March 4). Modern monetary nonsense. *Project Syndicate.* https://www.project -syndicate.org/commentary/federal-reserve-modern-monetary-theory-dangers-by-kenneth-rogoff -2019-03?barrier=accesspaylog

Summers, L. H. (2019, March 4). The left's embrace of modern monetary theory is a recipe for disaster. *Washington Post.* https://www.washingtonpost.com/opinions/the-lefts-embrace-of-modern -monetary-theory-is-a-recipe-for-disaster/2019/03/04/6ad88eec-3ea4-11e9-9361-301ffb5bd5e6_story .html

The Verge. (2019, February 12). *Bill Gates: His tax rate has been 70 percent — And it should be again.* https://www.theverge.com/2019/2/12/18220756/bill-gates-tax-rate-70-percent-marginal-modern -monetary-theory

Van Lear, W. (2002). Implications arising from the theory on the Treasury's bank reserve effects. *Journal of Post Keynesian Economics, 25*(2), 251–261. https://doi.org/10.1080/01603477.2002.11051358

William, S. J., & Taylor, R. (2022). *Sustainability and the new economics synthesising ecological economics and modern monetary theory.* Springer.

Wray, R. (1998). *Understanding modern money, the key to full employment and price stability.* Edward Elgar Publishing Ltd.

1

MODERN MONETARY THEORY'S VIEW OF THE ORIGIN OF MONEY AND ITS CRITICISMS

Introduction

The conception of the origin and nature of money is not – as some might perhaps think – a trivial or ornamental aspect of economic thought for historians or whimsical analysts, but is fundamental to explain the different views that exist on all other economic issues. In fact, it is relatively easy to guess which view of money an economist takes simply by looking at his or her stance on issues such as monetary or fiscal policy. This is because money is a central element in our economies and is therefore interrelated with all other economic elements. The conception of money shapes our understanding of the economic world around us and therefore conditions the responses we come up with to transform it. In other words, depending on the conception we have of money, we will develop one economic vision or another. For example, those who conceive of money as a commodity, which is by definition something finite and which must first be obtained in order to be used, will develop a logically very different view of the possibilities of public spending than those who conceive of money as an abstract and unlimited creation by the public authorities.

But the fact of conceiving money in one way or another does not only affect public spending policies but also taxes, bank credits, wages, social insurance, productive activities, and so on. Each part of the economic world around us will be interpreted differently depending on our particular conception of money. Hence the importance of considering the view of the origin and nature of money adopted by Modern Monetary Theory, because this is precisely what makes it so special in comparison with the rest of the economic views and also the theoretical basis used to develop the rest of its approaches. Contrary to more conventional views, which adopt a view of money as a commodity and as a natural evolution due to market forces, MMTers adopt a view of money as debt or credit that originated in a centralised way thanks to public authorities. We will begin by reviewing the former and then explain the latter in detail. We will then address the criticisms that this heterodox view receives, and finally we will draw our conclusions.

DOI: 10.4324/9781003371809-2

Vision of commodity money

One of the most widespread views in our society and throughout history (at least until very recently) conceives money as a commodity that we choose to measure the value of other commodities. This is what is basically known as the money-commodity view, and we can find traces of it already in the writings of Aristotle in Classical Greek times (Schumpeter, 1954, p. 100; Martínez-Echevarría & Crespo, 2011, p. 6). Despite its early origin, this approach has been dominant for millennia. In the words of Joseph Schumpeter: "whatever its weaknesses, this theory – Aristotle's – though always disputed, substantially predominated until the end of the nineteenth century and even later. It is the basis of the core of all analytical work done in the field of money" (Schumpeter, 1954, p. 100).

This view originally starts from the following account: in the early years of human civilisation the most common and widespread mechanism for carrying out economic transactions had been barter: the exchange of one commodity for another at the same moment. Thus, a blacksmith could, for example, give nails to a fisherman in exchange for a piece of fish. However, as economic exchanges became more complex due to civilisational development, bartering began to be a cumbersome and inefficient practice. On the one hand, it was difficult to move certain quantities of heavy and bulky goods to the places where exchanges took place, as well as to measure and separate them in order to achieve the specific quantity that matched the goods to be received in exchange. On the other hand, it was not easy to find someone who had the product one demanded and at the same time have what that person wanted in exchange. Moreover, knowing the equivalent prices between all the products being exchanged was almost impossible because the combinations were so numerous and because these relative prices varied constantly (Smith, 1994, pp. 56–57; Glyn, 1994, p. 15; Ingham, 2004b, p. 22; Samuelson & Nordhaus, 1975, pp. 274–276).

This account can be found in Adam Smith, the father of modern economics, in his famous book "The Wealth of Nations":

> But when the division of labor first began to take place, this power of exchanging must frequently have been very much clogged and embarrassed in its operations. One man, we shall suppose, has more of a certain commodity than he himself has occasion for, while another has less. The former consequently would be glad to dispose of; and the latter to purchase, a part of this superfluity. But if this latter should chance to have nothing that the former stands in need of, no exchange can be made between them. The butcher has more meat in his shop than he himself can consume, and the brewer and the baker would each of them be willing to purchase a part of it. But they have nothing to offer in exchange, except the different productions of their respective trades, and the butcher is already provided with all the bread and beer which he has immediate occasion for. No exchange can, in this case, be made between them. He cannot be their merchant, nor they his customers; and they are all of them thus mutually less serviceable to one another.
>
> *(Smith, 1994, pp. 56–57)*

To solve all these difficulties, it is considered that money emerged – in a completely decentralised and unplanned way – a specific commodity that would serve as a general equivalent among all other products and that, thanks to its natural properties, would facilitate and economise economic transactions by being lighter, easily transportable, divisible and storable. Smith continues:

In order to avoid the inconvenience of such situations, every prudent man in every period of society, after the first establishment of the division of labor, must naturally have endeavored to manage his affairs in such a manner, as to have at all times by him, besides the peculiar produce of his own industry, a certain quantity of some one commodity or another, such as he imagined few people would be likely to refuse to give him something in exchange for.

(Smith, 1994, pp. 56–57)

This, then, is the explanation for the shift from barter to commodity money. As Samuelson explains: "if we were to construct history along hypothetical and logical lines, we should naturally follow the barter era by the commodity-money era" (Samuelson, 1973, pp. 274–276). According to this account, the first commodities to be used as money were cattle, iron, salt, shells, dried cod, furs, grain, sugar, tobacco, nails, nails, etc., until progressively and through a natural evolutionary process driven by market forces, precious metals such as silver and gold were imposed as they presented much more appropriate characteristics to become money-merchandise (Samuelson, 1973, pp. 274–276). According to Stanley Jevons these characteristics were: prior utility, portability, indestructibility, homogeneity, divisibility, stability of value, and knowability (Jevons, 1896, pp. 30–40). As Adam Smith explained: "in all countries, however, men seem to have been impelled by irresistible reasons to prefer metals above all other commodities for this purpose" (Smith, 1994, pp. 56–57).

The most refined explanation about which merchandise manages to prevail over the rest as a general equivalent involves the evolutionary process proposed by Carl Menger through the concept of "saleability": "a commodity is more or less saleable according as we are able, with more or less prospect of success, to dispose of it at prices corresponding to the general economic situation, at economic prices" (Menger, 1892, p. 245). That is, the most liquid goods are those that are more easily interchangeable because in doing so their value will not vary much, unlike what happens with the less liquid goods. These differences in liquidity would be explained by the intrinsic characteristics of the interchangeable products: for example, a house is a much less liquid commodity than a piece of silver because the first cannot be easily sold without greatly reducing its price (because it is not easy to find to people interested in a non-transportable merchandise and as complex as a house), unlike what happens with a piece of silver (it is easy to find people interested in transportable goods, with little weight, mouldable, simple, etc.). In this way, there are incentives to use the most liquid goods in the exchanges, delivering them in exchange for the goods that are desired at that moment, since their high liquidity will imply that there are many more people interested in them. Ultimately, that liquid merchandise would be sued not so much for its intrinsic value, but for its value as exchangeable merchandise for other merchandise that would bring more value to the individual in particular. Since there are many commodities with different degrees of saleability, individuals gradually discovered which were the most liquid (through observation but also imitation) and, consequently, choosing the ones they would use for exchanges. In this way, and in the heat of individual decisions driven by economic interests, an evolutionary process was originated by which the less liquid goods were discarded in favour of the use of more liquid goods, until reaching an end point at which it would be exclusively used the most liquid merchandise of all in the corresponding social, geographical, and historical context. This merchandise is what becomes money.

More recent versions of money as a commodity can be found in Von Mises (1912), Brunner (1971), Alchian (1977), and Kiyotaki and Wright (1989), but the essence of the liquidity of commodities by their intrinsic characteristics proposed by Carl Menger is still maintained.

In short, according to this view of commodity money, money would be no more than a neutral instrument or veil used to facilitate mercantile exchanges (Schumpeter, 1994, p. 277; Menger, 1892, p. 12; Innes, 1913, p. 377; Tooke, 1844, pp. 4–5). As MMTer Randall Wray points out, from this point of view, money is defined primarily by its function as a medium of exchange (the good used as money serves to obtain any other product), leaving in the background its other functions as a means of payment (the commodity can be used to settle debts or pay taxes), as a store value (people can store it for a period of time in order to preserve its purchasing power, since they can use it in the future to purchase other products, pay taxes or pay off debts), and as a unit of measurement (the commodity is used to account for prices, taxes, economic values, debts, etc.) (Wray, 2015, p. 259).

As for the minting of money by states, this orthodox approach to commodity money considers that, due to the enormous market potential of precious metal commodities, governments devoted enormous efforts to acquire them and regulate their operation to the point of becoming monopolists in their manufacture. To this end, they created pieces of precious metal in a certain shape on which they stamped their symbol of power, persecuting and sanctioning any other type of forging. They thus ensured that their coins were the only ones allowed in economic transactions, thus monopolising the competence to create money (Innes, 1913, p. 377; Wray, 2010, p. 32).

In more recent times, in order to economise the use of metals and avoid their constant transportation, a new mechanism called "credit" would begin to be used. This credit would be simply a promise to pay money that under favourable circumstances had the same value as the metal money itself and took the form of banknotes, cheques, and even electronic notes. If money had arisen to avoid the cumbersome use of heavy and bulky materials, credit had arisen to avoid the cumbersome use of metallic coins (Innes, 1913, p. 377; Klein & Selgin, 2000; Friedman, 1969).

Marx's commodity money

As Joseph Schumpeter reminds us, the aforementioned view of commodity money "was for more than a century almost universally accepted – by Marx, implicitly, more than by anyone else" (Schumpeter, 1954, p. 338). Indeed, the German philosopher also conceived of money as a commodity that arose spontaneously in the course of the social development of production and trade as a universal medium of exchange. In his own words, money "arises naturally out of exchange and in exchange is its product" (Marx, 2007, pp. 93–94). Although Marx's view differs in some elements from the orthodox view presented above. As Costas Lapavitsas and Nicolás Aguila explain, the Marxist view of money

> does not rely on puerile notions of "primitive" barter societies. Rather, money emerges historically at the point of mercantile contact between pre-capitalist societies and fully develops under capitalist conditions. It is a social relationship that unfolds completely when capitalism dominates economic and social life.
>
> *(Lapavitsas & Aguila, 2020, p. 4)*

In other words, even if one shares the view of the spontaneous origin of money and its commodity status, the fundamental difference is that it is framed specifically in capitalist societies; it would not be a valid concept for other types of societies. As Michel Roberts explains:

> For Marx under capitalism money is the representation of value and thus of surplus value. (…). Money could not make exchange possible if exchangeability were not already inherent in commodity production, if it were not a representation of socially necessary abstract labor and thus of value. In that sense, money does not arise in exchange but instead is the monetary representation of exchange value (MELT), or socially necessary labor time (SNLT).
>
> *Roberts (2019, p. 4)*

Another noted difference is that there is no inherent metallism in the Marxist theory: although it is considered that money tends to gravitate towards precious metals due to their properties of divisibility, reconstitutability, durability, and portability, money necessarily develops beyond the commodity form and even becomes incorporeal. Therefore, it does not matter the form it takes; it will continue to be the universal equivalent spontaneously created through the exchange of commodities (Lapavitsas & Aguila, 2020).

However, despite this historical, social, and even philosophical contextualisation of money, it does not deviate too far from the orthodox view: there is some similarity in Menger's evolutionary process with Marx's dialectical method in the genesis of money. The money form in its embryonic state appears on the "margins" of communities, not within them. In the barter between communities as the relative price between pairs of goods, the first goods that were used as money were very diverse: from cattle, iron, or grain to salt, shells, dried cod, or skins. But why such a heterogeneity of things have been used for the same function? For Marx (1859 [1989], pp. 29–30) the commodity chosen to perform the function of mediating these exchanges in the first societies is the one that occupies a central position in the economy, that is, if the people are nomadic, the money function will be made by cattle or skins; if the people are fishermen, the dried cod. Over time, custom and habit spread to entrench the general equivalent in its role as money, dissolving its usefulness as use value and thus becoming money *stricto sensu*.

However, even this intermediate money form can continue to be consumed at any time as use value. A final step is necessary to reach the capitalist money form: the minting of gold and silver is the end point to this cumulative sequence that begins with the ordinary terms of trade until its developed form characterised by money. Precious metals such as silver and gold have characteristics that are much more appropriate to become commodity money. Menger (1892, p. 12) poses it as a natural evolutionary process driven by market forces that, certainly, is reflected in the genesis of Marx's money (Cruz et al., 2020b; Garzón et al., 2023).

In short, any money-commodity narrative falls into presenting money as the product of an evolutionary process driven by the economic interests of free individuals who interact in the market, either in groups or individually. It is a narrative that also arises in trade, in this case of communities and not of individuals, but whose meaning in logical terms implies nothing more than a reduction in the number of equations immersed in the postulation of why commodity will finally be positioned as equivalent. The indeterminacy problems remain unsolved (Cartelier, 1991, p. 257; Ingham, 2004a, pp. 263–264).

Finally, it is worth noting that some economists have criticised Marx's commodity money view precisely because it contradicts one of the central elements of his thinking; namely, the circuit of capitalist production (Graziani, 1997; Bellofiore & Realfonzo, 1997; Bougrine & Seccareccia, 2002). The argument presented is that, according to the Marxist view, capitalists use money to buy labour power for the purpose of producing commodities. Therefore, if money were a commodity, it would have to be the result of a prior productive process that would, in turn, require money to be realised, leading to a problem of infinite regression. The logical deduction resulting from this reasoning is that money cannot be a commodity but something very different.

Critique of the commodity money view

Although the commodity money view has been dominant throughout history, it has not been exempt from criticism or confrontations with other approaches. As early as the times of Classical Greece, philosophers like Plato conceived money as an arbitrary and abstract symbol whose value was independent of the material with which it was made (Schumpeter, 1954, p. 341). However, this conception was always a minority view, and there were not many significant records of it until the sixteenth century. Einaudi (1953) offered a detailed examination between the sixteenth and eighteenth centuries of a concept variously termed "imaginary money", "ideal money", "political money", "moneta numeraria", or "ghost money". Similar ideas can also be found in the works of Cipolla (1956, 1976). In the eighteenth century, John Law made one of the most well-known contributions to this perspective:

> the silver serving as money (…) is perfectly interchangeable with a cheaper material and, in the ultimate case, even with a material that has no value as a commodity, like printed paper, as money is not the value for which goods are exchanged, but the value through which they are exchanged.
>
> *(Schumpeter, 1954, p. 343)*

In the nineteenth century, this alternative approach to money gained significant momentum, especially during the debate between the Bullionists and the Greenbackers on the nature of money after the American Civil War. Carruthers and Babb pointed out that the Greenbackers were aware of the fact that the object used to measure money was not what it was actually relevant: "true money is not wealth any more than the deed for a farm is the farm itself; and there is no more use in having our money made of gold than in having our deeds drawn upon sheets of gold" (Carruthers & Babb, 1996, pp. 1569–1570). However, it was not until the end of the nineteenth century and the beginning of the twentieth century that this different money approach underwent a much more complete theoretical development and introduced itself as a serious alternative to the dominant vision. Within the intellectual debate that took place in the 1890s, which was called "Methodenstreit", a view of money opposed to the hegemonic one – at the time championed by the Austrian Carl Menger – was defended by the authors of the German Historical School with Gustav von Schmoller at the head (Louzek, 2011; Bell, 2001, p. 151; Ingham, 2004b, pp. 18–24).

One of the main drivers of this non-orthodox approach was Mitchell Innes, who in his 1913th essay "What is Money?" bluntly stated the following about the commodity money approach: "it may be said without exaggeration that no scientific theory has ever been put forward which was more completely lacking in foundation" (Innes, 1913, p. 383). This fierce criticism is based on the fact that although the money-commodity approach, settled on logical reasoning,[1] can seem quite intuitive, not only it is full of theoretical inconsistencies but it also goes against the available empirical findings (Hudson, 2004, p. 120; Wray, 2010, p. 40). Among the theoretical inconsistencies it highlights the seemingly strange fact that the sole market forces and the rational behaviour of its participants lead to a decentralised way for hundreds of thousands of people scattered across vast territories and in different communities to agree to use the same means of exchange and the same unit of account for hundreds of different products (Gardiner, 2004; Ingham, 2004a; Desan, 2013). In short, and in the words of MMTers Wray and Tymoigne (2005, p. 4), "orthodoxy has never been able to explain how individual utility maximizers settled on a single numeraire".

Besides that, there is an important theoretical contradiction in the money-commodity approach when considering money only as a trace of the transactions of products when at the same time it is recognised that it fulfils other functions – although they are considered secondary – as deposit of value, unit of account, and means of payment. If a particular commodity serves to treasure wealth, to measure economic value, and to pay taxes and settle debts, it seems difficult to think that it is limited to be a simple neutral instrument without implications for economic dynamics (Ingham, 2004b, p. 19; Tcherneva, 2016, p. 2). Another logical inconsistency lies upon assuming that back in those days some basic product worked as means of exchange since that would imply that such a product would be equally affordable for all the members of the community, including the producers of that particular good: "if the fishers paid for their supplies in cod, the traders would equally have to pay for their cod in cod, an obvious absurdity" (Innes, 1913, p. 378).

Regarding the lack of support for empirical evidence, it is pointed out that an appropriate analysis of archaeological remains, cuneiform writing, and numismatic studies would harm the conception of money arising through barter. One of the most reputable anthropologists, Caroline Humphrey, put it this way: "no example of a barter economy, pure and simple, has ever been described, let alone the emergence from it of money; all available ethnography suggests that there never has been such a thing" (Humphrey, 1985, p. 48). Although it is not denied that barter took place in primitive societies, it is nuanced that it took place for ceremonial exchanges, and it did not play a decisive role in day-to-day activities. As Graeber (2011a, p. 32) explains: "what all such cases of trade through barter have in common is that they are meetings with strangers who will, likely as not, never meet again, and with whom one certainly will not enter into any ongoing relations". Polanyi (1957) also points that barter took form as individual acts that do not necessarily lead to markets in societies where other forms prevail. This is suggested by the fact that the study of hundreds of archaeological sites has not allowed the identification of any physical space in which the exchanges of the products in the primitive settlements supposedly took place (Wray, 2010, p. 39; Graeber, 2011b).

On the other hand, there is ample empirical evidence which shows that credit – a much more efficient mechanism than using means of exchange – existed thousands of years before the use of precious metals as a means of exchange (Innes, 1913, p. 396; Goodhart, 1998; Wray, 2010, p. 40). Even one of the extreme defenders of the money-commodity approach, Carl Menger, admitted this fact without being fully aware of it, as Rallo (2017, p. 42) reminds us: "Menger himself (…) recognized that, before money even of spot barter, there already existed unilateral obligations among the members of a community, which (…) were clear cases of pre-monetary credit / debt".

The key to vault of the differences between both perspectives, which explains their total incompatibility, is that the heterodox view holds that the use of money does not require the presence of any merchandise or any physical element, since money is nothing more than a unit of measurement, an abstract concept created by the human being that cannot be perceived with the senses: "money (…) was a purely mental revolution. It involved the creation of a new intersubjective reality that only exists in the shared imagination of the people (…). Money is not a material reality: it is a psychological construct" (Harari, 2015, pp. 200–203).

Although from the money-commodity approach it can be agreed that money is an invention of human being, the important point is that while its defenders emphasise that this invention consisted in socially agreeing that a particular commodity served as a medium of general exchange, the promoters of this alternative approach emphasise that there is no need to use physical or tangible products since money is a fiction that is created and kept apart from any material reality, only thanks to the imagination of people. This fiction can then be represented somehow in a physical object to facilitate its management, but it is unnecessary to explain its existence and its implications.

Exactly the same happens with any other type of unit of measurement invented by the human being: distance, volume, or weight are fictions devised by humans that have no material reality, but for whose measurement tangible objects can be used (such as tape measures, marked volumes, scales, etc.). In the case of the magnitude that is measured with money: shells, metal coins, gold bars, banknotes, etc. can be used. But the existence of these physical tools does not define the essence of money, just as the existence of metric tapes does not define the essence of distance. The money-commodity approach confuses the concept of money as a unit of measure with the material thing that can be used for its measurement (Ingham, 2004a, p. 176; Wray, 2015, p. 267). In the words of Innes:

> The theory of an abstract standard is not so extraordinary as it first appears, and it presents no difficulty to those scientific men with whom I have discussed the theory. All our measures are the same. No one has ever seen one ounce or a foot or an hour. A foot is the distance between two fixed points, but neither the distance nor the points have a corporeal existence. We divide, as it were, infinite distance or space into arbitrary parts and devise more or less accurate implements for measuring such parts when applied to things having a corporeal existence.
>
> *(Innes, 1914, p. 155)*

But if, according to this interpretation, money is a unit of measure, what exactly does it measure?

Credits and debts

According to this alternative view, money is an abstract unit of measurement created by human beings to measure commitments and obligations (Fontana & Realfonzo, 2005, p. 6; Ingham, 2004b, p. 25). Money would be not any commodity; it would be "simply a non-tangible abstract unit in which obligations are created and discharged" (Henry, 2004, p. 93). These obligations or commitments always involve two agents who are connected by a direct link that turns one of them into a creditor and the other into a debtor: [credit] is simply the correlative of debt. What A owes to B is A's debt to B and B's credit on A. A is B's debtor and B is A's creditor. The words "credit" and "debt" express a legal relationship between two parties, and they express the same legal relationship seen from two opposite sides.

(Innes, 1913, p. 392)

In this social relationship, one of the parties gives value and the other receives it. The party that gives value is the creditor because the fact of giving value has conferred the right to receive the equivalent at some point in the future. The party that receives value is the debtor, by the fact that receiving value has conferred the obligation to give the equivalent at some point in the future (Graziani, 2003, p. 59; Gardiner, 2004, p. 149). For example, when the blacksmith delivers nails to the fisherman, he becomes the creditor of the fisherman, who is now debtor of the blacksmith. At some point in the future the fisherman will have to pay off his debt by giving the blacksmith an equivalent value. This may be by handing him a piece of fish or by carrying out any activity that the nail manufacturer values. What works as money is credit, not any commodity (Macleod, 1889, p. 72).

Innes explained it quite clearly as follows:

> The eye has never seen, nor the hand touched a dollar. All that we can touch or see is a promise to pay or satisfy a debt due for an amount called a dollar. (...) What is stamped on the face of a coin or printed on the face of a note matters not at all; what does matter, and this is the only thing that matters is: What is the obligation which the issuer of that coin or note really undertakes, and is he able to fulfill that promise, whatever it may be? (...) Credit and debt are abstract ideas, and we could not, if we would, measure them by the standard of any tangible thing. We divide, as it were, infinite credit and debt into arbitrary parts called a dollar or a pound.
>
> *(Innes, 1914, p. 155)*

The anthropologist David Graeber emphasises that the transactions that occurred in the early days of the human being took place through this recognition of credits and debts, and rarely through barter:

> obviously what would really happen, and this is what anthropologists observe when neighbors do engage in something like exchange with each other, if you want your neighbor's cow, you'd say, "wow, nice cow" and he'd say "you like it? Take it!" – and now you owe him one. Quite often people don't even engage in exchange at all.
>
> *(Graeber, 2011b)*

Due to its very nature, this recognition of credits and debts would be a much more useful and efficient tool for carrying out transactions than barter or the use of commodity money. In fact, Gardiner (2004, p. 30) assures that it is unlikely to think that barter was used in a generalised way because it presented many inconveniences that, by the way, were easily solved using credit. The first of these was the already mentioned, unlikely fact that the coincidence of needs and availability of products occurred at the same moment, something that is perfectly resolved with the use of credit (because you can settle the debt at a future time). The second one was the most important, and it referred to the fact that most productive activities involve a sequence of stages from the transformation of the first raw material to the sale of the finished product. This makes the person who produces the final goods to not have anything to offer to the producer of the raw material until the end of the process. That is why it used to happen that the producer of the final good provided a credit to the producer of the raw material in exchange for it, that is, he promised to provide value at a future time. The example that Gardiner accompanies to his explanation is quite clarifying in this regard:

> Let us assume that the huntsman is in need of a supply of arrows, but until he can hunt he has nothing to give in exchange. So he promises the fletcher ten haunches of venison in exchange for a supply of arrows. In modern terminology he is asking for "trade credit".
>
> *(Gardiner, 2004, p. 131)*

Credit, precisely because it has no corporeal existence, would be the most efficient mechanism to carry out exchanges (much more than any commodity) and, it is also, and above all, the most valuable type of property. After all, credit has no weight, it does not occupy space, it can be easily transferred to another agent, it can be more easily protected against any physical threat such as destruction or theft, and it is imperishable (Innes, 1913, p. 392; Wray, 2010, p. 40; Gardiner, 2004, p. 30).

As it can be seen, this line of thought emphasises the function of money as a unit of account (economic values are measured as a duty), leaving the rest of the functions in a second place (means of exchange, means of payment, and deposit of value). Given that money is used to measure commitments and obligations (credits and debts) between people, it can exist outside of spaces in which exchanges take place, something totally unthinkable according to the money-commodity approach. According to that view, money as a unit of account predates exchange since the first appearance of money took place in primitive hunter-gatherer societies in which there were no markets at all or anything like it (Parguez & Seccareccia, 2000, p. 101; Ingham, 2004b, p. 25; Wray, 2004, p. 225).

Primitive money

Many analysts point out that nowadays we do not have a particular way of knowing when or under what circumstances the use of money began, since they consider that this event dates from a prehistoric era before writing and there are no records that allow us to scrutinise the past with precision. As pointed out by Keynes (1930, p. 13): "the origins of money are lost in the mists of time". Hence, these analysts suggest being aware of the limits of our analysis and very cautious with the available evidence (Grierson, 1977, p. 12; Eagleton & Williams, 2007, p. 10; Mitchell et al., 2016, p. 44).

Notwithstanding the foregoing, if we consider that money is fiction that serves to measure obligations, we could say that the first type of money that was created was not used to facilitate the exchange of products but to articulate social relations through the measurement of engagements regulated and controlled by a higher authority in the context of primitive societies (Malinowski, 1921, p. 860; Polanyi, 1957, pp. 1181–1182, p. 198; Heinsohn & Steiger, 1983). These "primitive monies", following Dalton (1967, p. 185), "are used to create social relationships ... prevent group hostility and warfare ... elevate one's political position ... and restore peaceful social relationships between persons and groups disrupted by conflict".

Therefore, money, understood as a unit of account of obligations, would have appeared as an institutionalised practice within the framework of a system of pre-legislative obligations for the benefit of the interests of the community. These imposed obligations were personal and those affected were thus forced to perform certain actions or suffer certain punishments, which could be quantitative (deliver several objects, for example) or qualitative (mourn, lose a social status, etc.). Consequently, according to these analysts, money did not emerge from a pre-monetary market system but from the penal system (Grierson, 1977; Goodhart, 1998).

One type of penal system applied by these primitive societies and of which we have some evidence is the Wergeld system, based on the reparation of the victim or of his family (who became creditor) on the part of the guilty person (who became debtor). It was considered desirable that the guilty party was obliged to provide value to the victim's family to avoid a revenge that will make the situation even worse. And until the perpetrator did so, he would remain indebted (Hudson, 2004, p. 99; Wray, 2004, p. 227). Hence, the process of enforcement of the penalty equals "pacifying", which is the etymological root of the word "pay". If the culprit was condemned to deliver a head of cattle to the victim, in doing so he would pay off his debt and pacify the conflict. Hudson (2004, pp. 99–102) emphasises that it is no coincidence that words for debt in almost all languages are synonymous with "sin" or "guilt".

The fines or corresponding payments were made directly to the victims or to their families, not to public institutions. There were extensive lists of transgressions and fines for each transgression and, in general, these payments involved living and animated merchandise such as livestock or housemaids (Wray, 2004, pp. 9, 227). As discussed above, even one of the best-known exponents of the money-commodity approach, Carl Menger, was fully aware of the existence of these criminal systems – although he did not link them to the nature of money:

> long before barter appeared in history, or acquired a decisive importance to obtain goods, we already find several forms of unilateral obligations: voluntary donations or under more or less coercive pressure, taxes imposed forcibly, punishments of a patrimonial nature, the Wergeld, unilateral obligations derived from family relations, etc.
>
> *(Menger, 1909, p. 143)*

This normative order was inextricably linked to spiritual, magical, and, after all, religious beliefs. Obligations were not only of an institutional nature, but they also were a sacred penance, and those affected had to fulfil them if they did not want to be punished by divine forces beyond the punishment imposed by the tribal authority. According to Henry (2004, p. 89) and Semenova (2011b), debts and religion have always gone hand in hand; the origin of money cannot be understood aside from the religious beliefs. That would be why many of the words associated with money and debt have religious meanings, such as sin, retribution, redemption, "erasure and new account", Jubilee Year. As Wray (2015, pp. 151–152) remembers, in Aramaic, the language spoken by Jesus of Nazareth, the word used for "debt" is the same one as that one used for "sin"; and Christ is known as the Redeemer and the perpetrator, the one who steps forward to settle the debts that we cannot redeem; moreover, in the Bible it can be stated that the original Our Father prayed "Forgive us our debts as we also forgive our debtors"[2] (Mt 6, pp. 9–13).

But according to this money-debt approach, this primitive money underwent a very important transformation as societies became more complex. Specifically, it was the emergence of class society that marked the transition from a kind of money that served as a unit of account of marginal obligations to the sort of money that would begin to take up many more spaces of social life.

Money in class society

From the money-debt approach, money is a social relationship that establishes commitments and obligations, and this necessarily implies talking about some underlying inequality. After all, the link between a creditor and a debtor is not, by nature, horizontal but vertical, since the latter must provide value to the former. Consequently, the creditor holds a position of power against the debtor. Without this hierarchical link between them, there would be no social reason to comply with these obligations or any other mechanism to enforce the payment owed (Henry, 2004, p. 79).

It is considered that in primitive societies these vertical obligations only took a marginal place since these communities were characterised by the absence of hierarchical links. The obligations were reserved only for those special and isolated cases in which peace and social harmony were being put at risk. For the rest of the activities and relationships it did not make sense to use the imposition of obligations because in them predominated the principles of reciprocity and altruism. In tribal societies, the rule of hospitality derived from common property prevailed: "all had a right to subsistence that was collectively produced by its members on collectively held means of production" (Henry, 2004, p. 83). The exchanges of products followed the logic of reciprocity, mutual aid, and gifts. With the delivery of an object or the provision of a service nothing was expected in return since the welfare of everyone was comparable to the group welfare. Precisely for this reason, there was no need for a part of the society to follow up with what is owed to someone or who owes it (Henry, 2004, p. 93; Polanyi, 1957; Stanfield, 1986, p. 59). In fact, the value that was given to sharing the goods was so strong that they had no words to express their gratitude nor to indicate the satisfaction of receiving something from the hand of someone. Moreover, giving thanks could even be offensive by indicating a lack of trust and fraternity (Garrote, 2017, p. 23; Kottak, 1994, p. 176).

For this very reason it is considered that the barter did not make any sense in communities of these characteristics; because in the exchange of products, the valuation of themselves operates with the goal of that there is nobody losing nor earning more than the other party (Wray, 1990; Bell & Henry, 2001). Furthermore, there was no division of labour as we understand it today due to the small size of these primitive communities and to the roaming of their economic activity: "technical knowledge (excluding medicinal and / or mystical knowledge) was learned as part of the socialization process and they were not usually controlled by specialists who later exploited them for their own interests" (Lisón, 1999, p. 183). At the time, when humanity was organised in hunter-gatherer communities, the organisation of the division of labour was supposed to be an extension of family matters, with a "pater familias" firmly in charge of the rest of the members who were undoubtedly closely related to each other (Gardiner, 2004, p. 121). The different members of a group might specialise in different tasks but shared their goods and services through an economy of favours and obligations: "a piece of meat that was offered for free would carry with it the assumption of reciprocity: medical assistance, say" (Harari, 2015, p. 1197). Bartering was totally meaningless in communities where there was no division of labour and in which the principles of reciprocity and community predominated.

However, with the gradual establishment of the division of labour and, consequently, of the social classes, the panorama changed:

> early success in these activities [technological advances in agriculture] allowed the creation of a small and probably irregular economic surplus which made it possible to release some labour from direct production. But it was a thousand years from the dawn of agriculture to the first evidence of inequality.
>
> *(Henry, 2004, p. 84)*

The differentiation of work began to develop (although, at first it was social rather than individual, with a group of families specialised in a particular function) and that made the collective rights and obligations of the tribe to begin to collapse, and the inequality increased until finally a ruling class emerged (Wray, 2004, pp. 229–230).

Those groups that managed to acquire greater economic power and influence began to be able to establish bonds of authority and superiority with respect to the rest of the groups in areas that transcended the imposition of obligations for special cases, unlike it had been the case until then. And as these kinds of obligations became increasingly numerous, there was a greater need for the institutions dominated by the most powerful classes – namely, religion and government – to regulate them. This is tested by the evidence found in the archaeological findings of Mesopotamian civilisations: "the surviving records of an early agricultural/industrial society, that of Bronze Age Mesopotamia, show an organisation of economic activity very tightly regulated by the state, or by the local temple, which in turn was controlled by elite local families" (Gardiner, 2004, p. 129).

Henry (2004) illustrates this gradual transformation of society referring to the history of Egypt:

> the development of money in the third millennium (1) is placed squarely in the transition from egalitarian to stratified society, (2) is intertwined with the religious character of early Egypt, and (3) represents a fundamental change in the substance of social obligations between tribal and class societies.
>
> *(Henry, 2004, p. 80)*

And this development would be political and administrative, totally unrelated to the functioning of the market, since "the Egyptians had no vocabulary for buying, selling, or even money; there was no conception of trading at a profit" (Bleiberg, 1996, p. 14). Randall Wray sums up this story as follows: "if Henry is right, specialisation begat wisdom, begat status, begat religion, begat fines, fees, tribute, tithes and taxes paid to the Papacy" (Wray, 2004, p. 230).

But the archaeological studies used by opponents of commodity money do not just rely on the Egyptian case; they do so in the case of Mesopotamia as well.

Temples and palaces in Mesopotamia

The unit of account that Egyptians used in temples to regulate debts and transactions was called "deben", which was no more than a unit of weight (initially equivalent to 92 grams of wheat). Archaeological evidence shows that in Mesopotamia the analogous form of unit of account used in temples referred to barley, another cereal (Harari, 2015, p. 204; Powell, 1996). Seemingly none other unit of account but this one was chosen because in the existing agroindustry of subsistence agriculture cereal was the most important and used product of all.

The fact that the unit of account used to measure the tributes and all the economic relations that took place in the temple was the cereal grain does not mean that grain was used in all of those transactions; the grain was simply the unit of reference to pay debts and to exchange goods and services. It is evidenced by the fact that, for some workers in Mesopotamia, the monthly salary expressed in barley far exceeded the amount of barley that they could eat during that period:

> one sila was equivalent to approximately one litre of barley. A worker earned 60 silas a month and a worker 30 silas. A foreman could earn between 1,200 and 5,000 silas. Not even

the hungriest of the foremen could eat 5,000 liters of barley in a month, but he could use the silas he did not eat to buy all kinds of items.

(Harari, 2015, p. 204)

It is important to understand that it is not that this particular worker received all of that great amount of grain and then exchanged it for other products, but that once his inputs were recorded in terms of cereal grains, he could obtain other products simply by subtracting from his salary the quantity of barley that he needed. The worker did not have to receive the barley grains to obtain other products or to settle his tax obligations, since those were only the unit of account in which the price of the rest of the products and the value of the debts were expressed.

These records of obligations of the agents involved were recorded on any object that supports those annotations. There is abundant archaeological evidence supporting the fact that the inhabitants of Mesopotamia created permanent records on an indestructible material, the clay, since it "enhances infinitely the chances of worthwhile records surviving" (Gardiner, 2004, p. 135). In these tables were written down notches that represented the amounts of units of account that were owed and to be received by the agents involved (Eagleton & Williams, 2007, p. 17). This is how a system for recording and storing accounting data began to be developed (Englund, 2004; Harari, 2015, p. 141; Schmandt-Besserat, 1992; Nissen et al., 1993). The Babylonian clay tablets (shubati) of around the year 2,500 BC were "the recognition of indebtedness measured in an account money" (Innes, 1913, p. 396).

Therefore, the first texts of history "are boring economic documents that record the payment of taxes, the accumulation of debts and the possession of property" (Harari, 2015, p. 142). An example of these first messages found is: "a total of 29,086 measurements of barley were received over 37 months. Signed, Kushim" (Robinson, 1995, p. 36). To avoid the manipulation of these clay handwritten tables they were put into crates in which the most important information was repeated, in such a way as in order to know all the details the casing had to be broken, something that – with a view to avoid falsification or alteration of the table – was only done when the definitive agreement was reached (Innes, 1993, pp. 395–396; Wray, 2015, p. 155; Tcherneva, 2016, p. 14).

The civilisations of the Middle East were not the only ones that used writing to measure credits and debts. On the other side of the planet and without having contact with the civilisations of Europe, Africa, and Asia, the Incas also began to write down data related to the collection of taxes and the possession of property (Ascher and Rober, 1981).

In any case, the novelty would not be the registration of commitments and obligations, which had been happening in primitive societies for some time, but their articulation and regulation through the authorities of the temples in the context of a society of classes in which such obligations were much more numerous and complex. The annotation of commitments and debts is much earlier: authors such as Gardiner (2004, p. 150) situate this phenomenon 10,000 years ago. Others, such as Georges Ifrah (1994), go back to the ancient Stone Age, pointing out that only the invention of fire was a technological innovation prior to accounting. In some settlements of hunter-gatherers there were bones with very elaborate notches that survived, and which are understood by some scholars as evidence of a fairly sophisticated accounting method (Gardiner, 2004, p. 131). All of this goes in line with that money predates writing as it arose to measure credits and debts.

The novelty in the case of Mesopotamia would have been of a cognitive and symbolic nature. The tables were typical of a stratified society, created by a privileged social group to be recognised and to be used by the rest of the population that interacted with the temples (the laws and codes of conduct created from the temples did not affect the whole society, they were limited to the public sector and the part of the economy that was in connection with it). At the same time, the emergence of these clay tablets would have been an important and necessary step towards the systematisation of the records of economic relations that were becoming more extensive and complex: "the conceptual leap was to endow each token shape ... with a specific meaning" (Schmandt-Besserat, 1992, p. 161). The marks used in the past could not be understood outside the context in which they were recorded. The opposite was true for the Mesopotamian plates, whose meanings could be immediately understood by any person who was familiar with the system established by the temple authorities. The users of these tables could "manipulate information concerning different categories of items, resulting in a complexity of data processing never reached previously" (Schmandt-Besserat, 1992, p. 161). Over time, the increase in the number and types of obligations to be recorded led the system to become more complex, incorporating new brands that in turn represented a specific number of tables (Englund, 2004; Henry, 2004, p. 94).

Thus, a general scheme of price equivalences, which worked with weights and measures, was created. A system of interconnected elements coordinated the resource flows and allowed to articulate the debts that were owed to the public institutions. The production of tables and its administration, associated with the system of tributes that had supplanted the old tribal obligations, became the activity of the temples (Henry, 2004, p. 94). Under normal conditions, the old tribal way of allocating price would have been replicated in many of the rest of the transactions that took place in the economy (Wray, 2004, p. 9).

This accounting method was necessary to manage a complex administrative hierarchy: "barley and dates produced on land leased out by the temples were distributed as rations to non-agricultural labour employed in their workshops to weave cloth from the wool produced by the herds with which these institutions were endowed" (Hudson, 2004, p. 112). These payments did not have a fixed date in the calendar, but they were made to coincide with the time of harvest. Those who received the payment were obviously the temples but also the officials of the bureaucracy who had given loans to individuals with problems (Hudson, 2004, p. 116). According to Mederos and Lamberg-Karlovsky, la contabilidad se convirtió en una forma de "tecnología de control social" (Mederos y Lamberg-Karlovsky, 2004, p. 206).

All payment obligations as well as its cancellations had to be duly accounted for to make the distributive system to work correctly. A good organisation was essential to coordinate all economic and social relations: "the temples were the main instrument to supervise this cooperation, and they also became the instruments of industrial development" (Gardiner, 2004, p. 135). The temples had not only imposed the moral code that made enforceable obligations and maintained social peace thus allowing the system to work, not only had they developed the writing to register the accounts, but they also became industrial poles:

> in Mesopotamia temples employed the poor, the widows and the orphans in factories which produced textiles to be traded abroad for the commodities the region lacked, including silver, copper, tin and lead. They were, it seems, the major business centres.
>
> *(Gardiner, 2004, p. 135)*

Silver

Using cereals as a reference unit to measure the prices of other products and services had a significant problem: the yield of cereal crops varied drastically year after year, which affected their value in relation to the other products. Ideally, the value of the product that is used as a reference must not easily vary in terms of other objects, thus, these units of reference were not useful to meet that condition in comparison with other products that are permanent and that, by convention, can have an established value. Or to look at it from another perspective: when deciding to use a product as a measure of value is desirable that its intrinsic value is lower than its value as a means of exchange so that the latter is affected, as little as possible, by the demand and supply of the exchange good that takes place because of its intrinsic value. Thus, a commodity which we need to feed ourselves like cereal is not a good idea, since its use value for feeding could be very far from its value as a unit of measure. Obviously, the same cannot be said of silver and gold since they are not life needs (Gardiner, 2004, p. 133; Powell, 1996; Heinsohn & Steiger, 1983, p. 21).

According to the money-debt approach, there is no need for a real product that represents the unit of account of obligations and debts, because in the end, these are fictions and their management does not need physical embodiment. But at a time when not even a precise and manageable numbering system had yet been developed, everything seemed easier if those fictions could be correlated to something physical. It would have been more useful and practical to have a physical commodity to be traded, accounted, watched, known, beautiful, and transportable with which to facilitate the creation and settlement of debts and credits (Harari, 2015, p. 205). Archaeologists are still unclear about why silver was chosen (Hudson & Wunsch, 2004, p. 351), and this is recognised by MMTer Randall Wray: "¿so what were coins and why did they contain precious metal? To be sure, we do not know" (Wray, 2012, p. 165). However, it is speculated that the explanation is that silver played a central role in the gift system of palaces and temples and because it was on top of the pyramid of materials from a cultural perspective (silver was transformed into jewels, crowns, and other symbols of power) (Hudson, 2004, p. 123; Harari, 2015, p. 205; Eagleton & Williams, 2007, p. 19). In any case, what is clear is that the most popular medium of exchange for the last 5,000 years has been silver, or, from a money-debt perspective, "a promise to provide a quantity of silver, measured by weight" (Gardiner, 2004, p. 134).

But how was the cereal replaced by silver as a unit of account according to this perspective? The most mentioned theory points to the activity of the merchants of the time. Merchants should not be understood from a current perspective, as individuals who freely decide to trade, to do business: "the merchants in Bronze Age society were not completely free agents but appear to have been a body of people authorised by the state or temple to undertake some specific trading on behalf of the community" (Gardiner, 2004, p. 129). In fact, the word "merchant" (tamkarum) appears as an official title, not simply a freely chosen activity that anyone could take when it suited him (Gardiner, 2004, p. 129).

Following this approach, massive public institutions would have been essential to organise trade. Long-distance trade was promoted from the temples, whose leaders were interested in capturing precious metals and other raw materials from abroad to be able to incorporate them into their economic circuit. Existing records reveal that Babylonian merchants accepted clothing advances from the temple workshops in return for a promise of supplying a fixed amount of silver later on. From the temples, the merchants got documents that were nothing more than promises of payment to those who held them. The British Museum in London retains more than 600 records of this type (Hudson, 2004, p. 124; Gardiner, 2004, pp. 135–136). Likewise, everything suggests that these documents and the rights they enclosed could be transferred and therefore used in exchange for other products:

Promissory notes which do not mention the creditor by name, but refer to him as tamkarum, "the merchant/creditor". In a few cases such notes at the end add the phrase "the bearer of this tablet is tamkarum" (wabil tuppim sut tamkarum). This clause suggests the possibility of a transfer of debt-notes and of ceding claims, which would make it a precursor of later "bearer cheques".

(Veenhof, 1999)

Most of these first known records were created in public institutions over 3,500 years ago. However, it does not mean that this kind of promises was not created outside the temples, what happens is that they may simply have not been preserved (Eagleton & Williams, 2007, p. 21). After all, the temples and palaces "did not pursue cost containment: the bureaucrats' main concern was doubtless to protect themselves from accusations of embezzlement" (Gardiner, 2004, p. 129), which would be why the record of these promises was so solid and has survived until today.

Silver would have come through these trade flows and thus circulated through the economy. At first it would have worked as a measure and as deposit of value, especially to denominate debts, starting with those of which the temples were creditors. In this way, silver would have been replacing the vehicular role that barley had played until then by assigning values to internal resource flows and to debts owed by merchants and other individuals related to the temples and palaces. These prices were an intrinsic part of the system of weights and measures, with the heavy silver designated as the common denominator, and being also the reservation of sanctified value. Since the main flows of resources within public institutions were fees to feed the dependency of creditors' labour, and that the principal payments of the communities to the palace consisted of crops, silver would have become comparable to barley. The idea would have been to manage the prices of the essential transactions with which the various departments of the temples and palaces interacted between each other and with the economy in general: the value of the crops, the rents, the tariffs, and the purchases of basic products (Hudson, 2004, pp. 111–115).

The accounting prices, as well as the fines and obligations, would have continued to be added to the resources of the massive institutions, but this time expressed in relation to the weight of silver:

setting the value of a unit of silver as equal to the monthly barley ration and land-unit crop yield enabled it to become the standard measure of value and means of payment, although barley and a few other essentials could be used as proxies as their proportions were fixed.

(Wray, 2004, p. 9)

Despite starting as a measure and a deposit of value, as time goes by, silver would have been used as a personal tradable asset for exchange. The main way for most families to make money with silver was, evidently, selling the surplus produced on their own land or on the land leased to public institutions. However, the transactions were made through the accumulation and cancellation of debt balances, so truly silver would have not been entirely used as a means of payment: silver would have been used as a means to settle debts, mainly with the large institutions and its collectors. According to Hudson (2004, pp. 114–115), in small sales such as the beer service, the common practice was not to pay instantly but to write down the debt, as it is done in many bars today.

In any case, from the money-debt approach it is important to note that the use of silver as a means of change derived from its main and original function as a unit of account. It would have been through a process planned and designed in temples and palaces, that silver started to be used to carry out transactions in the private sphere. Indeed, according to Hudson (2004, p. 115), the fact that the silver was backed by public institutions was what gave people confidence when carrying out the exchanges, since it would always serve to pay off the debts owed to the temples and palaces.

General-purpose money

All the social and political phenomena described so far would explain how the primitive money that was exceptionally used in prehistoric communities was evolving according to this money-debt approach. The money used in class societies such as the Egyptian or the Mesopotamian one would have not been no longer just useful to measure a few specific obligations, it also would have been desirable to articulate many obligations and transactions that occurred in much larger and more complex economies in which interactions among many more agents took place. As it has already been pointed out, this transformation would have been due to the emergence of class society, the imposition of payment obligations on the entire population, and the development of temples and palaces as administrative, industrial, and commercial centres. But what finally allowed money to be widely used beyond the administrative centres would have been the monetisation of the obligations that were managed in those spaces. This last phenomenon is what would explain that primitive money finally became "general-purpose money": "it is the extensive transferability of debt and the creation of a hierarchy of acceptability that was crucially important in the development of the form of (circulating) credit money" (Ingham, 2004b, p. 185).

Although credit (and therefore its counterpart, debt) binds two parties through a payment commitment, the token – the physical object that can be used to represent its existence – can be transferred to third parties and even circulate throughout the economy. Therefore, it is possible for many credits to be created and liquidated thanks to the same token. For example, the first clay tablets that theoretically represented the obligations that were imposed on the population were not interchangeable in the community, but linked only to the debtor, they were not useful for anyone else. However, silver could circulate from hand to hand representing many different credits (and debts). In the first case Wray and Tymoigne speak of a "monetary instrument" and in the second case of a "monetary object" (Wray & Tymoigne, 2005, p. 5). The monetary instrument represents a particular debt, and the monetary object can represent many more. The process of converting a monetary instrument into a monetary object – that is, of converting a debt into a means of exchange – can be called "monetizing debt" (Gardiner, 2004, pp. 168–169; Ingham, 2004b, p. 185).

In the words of Ingham: "money, even in its virtual form as a book entry, only becomes an exchangeable 'commodity' after its quality of 'moneyness' has been constituted by the social relations between the issuers and users of money" (Ingham, 2004b, p. 179). That is why money always would mean credit, although credit would not be always money. Tribal obligations did not become money because of its general use, neither did so the first Mesopotamian clay tablets. But the silver measured in weight was used like general-purpose money: it would be a "token" that served to pay the tributes to the temples but that could be changed hands to create and to settle obligations between different economic agents. Despite the existence of primitive money, only the money originated through the internal accounting practices of the temples and palaces would have generated a general-purpose account money with which denominate prices, although other traditions could have developed the idea of money for special purposes and for measuring debts (Ingham, 2004b, p. 185; Wray, 2004, p. 229; Innes, 1913, p. 392).

This conception implies a drastic change with respect to the individualistic perspective of money as a commodity. Money would have not been a technological innovation that emerged in a decentralised manner and under the heat of market forces to overcome the impediments of barter; it would have been a social and centralised construct and a complex social practice that carries power and class relations, socially constructed meanings, abstract representations of social value, etc. (Wray, 2004, p. 231; Harari, 2015, p. 203). According to this approach, without the existence of the monetary mechanisms created, imposed, regulated, and supervised by the authorities, it would have been very difficult that transactions took place in a generalised manner. The silver would have been used to articulate all kinds of economic relations because, ultimately, the authorities accepted it as a tax payment. That is why the money and the law would have gone hand in hand forming the basic elements of economic progress and that would be why, only with a few and rare exceptions, every unit of account used throughout history and in every corner of the globe has been associated to a central authority (Gardiner, 2004, p. 130; Wray & Tymoigne, 2005, p. 4; Wray, 2010, p. 45).

The transformation of primitive money into general-purpose money would entail a constant transformation of creditors and debtors. In the case of the first clay tablets, the community would have been the debtor which had to pay tribute to the temples and palaces, to the creditors. But in the case of general-purpose money, the "tokens" such as silver would have been used to allow the exchange of all kinds of services and goods and therefore any person in possession of them would be entitled by the entire community. The individual who owned the silver would have not been the creditor of any specific person or institution but would have been recognised as a creditor by anyone who provided him with goods in exchange for his silver (Gardiner, 2004, p. 147).

When the record of a commitment is regulated and generalised in a community in a way that allows the use of it to obtain goods and services, it can be considered that the holders of these cards hold the title of creditors in front of the community, while the community holds the title of debtor in front of them. In Gardiner words, these tokens that the seller receives for his supply "are the measure of the credit he has given to the purchaser, and, more widely, they reflect the debt society as a whole owes him" (Gardiner, 2004, p. 147). In a similar way the sociologist Georg Simmel explained, at the beginning of the twentieth century:

> money is only a claim upon society. (...) The liquidation of the individual's liability may still involve an obligation for the community. The liquidation of every private obligation by money means that the community now assumes this obligation to the creditor.
>
> *(Simmel, 1907, p. 177)*

In other words, money would be "simply the right to demand a good or a service from another person" (Macleod, 1889, p. 67).

Consequently, from the money-debt approach, the sale is conceived in a way far from the conventional one: "a sale, according to this theory, is not the exchange of a commodity far some intermediate commodity called the 'medium of exchange', but the exchange of a commodity for a credit" (Innes, 1913, p. 391). When a person wants to sell something, he would not be looking for coins, gold or silver, what he would be looking for is to obtain credit, that is, the recognition that he should be provided with value in the future and in some way. The sellers would not want to treasure monetary objects, what they would want is to gather credit, which is what would help them to acquire products, pay taxes, or enjoy a service:

> a credit cancels a debt; this is the primitive law of commerce. By sale a credit is acquired, by purchase a debt is created. Purchases, therefore, are paid for by sales. The object of commerce is the acquisition of credits.
>
> *(Innes, 1914, p. 168)*

The instrument or the monetary object used would be irrelevant; it would be only a credit and debt thermometer that facilitates transactions, just as the important thing is not the measuring tape but the distance to be measured. The relevant issue would be the unit of account, which is a measure of the value of the goods, "but is not itself a commodity, nor can it be embodied in any commodity. It is intangible, immaterial, abstract. It is a measure in terms of credit and debt" (Innes, 1914, p. 159). According to this approach, when we "promise to pay" we do not commit to pay with silver or with other monetary objects, but we simply commit ourselves to cancel our debt by an equivalent credit expressed in terms of our abstract and intangible standards (Innes, 1914, p. 155).

Criticisms

The historical validity of the money-as-debt account, which would have emerged in the heat of public authorities in Mesopotamia and Egypt, has been questioned by many analysts. The central idea shared by these critics is that empirical evidence would indicate that precious metals were used as a medium of exchange throughout history and by all civilisations, so it would not fit that money was a political and centralised invention by the authorities of each community, since in that case it would be expected that each of them would choose a different medium of exchange and not a universal one. Instead, they argue that such evidence would rather prove that money was the decentralised result of market forces finding the most efficient medium of exchange due to its intrinsic characteristics and that only afterwards the public authorities would have appropriated its creation and regulation through their power.

Some critics consider the mentioned historical events to be imprecise or "a red herring in the debate" (Palley, 2015, p. 47). Some such as Mehrling have dismissively claimed that such history "is akin to that of the gold fanatics", but instead of putting the emphasis on the gold it puts it on the public authorities (temples and palaces), and that "it is speculative history at best" (2000, p. 402). Lapavitsas and Aguila (2020, p. 5) point out that the history of Egypt and Babylonia shows that the unit of account was different from the means of exchange, which would be a common feature of several monetary systems. Powell (1996) argues that also in Mesopotamia the choice of the means of exchange responded to the intrinsic characteristics of the chosen commodities, not to an arbitrary decision of the political and religious ruling class:

> all moneys in ancient Mesopotamia were potentially useful substances in their own right. In other words, with the possible exception of "axes" (to which we will refer at the end of this essay), we have no evidence of symbolic or representative moneys.
>
> *(Powell, 1996, p. 32)*

In the same vein, although regarding the wergild system, Caligaris and Starosta (2016) argue that when these practices are considered more closely, the units of account emerge as products of labour and their choice was not necessarily an arbitrary decision by public authorities. However, these notes do not go to the root of the matter and do not challenge the historical account presented, since, according to it, the authorities of the temples and palaces ended up using silver as a monetary instrument and unit of account basically because it was useful for trade with other peoples, but only after having unilaterally and politically created another type of money. The key question is whether money arose in a decentralised and evolutionary way thanks to market forces or whether it was created unilaterally by an authority in order to achieve its political objectives.

And it is on this aspect in particular that Juan Ramón Rallo (2017) takes a position:

> the most plausible hypothesis, and the one with the most historical support, is not that the temples and palaces unilaterally and centrally imposed silver as money on society as a whole after it was imposed on them by the monetary needs of international trade, but that this was an evolutionary process that even developed in parallel with the search for money by the private sector.
>
> *(Rallo, 2017, p. 54)*

In order to argue his position, he draws on the research of Jursa (2010), in which much emphasis is placed on the fact that silver was the predominant medium among Mesopotamian peoples beyond the economic and social sphere surrounding temples and palaces, which is presented as evidence that the use of silver arose in the private sector:

> A basic distinction must be drawn between transactions within the temple and transactions with the outside of the temple. Silver was the almost exclusive means of payment for all transactions beyond the confines of the temple. In terms of the number of transactions, these external exchanges accounted for between 30 and 50 percent of all economic activities carried out by the temples, as attested by documents. Essentially due to the importance of commercial agriculture (the main source of monetary income for the temples) and the hiring of workers who had to be paid in silver, the temples could not have functioned without monetised exchanges with the rest of the economy.
>
> *(Jursa, 2010, p. 775)*

This approach is also shared by Goetzmann (2016) and Palley (2018): the emergence of money in the ancient Near East was thanks to an extraordinary innovation whereby tokens were created to record private debt contracts, and those tokens then became money because they could perform the functions of money (in Mengerian terms, they had "saleableness"). Money first originated in this way in the private sector and was then appropriated by the authorities through their power. Many Keynesian-inspired economists take a very similar position, although without referring specifically to this moment in history, emphasising that private money, specifically bank money, preceded state money. For example, Parguez and Seccareccia point out that

> viable monetary systems existed during periods of economic history when taxes were quite insignificant. What matters, therefore, was not whether tax liabilities were of any

significance but rather whether, largely through the legal system, the state endorsed existing banks by allowing them to issue debts on themselves.

(Parguez & Seccareccia, 2000, p. 120)

Following a similar argument, Eladio Febrero points out that "private money predates state money" (Febrero, 2009, p. 524); Rochon and Vernengo point out that money is "a creature of banks rather than a creature of the state" (Rochon & Vernengo, 2003, p. 61); and Mehrling says that it is convincing that modern money has its historical origins in private money and that private finance is a better logical place to start when trying to understand it. Mehrling's central theoretical point is that "our government is our creation (...) Further, our state arises out of a thriving private civil society, not the reverse" (Mehrling, 2000, p. 402). In short, according to these critics, money was created spontaneously by the private sector through its ability to create debts and promissory notes without the intervention of public authorities, although their role may later be decisive in bringing it into widespread use.

This particular point has been contested by Tymoigne and Wray: "MMT is agnostic as it waits for a logical argument or historical evidence in support of the belief of critics that there is an alternative to taxes (and other obligations). We have not seen any plausible alternative" (Tymoigne & Wray, 2015, p. 10). They acknowledge that the private sector can theoretically create money without the need for public intervention, but that the historical record does not point in that direction: "private money-denominated IOUs developed for reasons other than the imposition of taxes, but history suggests that government provides the foundation upon which modern monetary systems developed" (Tymoigne & Wray, 2015, p. 29).

Moreover, to reinforce their argument, and this is something that will be discussed in more detail in the next chapter, they insist that the historical narrative alluded to has been repeated systematically throughout history:

when new countries are formed, their governments adopt a new money of account, impose taxes and other obligations in that unit, issue a new currency in that unit, and accept their own liabilities in tax payment. Whatever might have been the case in prehistoric times, with few exceptions we observe a familiar pattern throughout recorded history.

(Tymoigne & Wray, 2015, p. 29)

Conclusions

Modern Monetary Theory relies on anthropological and archaeological research to support its view of the origin of money, which is very different from the better-known metallist or evolutionary views of money-markets. The latter have important differences between them, but they share the central idea that money arose decentralised and spontaneously in the private sector. Whether as a technological innovation to overcome the drawbacks of barter (as in the money-commodity view presented by Adam Smith), as a general equivalent arising in the heat of the capitalist economic system (as in the Marxist view), as the result of the search for the most liquid commodity possible (as in the evolutionary view), or as a debt originated by commercial banks (as the Keynesian view), all these theories agree that money was a creation of private economic agents and that only after that the state appropriated it through minting and its power. The Modern Monetary Theory, on the other hand, places the origin of money in the establishment of a unit of account by political and religious authorities during prehistoric times, with which they articulated the social and economic relations that took place under their dominion.

This is an antagonistic view to the dominant approaches, which is why it has received numerous criticisms, although these have certainly been more theoretical than empirical or historical. In any case, it is important to bear in mind that it is virtually impossible to know with certainty what happened so many thousands of years ago, so we need to be cautious about the claims of any approach to the subject, however much it may rely on certain historical records.

And yet, I will argue that the MMT view can be integrated with views that conceive of money as a creation of the private sector: by turning to the term "control space", as we argue in detail in Garzón et al. (2023). This notion refers to the geographical area over which an authority exercises sufficient power and control to be able to regulate social relations at its discretion. This space of monetary control is precisely the one that defines the areas in which the postulates of the two different approaches are applicable: the MMT vision would suitably adjust to those operations that take place within the corresponding space of control, while the evolutionary approach would serve to analyse the operations that take place between different spaces of control. The available empirical evidence would corroborate this idea: the first civilisations – such as Mesopotamia and Egypt – used money created and regulated by the authorities (which is consistent with the MMT), but this only occurred for those monetary operations that took place within those communities – their space of control; for the rest of the monetary operations, barter was chosen as a way of articulating commercial exchanges. As time went by, barter evolved towards the use of money-merchandise outside the spaces of control (which is coherent with the evolutionary approach), until the intensification of relations (commercial and military, especially) between different peoples and civilisations finally pushed the authorities to create their money from the same material that was used as money-merchandise.

The historical evidence that would support this thesis would be the following. In primitive societies barter would only have taken place between different communities, not within them. Following David Graeber:

> The economists' barter scenario may be absurd when applied to transactions between neighbours in the same small rural community, but when it is a transaction between the resident of that community and a passing mercenary, it suddenly starts to make a lot of sense. Thus, for much of human history, a bar of gold or silver, sealed or unsealed, has served the same function as the contemporary drug dealer's suitcase full of unmarked notes: an object with no history, valuable because it is known that it will be accepted in exchange for other goods almost anywhere, no questions asked.
>
> *(Graeber, 2011a, p. 213)*

Without rules or institutions articulated by the authorities, or without their direct and easy supervision, trade between villages operated through barter. And although this process operated primarily at the inter-community level, its impact was by no means minor. As anthropologists Humphrey and Hugh-Jones sum up:

> Barter is important partly because of its ubiquity. It is not just the rare and perhaps dubious cases of silent trade (…) or a few insignificant exchanges at the margins of groups, but entire trading systems have been based on barter as the primary mode of exchange (…). These systems cut across Australia, link the Andes with the jungle, the Amazon and the Orinoco,

and are documented in native North America, pre-Columbian Mexico, Central Asia, Siberia and many other places. Anthropology's previous preoccupation with "societies" as bounded units has led to a disastrous undervaluation of socio-economic relations between groups, which are in fact essential to the reproduction of cultures!

(Humphrey & Hugh-Jones, 1992, p. 3)

We assume that the evolutionary process concerning money took place in those spaces with little or no political influence. As relations between different political communities became more intense – mainly through warfare and trade – the number of transactions outside the spaces of control increased, so cash could become more important.

Van De Mieroop argues that silver developed as a unit of value and medium of exchange in Mesopotamia because the political structure until the end of the second millennium was fragmented into city-states that had to trade with each other and had to trade abroad to obtain key goods. Silver was important because it was a widely accepted currency beyond the relatively limited borders of the early Near Eastern states.

(Goetzman, 2016, p. 59)

The progressive extension of trade relations, as well as invasive manoeuvres, involved the spread of the use of precious metals as a medium of exchange, first within Eurasia – specifically with the homogenisation of the Lydian and Chinese monetary system – and later across the globe:

Muslim and European merchants and conquerors gradually extended the Lydian system and the gospel of gold to the farthest corners of the earth. By the end of the modern era, the entire world was a single monetary zone, based primarily on gold and silver.

(Harari, 2015, p. 207)

Consequently, international trade and payments became a practice that responded to evolutionary or metallist postulates: not using the currency created by the authorities as was the case within communities, but exchanging one commodity for another that functioned as a medium of exchange and did not respond to social institutions regulated by any authority: "people still spoke in incomprehensible languages, obeyed different rulers and worshipped different gods, but all believed in gold and silver and gold and silver coins" (Harari, 2015, p. 207). Therefore, it seems more plausible to think that it was this external, progressively ascending influence that would explain why the authorities began to manufacture their means of payment from precious metals such as gold and silver. In this way, they managed not only to be accepted within their sphere of control but also beyond it.

   In any case, this fact would not invalidate the MMT perspective, but would place it in a very specific sphere: the space of control. The introduction of silver in the monetary system within the community does not mean that the money created by the authorities disappeared since the authorities were still able to create their debts and without any kind of financial limitation. The main difference is that from then on, they would use the material of commodity money as a protagonist in international mercantile relations, thus significantly conditioning the establishment of its value. In effect, the value of the authorities' money could no longer be established unilaterally by its issuer by resorting to certain units of account but was strongly influenced by the value to which the relations maintained with other spheres of control. Consequently, the postulates of the two approaches are not incompatible in explaining the creation of money but would coexist through the filter of the delimitation of the space of monetary control.

There are other different analyses of the nature of money that could be well understood with this control space thesis, such as Lawson (2019, 2022). According to this approach, what defines that something can become money is its social positioning, that is, that it is accepted by the whole community due to its social relevance and status; so anything could become money depending on the particular social context. In his own words:

> A kind of thing, whatever the latter may be, can be incorporated in the money process only where a community, perhaps through the declarations or implicit agreement of some authority, positions it as money, whereupon the abilities of community participants to use it, qua money, to discharge debts, derive from community agreed rights and obligations, and do not depend on the kind of thing that occupies the money position. So certain commodities, just like forms of debt, may be (and indeed have been) positioned, and so incorporated, as a community's money.
>
> *(Lawson, 2019, p. 117)*

Consequently, this thesis on the social positioning of money is perfectly compatible with the thesis of control space: while within societies what was positioned as money was the unit of account created by the authorities, beyond the authorities, the most efficient commodity for transactions was positioned as money.

In short, this particular theoretical approach based on space control does not resolve the debate, but I do believe that it provides a new perspective that enriches it and that, perhaps, will convince some people.

In any case, some may find this historical debate irrelevant. After all, money may have had an origin and nature in the past that has nothing to do with the present. This is precisely what the economist Abba Lerner referred to: "whatever may be the history of gold, at the present time, in a normally well-working economy, money is a creature of the state" (Lerner, 1947, p. 413) or Keynes himself, who recognised that "this right is claimed by all modern states and has been so claimed for some four thousand years at least" (Keynes, 1930, p. 44). Consequently, even if the MMT view of the origin of money is not accepted, this would not be enough to discredit its postulates on the nature of money, since, even if they were not accurate for ancient times, they could be perfectly valid in the present. Therefore, in the following chapter we will abstract from historical events and focus on the nature of money according to MMT and the criticisms it receives.

Notes

1 In fact, Samuelson himself recognised that the well-known story of the emergence of money was "hypothetical and logical" (Samuelson & Nordhaus, 1975, pp. 274–76) and Kevin Dowd (2000) described this explanation as a "conjectural history".
2 After a request by Pope John Paul II for the text to be homogenised in all regions, the phrase became as follows: "Forgive us our trespasses as we forgive those who trespass against us".

References

Alchian, A. (1977). Why money? *Journal of Money, Credit, and Banking, 9*(1), 133–140.
Ascher, M., & Ascher, R. (1981). *Mathematics of the Incas. Code of the Quipu*. Dover.

Bell, S. (2001). The role of the state and the hierarchy of money. *Cambridge Journal of Economics*, *25*(2), 149–163.

Bell, S., & Henry, J. (2001). The limits of monetary economies. *Review of Social Economy*, *2*(59), 203–226.

Bellofiore, R., & Realfonzo, R. (1997). Finance and the labor theory of value: Toward a macroeconomic theory of distribution from a monetary perspective. *International Journal of Political Economy*, *27*(2), 97–118.

Bleiberg, E. (1996). *The official gift in Egypt*. University of Oklahoma Press.

Bougrine, H., & Seccareccia, M. (2002). Money, taxes, public spending, and the state within a circuitist perspective. *International Journal of Political Economy*, *32*(3), 58–79.

Brunner, K. (1971). The uses of money: Money in the theory of an exchange economy. *American Economic Review*, *61*, 784–805.

Caligaris, G., & Starosta, G. (2016). Explicación Sistemática y Análisis Histórico en la Crítica de la Economía Política. Un Aporte Metodológico a la Controversia Sobre la Naturaleza. In M. Del Dinero, R. Escorcia Romo, & M. L. Robles Báez (Eds.), *Dinero y Capital. Hacia Una Reconstrucción de la Teoría de Marx Sobre el Dinero* (pp. 123–158). Universidad Autónoma Metropolitana-Unidad Xochimilco and Editorial Itaca.

Carruthers, B., & Babb, S. (1996). The color of money and the nature of value: Greenbacks and gold in postbellum America. *American Journal of Sociology*, *101*(6), 1556–1591.

Cartelier, J. (1991). Marx's theory of value, exchange and surplus value: A suggested reformulation. *Cambridge Journal of Economics*, *15*(3), 257–269.

Cipolla, C. (1956). *Money, prices, and civilization in the Mediterranean world: Fifth to seventeenth century*. Princeton University Press.

Cipolla, C. (1976). *Before the industrial revolution: European society and economy* (pp. 1000–1700). W.W. Norton & Company, Inc.

Cruz, E., Parejo, F. M., & Rangel, J. F. (2020). El Dinero moderno y el enfoque cartalista institucional. *Revista de Economía Institucional*, *22*(43), 57–78.

Dalton, G. (1967). Primitive money. In G. Dalton (Ed.), *Tribal and peasant economies* (pp. 254–281). University of Texas Press.

Desan, C. (2013). *Creation stories: Myths about the origins of money* (Working Paper 13-20). Harvard Public Law.

Dowd, K. (2000). The invisible hand and the evolution of the monetary system. In J. Smithin (Ed.), *What is money?* (pp. 139–141). Routledge.

Eagleton, C., & Williams, J. (2007). *Historia del dinero*. Ediciones Paidós Ibérica.

Einaudi, L. (1953). The theory of imaginary money from Charlemagne to the French Revolution. In F. C. Lane & J. C. Riemersma (Eds.), *Enterprise and secular change: Readings in economic history* (p. 494). Richard D. Irwin, Inc.

Englund, R. (2004). Proto-cuneiform account-books and journals. In M. Hudson & C. Wuncsch (Eds.), *Creating economic order: Record-keeping, standardization, and the developments of accounting in the ancient near east* (pp. 23–46). CDL Press.

Febrero, E. (2009). Three difficulties with neo-chartalism. *Journal of Post Keynesian Economics*, *31*(3), 523–541. https://doi.org/10.2753/PKE0160-3477310308

Fontana, G., & Realfonzo, R. (Eds.). (2005). *The monetary theory of production: Tradition and perspectives*. Palgrave Macmillan.

Friedman, M. (1969). *The optimum quantity of money and other essays*. Aldine Pub. Co.

Gardiner, G. W. (2004). The primacy of trade debts in the development of money. In Law Review Wray (Ed.), *Credit and state theories of money* (pp. 128–172). Edward Elgar.

Garrote, J. C. (2017). *Reflexiones sobre el origen y la naturaleza del dinero. El Dinero moderno como una extensión del dinero primitivo*. Final Degree Project. University of Extremadura.

Garzón, E., Cruz, E., Medialdea, B., & Sánchez, C. (2023). The 'control space' of the state: A key element to address the nature of money. *Review of Radical Political Economics*, *55*(3), 448–465.

Glyn, D. (1994). *A history of money: From ancient times to the present day*. University of Wales Press.

Goetzmann, W. N. (2016). *Money changes everything: How finance made civilization possible*. Princeton University Press.

Goodhart, C. (1998). The two concepts of money: Implications for the analysis of optimal currency areas. *European Journal of Political Economy, 14*(3), 407–432.

Graeber, D. (2011a). *Debt: The first 5,000 years*. Melville House.

Graeber, D. (2011b). *What is debt? – An interview with economic anthropologist David Graeber*. Naked Capitalism.

Graziani, A. (1997). The Marxist theory of money. *International Journal of Political Economy, 27*(2), 26–50.

Graziani, A. (2003). *The monetary theory of production*. Cambridge University Press.

Grierson, P. (1977). *The origins of money*. The Athlone Press.

Harari, Y. N. (2015). *Sapiens*. Debate.

Heinsohn, G., & Steiger, O. (1983). Private property, debts and interest, or: The origin of money and the rise and fall of monetary economies. *Studi Economici, 21*, 3–56.

Henry, J. F. (2004). The social origins of money: The case of Egypt. In Law Review Wray (Ed.), *Credit and state theories of money* (pp. 79–98). Edward Elgar.

Hudson, M. (2004). The archaeology of money: Debt versus Barter. In Law Review Wray (Ed.), *Credit and state theories of money* (pp. 99–127). Edward Elgar.

Hudson, M., & Wunsch, C. (2004). *Creating economic order*. CDL (Cuneiform Digital Library) Press.

Humphrey, C. (1985). Barter and economic disintegration. *Man, 20*(1), 48–72. https://doi.org/10.2307/2802221

Humphrey, C., & Hugh-Jones, S. (1992). *Barter, exchange and value: An anthropological approach*. Cambridge University Press.

Ifrah, G. (1994). *The universal history of numbers*. The Harvill Press.

Ingham, G. (1996). Money is a social relation. *Review of Social Economy, 54*(4), 507–529.

Ingham, G. (2004a). The emergence of capitalist credit money. In Law Review Wray (Ed.), *Credit and state theories of money* (pp. 173–222). Edward Elgar.

Ingham, G. (2004b). The nature of money. *Economic Sociology: European Electronic Newsletter, 5*(2), 18–28.

Innes, A. M. (2004a[1913]). What is money. In Law Review Wray (Ed.), *Credit and state theories of money* (pp. 14–49). Edward Elgar.

Innes, A. M. (2004b[1914]). The credit theory of money. In Law Review Wray (Ed.), *Credit and state theories of money* (pp. 50–78). Edward Elgar.

Jevons, W. S. (1896). *Money and the mechanism of exchange*. Appleton and Company.

Jursa, M. (2010). *Aspects of the economic history of Babylonia in the first millennium BC: Economic geography, economic mentalities, agriculture, the use of money and the problem of economic growth*. Ugarit-Verlag.

Keynes, J. M. (1976[1930]). *A treatise on money, volumes I and II*. Brace & Co.

Kiyotaki, N., & Wright, R. (1989). On money as a medium of exchange. *Journal of Political Economy, 97*(4), 927–954.

Klein, P. G., & Selgin, G. (2000). Menger's theory of money: Some experimental evidence. In J. Smithin (Ed.), *What is money?* (p. 217). Routledge.

Kottak, C. (1994). *Antropología*. McGraw-Hill.

Lapavitsas, C., & Aguila, N. (2020). Modern monetary theory on money, sovereignty, and policy: A Marxist critique with reference to the Eurozone and Greece. *Japanese Political Economy, 46*(4), 300–326.

Lawson, T. (2019a). *The nature of social reality: Issues in social ontology*. Routledge.

Lawson, T. (2022). Social positioning theory. *Cambridge Journal of Economics, 46*(1), 1–39.

Lerner, A. (1947). Money as a creature of the state. *American Economic Review, 37*(2), 312–317.

Lisón Arcal, J. (1999). El mito del trueque. *Sociedad y utopía, Revista de ciencias sociales*, 1, extra, 181–187.

Louzek, M. (2011). The battle of methods in economics. The classical Methodenstreit – Menger vs. Schmoller. *American Journal of Economics and Sociology, 70*(2), 439–463.

Macleod, H. D. (1969[1889]). *The theory of Credit* (Vol. 1). Edizioni Bizzarri.

Malinowski, B. (1921). The primitive economics of the Trobriand islanders. *The Economic Journal, 31*(121), 1–16.

Martínez-Echevarría, M. A., & Crespo, R. (2011). Aristóteles y el pensamiento económico: una introducción. *Revista Empresa y Humanismo, 14*(2), 5–9.

Marx, K. (1989[1859]). *Contribución a la Crítica de la Economía Política*. Editorial Progreso.

Marx, K. (2007). *Elementos fundamentales para la crítica de la economía política (Grundrisse) 1857–1858*. Siglo XXI editores.

Mederos, A., & Lamberg-Karlovsky, C. (2004). Weight systems and trade networks in the old world (2500-1000 bc). In M. Hudson & C. Wunesch (Eds.), *Creating economic order: Record-keeping, standardization, and the developments of accounting in the ancient near east* (pp. 199–214). CDL. https://www.academia.edu/1272595/Weight_Systems_and_Trade_Networks_in_the_Old_World_2500_1000_BC_

Mehrling, P. (2000). Modern money: Fiat or credit? *Journal of Post Keynesian Economics, 22*(3), 397–406.

Menger, C. ([1909]2013). *El dinero*. Madrid: Unión Editorial.

Menger, K. (1892). On the origin of money. *The Economic Journal, 2*(6), 239–255.

von Mises, L. (1934). The theory of money and credit. 1912. (H. E. Batson, Trans.). Alden.

Mitchell, W., Wray, L. R., & Watts, M. (2016). *Modern monetary theory and practice: An introductory text*. Centre of Full Employment and Equity.

Mitchell, W., Wray, L. R., & Watts, M. (2019). *Macroeconomics*. Red Globe Press.

Nissen, H. J., Damerow, P., & Englund, R. K. (1993). *Archaic bookkeeping: Writing and techniques of economic administration in the ancient near east*. Chicago University Press.

Palley, T. (2015). The critics of Modern Money Theory (MMT) are right. *Review of Political Economy, 27*(1), 45–61.

Palley, T. (2018). *Modern Money Theory (MMT) vs. structural Keynesianism. Thomas Palley – Economics for democratic and open societies*. https://thomaspalley.com/?p=1145

Parguez, A., & Seccareccia, M. (2000). The credit theory of money: The monetary circuit approach. In J. Smithin (Ed.), *What is money?* (pp. 101–123). Routledge.

Polanyi, K. (1957). The semantics of money-uses. In G. Dalton (Ed.), *Primitive, archaic and modern economies* (pp. 175–203). Beacon Press.

Powell, M. (1996). Money in Mesopotamia. *Journal of the Economic and Social History of the Orient, 39*(3), 224–242.

Rallo, J. R. (2017). *Contra la Teoría Monetaria Moderna*. Deusto.

Roberts, M. (2019). Modern monetary theory: A Marxist critique. *Class, Race and Corporate Power, 7*(1), Article 1. https://doi.org/10.25148/CRCP.7.1.008316. https://digitalcommons.fiu.edu/classraceco rporatepower/vol7/iss1/1

Robinson, A. (1995). *The story of writing*. Thames and Hudson.

Rochon, L. P., & Vernengo, M. (2003). State money and the real world: Or chartalism and its discontents. *Journal of Post Keynesian Economics, 26*(1), 57–68.

Samuelson, P. (1973). *Ciencias económicas* (9th ed.). McGraw-Hill.

Samuelson, P., & Nordhaus, W. D. (1975). *Economics*. McGraw Hill.

Schmandt-Besserat, D. (1992). *Before writing, volume one: From counting to cuneiform*. University of Texas Press.

Schumpeter, J. A. (1954). *Historia del análisis económico*. Editorial Ariel.

Semenova, A. (2011a). Would you Barter with god? Why holy debts and not profane markets created money. *American Journal of Economics and Sociology, 70*(2), 376–400.

Semenova, A. (2011b). *The origins of money: Evaluating chartalist and metallist theories in the context of ancient Greece and mesopotamia* (PhD Thesis). University of Missouri–Kansas City.

Semenova, A. (2014). Carl Menger's theory of Money's origins: Responding to revisionism. *European Journal of the History of Economic Thought, 21*(1), 107–141.

Simmel, G. (1978[1907]). *The philosophy of money.* Routledge (Original work published 1907).

Smith, A. (1994). *La Riqueza de las Naciones.* Alianza Editorial.

Stanfield, J. R. (1986). *The economic thought of Karl Polanyi: Lives and livelihood.* Macmillan.

Tcherneva, P. (2016). *Money, power and monetary regimes* (Working Paper No. 861). Levy Economics Institute.

Tooke, T. (1844). *An inquiry into the currency principle.* Longman, Brown, Green and Longmans.

Tymoigne, E., & Wray, L. R. (2015). Modern money theory: A reply to Palley. *Review of Political Economy, 27*(1), 24–44.

Veenhof, K. R. (1999). Silver and credit in old Assyrian trade. In J. G. Dercksen (Ed.), *Trade and finance in ancient Mesopotamia (MOS studies 1)* (pp. 55–83). https://www.nino-leiden.nl/publication/trade -and-finance-in-ancient-mesopotamia

von Mises, L. (1934). *The theory of money and credit.* Alden.

Wray, L. R. (1990). *Money and Credit in Capitalist Economies: The Endogenous Money Approach.* Aldershot, UK: Edward Elgar.

Wray, L. R. (Ed.). (2004). *Credit and state theories of money.* Edward Elgar.

Wray, L. R. (2010). Alternative approaches to money. *Theoretical Inquiries in Law, 11*(1), 29–49.

Wray, L. R. (2012). *Modern money theory: A primer on macroeconomics for sovereign monetary.* Palgrave Macmillan.

Wray, L. R. (2015). *Teoría Monetaria Moderna: Un manual de macroeconomía sobre los sistemas soberanos monetarios.* Lola Books.

Wray, L. R., & Tymoigne, É. (2005). *Money; An alternative story* (Working Paper 45). Levy Economics Institute.

2

MODERN MONETARY THEORY'S VIEW OF THE NATURE OF MONEY AND ITS CRITICISMS

Introduction

In the previous chapter we discussed the Modern Monetary Theory's (MMT's) view of the origin of money, which inevitably led us to also discuss their view of its essence, albeit only partially (e.g. the concept of money-debt or its link with public authorities). In this chapter we will delve in detail into the approach used by MMT to conceive and analyse the nature of money, which is completely chartalist (or neo-chartalist, depending on how you look at it).

The beginnings of chartalism

We owe the term "chartalism" to the German economist George Friedrich Knapp, who in 1905 argued that practically all forms of money in history had been created by a state or an authority: "chartality has developed … for the State says that the pieces have such and such an appearance and that their validity is fixed by proclamation" (Knapp, 1924, p. 36). This view would thus contradict the then hegemonic – and already mentioned in Chapter 1 – evolutionary view of money of Carl Menger (1892), who considered money to be a decentralised and natural outcome of market forces. For Knapp, money is not a creature of the market, but a creature of the state. But, according to Wray (2000) and Tcherneva (2006, p. 76), not simply a creature of the law, as some authors such as Joseph Schumpeter (1954, p. 1090) and Davison (1972) might argue, understanding that money is accepted because legislators decide what kind of money should be used, but specifically a creature of the state's taxing power: the state establishes the money of account when it determines what will be "accepted at public pay offices" (Knapp, 1924, pp. 7–8), rather than through "jurisprudence". In other words, money would be accepted because it is necessary in order to pay taxes.

In fact, although we owe the term chartalism to Knapp, this conception of money had already been put forward by other authors. For example, Adam Smith himself in his masterpiece "The Wealth of Nations" wrote: "a prince, who should enact that a certain proportion of his taxes should be paid in a paper money of a certain kind, might thereby give a certain value

DOI: 10.4324/9781003371809-3

to this paper money" (Smith, 1994 [1776], p. 312), which is in line with the chartalist conception that taxes lead to money. Another example: the famous Russian novelist Leo Tolstoy wrote in 1886, in his essay "What Then Must We Do?", the following:

> any particular kind of money; it only obtains currency among people when it is forcibly demanded of them all. (...) And what then acquires value is not what is most convenient as a medium of exchange but what the government demands.
>
> *(Tolstoy, 1935 [1886], p. 66)*

In any case, this primitive conception of chartalism did not have much repercussion or diffusion, since not many other references to it are known. Some of them are pointed out by MMTer Forstater (2006), who reports that Say and John Stuart Mill too recognised that paper had value because it was "made efficient to discharge the perpetually recurring claims of public taxation" (Say, 1964 [1880], p. 280) and because the state had consented "to receive it in payment of taxes" (Mill, 1848, pp. 542–543). Furthermore, Mill pointed out that the sovereign state issuing the currency could arbitrarily fix its value and quantity (Mill, 1848, pp. 542–543).

But what gave chartalism a big boost was undoubtedly the publication of Knapp's book in 1905, although initially only in German-speaking regions (Ehnst, 2019), as it was not translated into English until 1924, incidentally, thanks to John Maynard Keynes, who was favourable to his thesis: "Knapp accepts as 'money', I think rightly, anything which the state undertakes to accept in its offices of payment, whether or not it is declared to be legal tender among the citizens" (Keynes, 1930, p. 6). The British economist thought that fiat money has to be explained in a chartalist logic:

> the age of chartalist or State money was reached when the State claimed the right to declare what thing should answer as money to the current money of account – when it claimed the right to enforce the dictionary but also to write the dictionary.
>
> *(Keynes, 1930, p. 5)*

Many German authors – among them well-known ones such as Knut Wicksell and Georg Simmel – gave their opinion on Knapp's thesis, although the general tone was one of scepticism and hostility (Ehnts, 2019). Precisely because of this geographical isolation of Knapp's work, another brilliant economist, in this case British – and already mentioned in the previous chapter – apparently independently reached similar conclusions: Mitchell Innes (1913, 1914, 1932). Curiously, his 1913 article was responded to by Keynes only a year later, showing his agreement with many of his ideas (Keynes, 1914). We have already advanced in the first chapter that Innes argued that money was not at all – nor was it referenced in – an object, but that it was a magnitude to measure debts and commitments; but to this he added that if such money was widely used it was because states took care of it using their tax prerogative. He focused mainly on the credit nature of money and never used the term chartalism (there is no indication that he was familiar with Knapp's work), but there is no doubt that he shared this view, as we can deduce from the following words:

> a government issue of money must be met by a corresponding tax. It is the tax which imparts to the obligation its "value". A dollar of money is a dollar, not because of the material of which it is made, but because of the dollar of tax which is imposed to redeem it.
>
> *(Innes, 1914, p. 165)*

Some years later, the prominent economist Abba Lerner was also a clear advocate of such an approach. In his 1947 article "Money as a Creature of the State", he stated that

> everyone who has obligations to the state will be willing to accept the pieces of paper with which he can settle the obligations, and all other people will be willing to accept these pieces of paper because they know that the taxpayers, etc., will accept them in turn.
>
> *(Lerner, 1947, p. 313)*

Everything suggests that at that time the chartalist thesis was widely supported, as can be deduced from the definition of money in the 1946 Encyclopaedia Britannica:

> If the government announces its willingness to accept a certain means of payment in the settlement of taxes, taxpayers will be willing to accept this means of payment because they can use it to pay taxes. Everyone else will then be willing to accept it because they can use it to buy things from the taxpayers, or to pay debts to them, or to make payments to others who have to make payments to the taxpayers, etc.
>
> *(Lerner, 1946, p. 693)*

Another prominent economist who adopted chartalism, albeit some decades later, was Hyman Minksy, who, according to Randall Wray (1998, p. 38), acknowledged in a private conversation that he owed an intellectual debt to chartalism and especially to Knapp. In his famous 1986 book "Stabilizing an unstable economy", Minsky wrote:

> in an economy where government debt is a major asset on the books of the deposit-issuing banks, the fact that taxes need to be paid gives value to the money of the economy … [T]he need to pay taxes gives value to the money of the economy … [T]he need to pay taxes means that people work and produce in order to get that in which taxes can be paid.
>
> *(Minsky, 1986, p. 231)*

This is a very clarifying precision: what gives value to money is not taxes directly, but the work that people need to do in order to pay taxes.

Finally, the chartalist view has been supported even from neo-Keynesian positions. Nobel laureate James Tobin wrote in his textbook (co-authored with Steven Golub):

> by its willingness to accept a designated asset in settlement of taxes and other obligations, the government makes that asset acceptable to any who have such obligations, and in turn to others who have obligations to them, and so on.
>
> *(Tobin & Golub, 1998, p. 27)*

And despite all this, chartalism has always been a minority and little-known view, which only MMT has been able to recover and extol thanks to its outstanding popularity.

Neo-chartalism (or MMT chartalism)

There has always been a lively debate about what really gives money its value (see, e.g., Louzek, 2011); if it is simply an abstract invention of the state that it creates at free will and without constraint, why does it have value? Why do people use it? And there are many different views on this. For example, the money-commodity view and especially its metallist variants consider that it is because money is made of or referenced to something that it does have value. There are other explanations that speak of an infinite loop of acceptability, i.e. that a person accepts money from the state because he knows that other people will accept it in exchange for the sale of goods and services, and those people will accept it in turn because they know that other people will do the same, and so on indefinitely. Other analysts argue that money has value because society has made it so by positioning it as a useful element for transactions and payments (see, e.g., Lawson, 2019, 2022). There are other views that argue that people accept the state's money insofar as the state manages it as a financial asset that provides a certain return to its holder (see, e.g., Rallo, 2017). And there are also others, such as the economist Joseph Schumpeter (1954), who point out that the acceptability of money is due to a legal issue: legislators decide what kind of money should be used.

But, as we have seen, chartalism offers a different answer to this question: what gives money its value is that the state forces people to pay taxes using that money. This makes people demand money from the state to pay those taxes and thus avoid legal reprisals.

Probably due to the growing number and importance of the archaeological research mentioned in the previous chapter that was in line with the chartalist view, in recent years this approach has received much more attention than in the past and several researchers have been bringing different contributions to the academy, both exclusively theoretical and historical. In fact, this is where we can find the origin of Modern Monetary Theory: in 1995 Warren Mosler (1995) explicitly combined the chartalist approach to money with the credit-money or debt-money view, laying the foundations of the theoretical framework we are concerned with in this book, which was soon further developed by Randall Wray (1998, 2014).

Among the historical research (for stages other than those of the Ancient Ages that we collected in the previous chapter) several stand out. MMTers Semenova and Wray (2015) focused on the connection between the chartalist view and the shaping of class society and the origin of money in ancient Greece, identifying parallels with Henry's (2004) aforementioned research on ancient Egypt. Both Pavlina Tcherneva (2002) and Mathew Forstater (2005), also proponents of MMT, argue that 19th-century European empires used taxation to force the indigenous populations of African colonies to work the land, since the only way for them to pay taxes denominated in the currency of the empire concerned was to collect a wage in exchange for contributing to production, which is entirely in line with the chartalist view. The money of the European empires began to be demanded and valued by the indigenous people simply because they needed it to pay the corresponding taxes, not for any other reason; if they had not been taxed, they would never have used the imperial currencies.

The link between colonisation and taxes exacted in imperial currencies, often referred to as monetisation of economic and social relations, was explored by other researchers such as Raymond Buell (1928), Walter Rodney (1972), Lovejoy (1974), Karl Polanyi (1977), Claude Ake (1981), Yolande Thomas (1984), and Perr Vries (2002), and not only focusing on colonial Africa but also on the Eurasian continent. In fact, as White (1996) develops, Karl Marx himself considered that this monetisation of taxes was key in the process of original accumulation and, therefore, in the development of the capitalist system:

the lands of the Russian and Indian communistic communities, which had to sell a portion of their product, and an ever-growing one at that, to get money for the taxes exacted by a merciless state despotism – often enough by torture.

(Marx, 1991, p. 860)

According to White: "the main reason which compels the worker to resort to the capitalist is to pay his taxes (…) the system of taxation in Russia was responsible for turning workers into proletarians" (White, 1996, p. 249). Indeed, some like Buell consider that taxation was the only way to put non-monetised communities to work: "one Governor, Sir Perry Girouard, is reported to say: 'We consider that taxation is the only possible method of compelling the native to leave his reserve for the purpose of seeking work'" (Buell, 1928, p. 331).

However, analysts such as Ake, Rodney, and Lovejoy point out that this phenomenon was not specific to the colonial era, but even preceded it. In Lovejoy's words for the Nigerian case:

Emirates [of Nigeria] paid their levies in cowries as well, so that the taxation system effectively assured that people participated in the market economy and used the currency, a policy remarkably similar to the one which the later colonial regimes pursued in their efforts to see their own currencies accepted.

(Lovejoy, 1974, p. 581)

In terms of purely theoretical research, the following stand out: Aschheim and Tavlas (1997) and Goldberg (2012) introduced chartalist money into a macroeconomic general equilibrium model, thus forming an alternative to ahistorical and only logical attempts to add money to a model that does not need it; Charles Goodhart (1998) relied on chartalism to elaborate a very harsh critique of the Optimal Currency Area paradigm and position himself against the creation of the single currency in the European Community, outlining some alternatives based on a different conception of money; Wray explored the connection between the early chartalist contributions of Knapp and Innes with the theoretical approaches of Joseph Schumpeter and John Maynard Keynes, and followed this up with the works of Abba Lerner, Hyman Minky, and Geoffrey Ingham (Wray, 2014); Stephanie Bell, John F. Henry, and Randall Wray (2004) used chartalism to challenge John Locke's exchange-based position, challenging his moral restrictions on property and undermining his theoretical defence of the accumulation process.

Thanks to this progressive and recent theoretical development, the current postulates of chartalism (or neo-chartalism) as used by MMT have become well defined. It would all start with the determination of a unit of account and the demand for tax obligations in that same unit of account: "taxes drive money. The government first creates a money of account (such as the dollar), and then imposes tax obligations in that national money of account" (Mitchell et al., 2019, p. 137). At this very moment, a money emerges that will be accepted and valued by the public. In Randall Wray's words:

The government first creates a money of account […] and then imposes tax obligations in that national money of account. […]. The government is then able to issue a currency that is also denominated in the same money of account […]. It is not necessary to "back" the currency with precious metal, nor is it necessary to enforce legal tender laws that require acceptance of the national currency [...] all the sovereign government needs to do is to promise "This note will be accepted in tax payment".

(Wray, 2012, p. 50)

Consequently, the essence of state money lies neither in the ability to create laws nor in the ability to print money, but in the government's ability to create the promise of the last resort (Ingham, 1998), i.e. to collect taxes and declare what will be accepted in payment offices for extinguishing the debt owed to the state (Tcherneva, 2006).

On the basis of this demand for taxes on the created unit of account, the public would have to set to work to obtain the monetary objects in which the unit of account is embodied, pay the taxes with them, and thus avoid legal sanctions. This would also imply that the economic agents would exchange products and make payments to each other with these monetary objects since they would always be useful because they would always have to pay taxes with them. The result of this would be that people would produce more goods and services, many of which would find their way into the hands of the relevant authorities. In the words of Warren Mosler and Mathew Forstater (1989):

> The monetary circuit begins with the vertical component, when the State describes that which it will accept for payment of taxes. The head tax is payable only in units of that currency. This causes taxpayers to offer goods and services in return for units of the currency. The State is now able to use its currency to purchase goods and services. This process results in the monetization of transactions in the State's currency. Taxpayers are continuously offering goods and services for sale, and soon other private sector agents who desire that which is offered for sale, seek the means of obtaining units of the currency demanded by the sellers.

This condition of taxation would be sufficient, according to MMT, to trigger the whole process described, since "as long as there is someone in the economy who is required to pay taxes denominated in the state's currency, that money will always be accepted" (Tcherneva, 2006, p. 76).

Taxes

Following the neo-chartalist approach, taxes do not serve to collect money. After all, if money is created by the state at its own free will and without limits because it is an abstract element, it is logical that it does not need to collect it. In fact, it could only collect it once it had created it, so the logical order would be: the state first create money, and then collect it, not the other way around. In Wray's words:

> once government has spent, then the fiat money is available to be transferred to the government to meet tax liabilities. As a matter of logic, the public cannot pay fiat money to the government to meet tax liabilities until the government has paid out fiat money to the public.

(Wray, 1998, p. 80)

Or to put it another way: "new created-money is the source of all government financing" (Bell, 1998, pp. 2–3).

Moreover, it is not only that the state does not need taxes to spend, but that collecting taxes would not serve that purpose, since taxes would not increase its spending capacity, but would simply destroy the money it had previously created through spending: "[revenues from taxes and bond sales] are not even capable of financing government spending since their collection implies their destruction" (Bell, 1998, p. 3).

The thesis that taxes do not finance public spending is not unique to MMT or neo-chartalism. Even a president of the New York Federal Reserve, Beardsley Ruml, explained in detail in 1946, in a paper provocatively entitled "Taxes for revenue are obsolete", that taxes were no longer necessary to finance the state (Ruml, 1946). And his thesis was well known even to Milton Friedman himself, who also considered that taxes were not necessary for the state to spend (Friedman, 1948). On the other hand, this idea is also shared by European economists who subscribe to the monetary circuit theory presented by Augusto Graziani (1990). In the words of Hassan Bougrine and Mario Seccareccia, who subscribe to this theory:

> [taxes] cannot be collected at the beginning of the [budget] period since the revenues from which they are drawn have not yet been distributed (...) According to the chartalist theory, money must be spent before it is collected as taxes.
>
> *(Bougrine & Seccareccia, 2002, p. 156)*

However, all this is not to say that taxes are useless to neo-chartalists. As we have already seen, what gives value to money from a chartalist point of view is the imposition of taxes, so taxes are necessary for the currency to be demanded and for economic agents to carry out productive activities in order to earn the money they need to pay those taxes. The curious thing about this view is that "taxes are considered an incentive, rather than an impediment, to economic activity" (Kregel, 2020, p. 2) as is central from orthodox views of economics. We also saw in Chapter 1 that this institutional set-up would have been applied in prehistoric times so that temple and palace authorities could centralise real resources and then distribute them according to their own political considerations. Consequently, another fundamental function of taxation would be to enable the redistribution of real resources by the authorities: "taxation is the *motor* behind the transfer of real resources from subjects to authority. Money is the *vehicle*" (Tcherneva, 2016, p. 6). If taxes did not exist, private economic agents would have no need to sell labour or products to the authorities, so the authorities would not be able to purchase anything (and thus not be able to redistribute anything either). MMT extrapolates this historical account to the present day: current tax systems allow the public sector to absorb real resources from the private sector (labour, materials, energy supply, etc.), and then redistribute them back to the same sector, but in the form of public goods, services, and benefits. As Pavlina Tcherneva explains:

> the modern state, as in ancient Greece, continues to serve a redistributive function in the economy, where it collects real resources (labor) from the private sector, and then redistributes them back to the private sector "more equitably" in the form of infrastructure, public education, government research and development, and via any other social welfare functions it has been asked to fulfill by voters. The role of taxation in modern market economies remains the same as in ancient times: it is not a "funding mechanism", but a "real resource transfer mechanism".
>
> *Tcherneva (2016, p. 9)*

But the functions of taxes would not stop there. They would not only serve to give value for money and redistribute real resources but would have other important functions. The aforementioned former Federal Reserve Chairman Ruml explained this in a prescient way in 1946. Firstly, taxes would also serve to destroy money, reduce the economic capacity of the population, and thus affect the economy and the value of the currency, since economic agents, by paying taxes, would be left with less money to consume or invest. Consequently, the state could use taxes to stabilise the economy and the value of the currency.

Another important function of taxes highlighted by Ruml would be to penalise or favour certain behaviours; for example, tobacco taxes are set for health reasons to discourage smoking, or green taxes are set for ecological reasons to discourage pollution. Another function would be to help certain businesses; for example, tariffs raise the price of imported products, which is good for a domestic industry that competes on price with those products. And the last function of taxes that Ruml pointed out is that they would help to value certain goods and services produced by the state; for example, social contributions is a tax that helps citizens to value the social benefits provided by the social security system, such as unemployment or pensions.

These points are shared and underlined by supporters of MMT (Wray, 2012, 2016; Fazi & Mitchell, 2018; Kelton, 2020, p. 48). In the words of Thomas Fazi and William Mitchell (2018):

> Taxation is first and foremost a way to redistribute economic (and therefore political) power between classes, as well as a means to alter the allocation of resources away, for example by encouraging or discouraging certain industries and/or products (think taxes on alcohol or carbon taxes).
>
> *(Fazi & Mitchell, 2018)*

Kelton notes that "states can use taxes to encourage or discourage certain behaviours. In this way, they can improve public health, combat climate change or discourage risky speculation in financial markets by enacting a tax on tobacco, carbon or financial transactions" (Kelton, 2020, p. 48).

However, some have pointed out that MMT pays a lot of attention to two of the main functions outlined above – giving value to the currency and withdrawing money from the economy to stabilise its value – but has largely neglected the other functions despite their importance in achieving certain social goals (Murphy, 2015, 2019; Avi-Yonah, 2011; Holt, 2017; Roth, 2019; Baker & Murphy, 2020). Indeed, based on this critique, the economist Murphy, sympathetic to MMT, has proposed to develop

> a modern theory of taxation (MTT) that, building on the understanding derived from MMT that tax is not a tool for government revenue maximisation, and can deliver new perspectives on the use of tax as a critical instrument in economic and social policy management.
>
> *(Murphy, 2019, p. 138)*

Another interesting contribution is that of Holt (2017), who uses in his work the chartalist thesis of MMT to propose policies that avoid some distributional conflicts and foster a sense of fairness.

Indeed, the redistributive nature of taxation has not been much addressed by MMT. Some positions can be found on the part of its founders, but they are purely personal and, in fact, may be contradictory to each other: while Randall Wray is of the opinion that "MMT is not opposed to using taxes on high incomes and high wealth in an attempt to reduce inequality" (Wray, 2012, p. 146), or Thomas Fazi and William Mitchell consider that tax havens should be closed "not with the aim of 'raising more money' but of creating a more equitable society" (Fazi & Mitchell, 2018), or Stephanie Kelton states that "there are very good reasons to tax the richest more and it is something that needs to be done (...) to help rebalance the balance of power" (Wray, 2012, p. 146), or Stephanie Kelton states that "there are very good reasons to tax the richest and it is something that needs to be done (...) to help rebalance rebalance the distribution of income and wealth" (Kelton, 2020, p. 89), Warren Mosler is self-recognised as "a strong supporter of the core Tea Party values of lower taxes, limited government, competitive market solutions, and a return to personal responsibility" (Mosler, 2010). The latter is what has led some heterodox economists such as Epstein (2019) to be suspicious of the ideological positioning of MMT, understanding that it may be a tool that serves the interests of the wealthy classes. This is also shared by some members of civil organisations in favour of achieving greater tax justice, such as the Tax Justice Network or ATTAC, as they note with alarm how the MMT ignores or leaves in a secondary place what for them is the cornerstone for achieving more equitable and prosperous societies.

At this point, it should be clearer to understand why it was said that the view on the origin and nature of money has important implications for economic policy. Viewing money as a commodity – or as functioning as a commodity – that arose spontaneously in the heat of market transactions inevitably leads to the idea that the state needs to collect or otherwise obtain it before it can use it. Only when money is conceived of as a debt that the state issues at will can one come to the conclusion that taxes are not necessary to finance public expenditure. Taking a stand on a simple, seemingly unimportant theoretical aspect really changes everything.

Criticisms

The chartalist or neo-chartalist approach has been one of the most criticised aspects of MMT, both from orthodox and heterodox – including post-Keynesian and Marxist – approaches. This shows that chartalism is a minority perspective that has failed to convince many analysts. The orthodox critique is quite simple and not worth elaborating on: money would not be a creature of the state but of the market, since it would have arisen spontaneously in the private sector thanks to the mercantile activities carried out among the different economic agents. Consequently, taxes would not drive money but simply collect it so that the state could spend it.

On the other hand, heterodox criticisms of chartalism are much more complex and enriching. In the following, we will review the most important of them, focusing on two key and interrelated aspects of chartalism: the extent to which taxation drives money, and the extent to which the state can determine its value.

Criticisms of taxation driving money

Some economists have questioned MMT's interpretation of the writings of the father of the term chartalism, Georg Friedrich Knapp, on the grounds that he did not actually argue that money is driven by state taxation. For example, post-Keynesian economists Rochon and Vernengo (2003) point out that Knapp did not so much emphasise taxation as the main cause of the acceptability of money, but that this would correspond more to Lerner. According to them, Knapp would have merely "suggested that money is the creature of the state because the latter determines the unit of account" (Rochon & Vernengo, 2003, p. 59). For his part, the economist Juan Ramón Rallo (2017) takes an extract from Knapp's original book to argue that he understood that what gives value to money is not taxes but the legal organisation of a community of payments, not necessarily the state:

> Each payment community can create its own unit of value for itself. The state can do this because it is a community of payments, not because it is the state. The state is only the most familiar and the oldest of the payment communities, but it is not the only one. It is the legal organisation of a community of payments that creates the unity of value. This is an important extension of the point of view with which we started the book: that the state is the only community of payments.
>
> *(Georg Friedrich Knapp, 1905, quoted in Rallo, 2017)*

And it is true that one cannot find in Knapp's writings any strong assertions in support of the idea that it is taxes that give value to money, as other chartalists such as Mitchell Innes or Abba Lerner made clear.

In any case, this idea pointed out by Knapp that the state is not the only institution that can create money is not necessarily a challenge to chartalism according to MMT proponents Eric Tymoigne and Randall Wray (2013), who already addressed this issue when it was raised by Thomas Palley (2012). The latter harshly criticised chartalism by pointing out that "unfortunately, MMT sets up unnecessary controversy by asserting that the obligation to pay taxes is the exclusive reason for the development of money" (Palley, 2015a, p. 2), since the private sector can create money spontaneously, and for this he gives the example of innovations such as Bitcoin, which "has absolutely nothing to do with the state and cannot be used to pay taxes, but is acquiring 'moneyness'" (Palley, 2015b, p. 60).

Eric Tymoigne and Randall Wray's response (2013) clarified that it is not the case that taxation is a necessary condition for money to exist, but merely sufficient:

> MMT does argue that imposition by authorities of obligations (including taxes, fines, fees, tithes and tribute) is logically sufficient to "drive" acceptance of the government's currency (...) But to be clear, MMT does not argue that taxes are necessary to drive a currency or money – critics conflate the logical argument that taxes are sufficient by jumping to the conclusion that MMT believes there can be no other possibility.
>
> *(Tymoigne & Wray, 2013, pp. 9–10)*

In any case, most critics of chartalism do not even accept the idea that taxes are sufficient to give rise to money and endow it with value but find other explanations for it, however much the state may play an important role in such a phenomenon. Most post-Keynesian economists and those who subscribe to the theory of the monetary circuit consider that the origin of money is to be found in private finance. Their criticisms are presented below in basically chronological order.

Parguez and Seccareccia (2000), based on the monetary circuit theory proposed by Graziani (1997), argue that throughout history, viable monetary systems existed at times when taxes were quite insignificant, and that it was the circulation of bank liabilities, permitted and supported by states, that allowed most transactions: "what matters, therefore, was not whether tax liabilities were of any significance but rather whether, largely through the legal system, the state endorsed existing banks by allowing them to issue debts on themselves" (Parguez & Seccareccia, 2000, 120). In other words, money was not accepted and used because it had to pay taxes on its unit of account, as the chartalist version maintains, but because the state supported the operation of the banks through its laws, which were the ones who put into circulation most of the money used.

Perry Mehrling is of the same opinion, pointing out that "private finance is a better logical place to start when trying to understand modem money" (Mehrling, 2000, 402). According to his view, the state is a creation of the citizens, so it is only able to impose taxes as long as the citizens allow it to do so.

Rochon and Vernengo (2003) hold a similar view: for them the main explanation for the existence and acceptability of money does not lie in the state's ability to tax the relevant unit of account, since there is no need for a powerful or taxing state for money to circulate and the economy to function: "one can certainly presume that firms will produce even if states are relatively weak, and hence unable to tax or force payment in a particular token" (Rochon & Vernengo, 2003, p. 61). Their main explanation for the existence and acceptability of money lies in the conditions created by institutions that bridge the present and the future by allowing economic agents to be willing to use money: "it is the fact that bank loans must be repaid that ensures the utilization of bank money, and money becomes a creature of banks rather than a creature of the state" (Rochon & Vernengo, 2003, p. 61). But this is not to say that the state cannot play an important role: "taxes and state money *may enter* the circuit later, and prove important to the extent that banks actually decide to provide credit in state money" (Rochon & Vernengo, 2003, p. 61, my emphasis). Therefore, according to their view, the state and taxes may be important in the acceptability of money, but only as subsequent and subordinate elements to private credit and, in any case, without being necessary for it.

Eladio Febrero (2009) also considers that money is not accepted because the state imposes taxes, but because it is basically a social convention in which private banks play a central role as the main creators and dynamisers of money: "in the real world as well, money is accepted, first, because it is a social convention and, second, because there are always people, directly or indirectly indebted to banks and they can use it to cancel pending debts" (2009, pp. 524–525). However, he also qualifies that state taxes intensify the acceptability of money:

> when agents are also indebted to the state, because of taxes, this increases the acceptability of money. And this may be the "ultimate" motive to accept money in a transaction when the state issues its own money to monetize public spending.
>
> *(Febrero, 2009, p. 525)*

In any case, Febrero also seems to place the origin of the acceptability of money in society in general and in banks in particular, relegating the state to second place.

But there are other views that question chartalism without the need to focus on bank credit. Colander (2019) is one of the economists who admits that the origin of money, understood as an accounting system for recording and cancelling debts, could respond to the account presented by chartalism, but that in his opinion it "evolved from the bottom up along the lines proposed by Martin Shubik (Shubik & Smith, 2016), not from the state down" (Colander, 2019, p. 64). In any case, whatever its origin, Colander shares Henry Macleod's (1899) thesis that money is a creature of society, not necessarily of the state:

the state is not necessarily involved with the essence of money. Any large agent with outstanding debt, for example the church, who was willing to accept payment of that debt in fulfillment of an obligation to it, could have created an alternative credit money. Money is a creature of society, not of the state.

(Colander, 2019, p. 64)

That is, although money is credit and the state can create credit, so could other economic agents. The truth is that MMT at no point denies that, in fact, in Chapter 5 we will see that it shares precisely such a view; the difference is that MMT places state money at the pinnacle of all types of money that exist, so that all forms of private money created by economic agents would be subordinated to the money issued and regulated by the state.

Colander (2019) also considers that at present state money dominates private money, but that this need not be the case in the future: "in a globalized economy, with advanced computational and information processing tools, we can expect competition among state and private monies and units of account in ways that we have not seen before" (Colander, 2019, p. 66). However, from a chartalist and MMT point of view, such a future in which private money takes precedence over public money does not seem at all likely (Garzón et al., 2023a).

A similar – albeit more precise – view, which also does not share the chartalist postulates, is Lawson's (2019) theory of money positioning. According to Lawson, money in general is never a debt in the sense suggested by MMT, so it would not be entirely correct for taxes to explain the overall demand for currency. In their own words:

Currency is not after all a form of debt but rather positioned debt, with its uses governed by (state-influenced) community accepted rights and obligations. In consequence, there is no redeeming of currency anyway, and so no puzzle (about how redeeming is be achieved) to be solved. Instead, it is the community accepted rights and obligations themselves that determine that the government must accept the community's currency, or money, when it is offered in payment of taxes. That basically is the whole story. No additional dubious government promise of any sort is required.

(Lawson, 2019, p. 121)

Therefore, since state money is not a debt to be redeemed through taxation, taxation would play no role in determining money, however much the state influences in an important way the rights and obligations of the community that govern money.

In a similar vein, the Keynesian economist Prates (2020) points out, building on Davidson's (1972) thesis, that the acceptability of money is not only driven by taxes as the chartalist view points out but also by contracts and monetary conventions:

money is money of account, a credit–debt relation and an asset, being accepted because it is both a convention and a creature of the state. Since taxes are a class of monetary contracts, the version of the "state theory of money" focusing on contracts (led by Davidson, 1972) is more general than the "taxes-drive-money view" (that is, MMT).

(Prates, 2020, p. 501)

On the other hand, we encounter the admittedly different criticisms of Marxist economists. They consider that money does not originate in the prerogative of the state to impose taxes as the Chartalist thesis claims but arises spontaneously in the course of the social development of production and trade as a universal medium of exchange (Marx, 1894; Winczewski, 2021). For this, no state intervention or regulation is needed:

> money is a commodity that emerges spontaneously and proceeds to act as the organizer of the total social labor, when production is dominated by private, autonomous, and independent units. It is an endogenous creation of markets that does not require any external authority to bring it into existence.
>
> *(Lapavitsas & Aguila, 2020, p. 6)*

Consequently, for Marxists money is not a creature of the state, but of the private capitalist sector, including banks: "MMT creates the illusion that this whole process starts and ends with the government when it really starts within the capitalist sector including the banking system" (Roberts, 2019, p. 9).

As can be seen, Marxist economists agree with more orthodox approaches – no doubt because of their common view of money as a commodity – that money originates in the heat of commercial exchanges, however much they put the focus on the capitalist system and not on the individual as the orthodox do; but they also agree with post-Keynesian economists that private banks play a crucial role in the origin and mobilisation of money. In fact, Marxists focus on the fact that 96% of the money in circulation is the result of the creation of private institutions, so they recognise the primacy of this sector (Booth, 2019): "the capitalist economy does not need the state to supply it with money – it can create credit money privately and endogenously" (Lapavitsas & Aguila, 2020, p. 8).

Now, Marxists also recognise the powerful role of the state in the regulation of money, but they historically confine it to the fiat money era, not to other epochs. The error of MMT would therefore be that they arbitrarily transfer the view on the fiat money era to the whole of economic history (Shaikh, 2016, pp. 687–688), in which "the demand for money was always a token created by the state" (Winczewski, 2021, p. 12), whereas Marxists would recognise the historical diversity of monetary forms (Lapavitsas, 2016, p. 235).

Many of the critics of chartalism often support historical evidence. For example, Mayhew (2019) doubts that the process of money creation has historically been as chartalism describes; namely, first states establish a unit of account, then tax it, and finally money denominated in those units acquires value. His argument is that Western states established their units of account at the same time as the monetisation of these units developed, not before:

> in the U.S., in the U.K. and generally in Western history the development of units of account and the growth of monetization were more or less simultaneous processes. In Western Europe, the growth of nation states and of taxation followed.
>
> *(Mayhew, 2019, p. 131)*

However, proponents of MMT have responded forcefully to these criticisms by pointing out that, even in the past, money was also chartalist and of a credit nature, not only because the metal currencies used were nothing more than a monetary instrument of the debt of the authorities, but also because many other systems of debt compensation than currencies were used. For example, Randall Wray (2004) draws on the writings of Mitchell Innes to argue that in medieval times tallysticks were widely used for trade and even tax payments, which were simply pieces of wood with symmetrically pointed notches on both sides and which were divided so that the two parties to the agreement kept the corresponding accounting records:

> For many centuries, how many we do not know, the principal instrument of commerce was neither the coin nor the private token, but the tally,* (Lat. talea. Fr. taille. Ger. Kerbholz), a stick of squared hazel-wood, notched in a certain manner to indicate the amount of the purchase or debt. The name of the debtor and the date of the transaction were written on two opposite sides of the stick, which was then split down the middle in such a way that the notches were cut in half, and the name and date appeared on both pieces of the tally. The split was stopped by a cross-cut about an inch from the base of the stick, so that one of the pieces was shorter than the other.
>
> *(Innes, 1913, p. 394)*

Actually, that these tallysticks were used for trade would only reveal the credit nature of money, not the chartalist one. But Mitchell Innes also explained that these instruments were also used to pay taxes, and offered some empirical evidence to support his thesis:

> This is well seen in medieval England, where the regular method used by the government for paying a creditor was by "raising a tally" on the Customs or on some other revenue-getting department, that is to say by giving to the creditor as an acknowledgment of indebtedness a wooden tally. The Exchequer accounts are full of entries such as the following: "To Thomas de Bello Campo, Earl of Warwick, by divers tallies raised this day, containing 500 marks delivered to the same Earl". "To … by one tally raised this day in the name of the Collectors of the small customs in the Port of London containing $40. The system was not finally abandoned till the beginning of the nineteenth century."
>
> *(Innes, 1913, p. 398)*

For Innes, this tallystick was simply a technological descendant of the Babylonian clay Tablet, as well as an ascendant of the modern banknote (Innes, 1913, p. 403). In other words, it would not matter what material the monetary instrument used was made of, but only that it served to discharge debts. According to Wray, "coins were typically a nearly insignificant part of the 'money supply', and most tax collections brought in far more hazelwood tally sticks than coins" (Wray, 2016, p. 4). The use of precious metal coins would be explained simply because "they outlasted the sovereigns that issued them and many of them contained bright shiny metal that blinds reason" (Wray, 2016, p. 5), not because of their intrinsic value.

On the other hand, Randall Wray (2016) also draws on Grub's (2015) analyses of the early American colonial experience to support the credit and chartalist nature of money in earlier times. In the colony of Virginia, the authorities created their own paper money which they equated with the currency of the metropolis and on which they levied taxes in order to expand their political room for manoeuvre, not to bring in more money. In fact, when the authorities collected their paper money, they did not use it to spend, but burnt it: "the taxes were not to 'raise revenue', indeed, when the paper notes were received in tax payments, they were burnt, not spent" (Wray, 2016, p. 7). This would be in line with the chartalist postulates that taxes do not serve to finance spending, but to give value to the currency and mobilise real resources, as well as to destroy the money created through spending.

Against this display of historical cases, some have pointed out that these experiences refer to economies with very different institutions from today's, and therefore would not be useful to explain the present economic reality. For example, Mehrling (2000) points out that

> the government of a country like the United States bears very little resemblance to a colonial governor who imposes taxes in order to monetize a primitive economy. For most of its history, the United States has been characterized by a rather strong private economy and a rather weak central government, punctuated by moments of increased government power during national crises such as wars. It is no accident that we did not achieve a permanent central bank until 1913.
>
> *(Mehrling, 2000, p. 402)*

Other analysts, such as Huber (2014), point out that, although in the past authorities were able to spend before collecting thanks to certain accounting instruments, "with regard to contemporary settings, however, there is no such evidence. Today, it is primarily the banks that decide if and how much money to create" (Huber, 2014, p. 47).

And yet, some others, such as Rochon and Vernengo, take just the opposite view: although they consider that throughout history banks and other financial institutions would have played the leading role, today, due to the institutional design of modern economies, "Modern money is chartal money no doubt" (Rochon & Vernengo, 2003, p. 66).

The latter has been used by Tymoigne and Wray to protect themselves from criticism by considering that, even if in the past money would not have been chartalist, the important thing is that today it would be:

> even if the "origins" of money are hidden in the "mists of time", we can look around the modern world and note that almost without exception each national government adopts its own money of account, imposes tax obligations in that unit, and issues currency as well as central bank reserves also denominated in that unit.
>
> *(Tymoigne & Wray, 2013, p. 10)*

Another typical criticism of chartalism is that there are developing economies – usually in Latin America – where, despite the fact that states tax in their currency, the currency does not achieve widespread acceptability. For example, Grishchenko et al. (2021) point out that

> it is not clear how the value of money and the level of taxation relate to each other, how differences in the demand for money manifest themselves in countries with different levels of taxation, etc.; there are examples of Latin American countries where the demand for domestic money fell even though they were the only ones accepted for tax purposes.
>
> *(Grishchenko et al., 2021, p. 13)*

Precisely in this respect there is an interesting historical study: that of Kauko (2018), which is located in the Finnish experience after the Russo-Swedish war in 1808–1809. The Finnish government, having become a Grand Duchy under Russia, tried to replace the Swedish currency – by then in circulation – with Russian currency. According to his conclusions, taxation was an efficient tool to make roubles valuable and accepted, as "tax collectors as private individuals were able to sell Russian money to taxpayers because roubles were needed for tax payments.

As tax-day approached, the market rate for roubles strengthened" (Kauko, 2018, p. 14). In fact, government expenditures in Russian currency managed to displace other means of payment in trade between private parties, which is also supported by the findings of Neovius (1899) and Piping (1961):

> the Russian army and military personnel paid in roubles, thereby putting them into circulation. Taxes were often paid in roubles in southern Finland during and immediately after the war, simply because the Russian army had been spending money in those areas.
>
> *(Kauko, 2018, p. 14)*

However, Kauko also concludes that the tax tool was not enough to make the Russian currency displace the Swedish currency, as it continued to be used to a significant degree:

> Due to a resilient trade surplus with Sweden and the resulting flood of Swedish money into Finland, bans on the riksdaler were largely ineffective. Taxation proved a particularly clumsy tool for leveraging the switch to roubles. Taxpayers almost forced the government to accept payments in a foreign currency. Even the government had to use Swedish money. Issuing roubles was of limited use.
>
> *(Kauko, 2018, p. 1)*

Kauko (2018, p. 15) concludes by asking why the currency exchange in the 1840s finally succeeded. In his opinion, it was not because of the imposition of tribute, but because a more attractive exchange rate was established than in previous attempts and because the silver standard and network effects lent greater credibility.

Consequently, this experience would support the chartalist thesis insofar as taxation gives validity to a currency, but would not support it insofar as it does not have to achieve the exclusive use of the currency. This perhaps suggests to us that the degree of taxation is important, something Rochon and Vernengo (2003) point out using a passage from the Chartalist Abba Lerner: "before the tax collectors were strong enough to earn for the State the title of creator of money, the best the State could do was tie its currency to gold or silver" (Lerner, 1947, p. 314). According to them, money is a creature of the state only after tax collection becomes relevant. This connects us to the next type of criticism.

Criticisms of the determination of the value of money

Beyond the criticisms of "taxes drive money", there is another type of criticism that focuses more on questioning the state's ability to establish the value of the money it creates. One of the first criticisms in this sense comes from Joseph Schumpeter, who, while acknowledging that taxing a token may confer a certain value on it, in no way determines its value:

> Had Knapp merely asserted that the state may declare an object or warrant or token (bearing a sign) to be lawful money and that a proclamation to this effect that a certain pay-token or ticket will be accepted in discharge of taxes must go a long way toward imparting some value to that pay-token or ticket, he would have asserted a truth but a platitudinous one. Had

he asserted that such action of the state will determine the value of that pay-token or ticket, he would have asserted an interesting but false proposition.

(Schumpeter, 1954, quoted in Roberts, 2019, p. 5)

As can be seen, Schumpeter validates the chartalist thesis that taxes drive money, although he denies that such action completely determines its value, however much it may affect it to some degree.

The Marxist approach is probably the most critical of the state's determination of the value of money (Roberts, 2019; Winczewski, 2021). According to this view, the state is the social agent most capable of sustaining and influencing the unit of account of money, but it has no direct power over the spontaneously operating measure of value, which would be what matters when talking about money. In the words of Lapavitsas and Aguila:

There are no tribal assemblies, priests of Babylon, and state bureaucrats engaging in extraordinary mental feats to commensurate commodities (and a myriad other human relations). Commensuration emerges spontaneously through regular production and exchange as diverse human labors are made equivalent to each other in practice. The abstraction is real, though it took the establishment of capitalism and the genius of classical political economy for it to be recognized. It provides the material bedrock of the money commodity on which the state is able to fix the unit of account.

Lapavitsas and Aguila (2020, p. 7)

Finally, post-Keynesian authors have also been particularly critical of this point. For example, according to Eladio Febrero (2009), the state cannot fully declare what it can use to pay taxes "because there are some factors (workers struggling for higher wages, or energy and raw material shortages) affecting the purchasing power of state money" (Febrero, 2009, p. 524). In other words, there are economic phenomena beyond the state's control that determine the value of essential products in the economy, so that it would be impossible for the state to determine their value on the basis of its prerogative to tax and create money.

However, these criticisms do not seem very fortunate, because, in fact, neither the original chartalists nor the neo-chartalists of the MMT seem to speak at any point about the degree of value that taxes confer on money; they simply argue that taxation gives acceptability and value to money, but not by how much. The concrete value of money will depend on the criteria used to define and measure it. It is not the same to measure the value of money in comparison to some products as to others, and this is central to the MMT vision. For example, the founder of MMT, Warren Mosler, and other strong proponents of this theoretical framework, such as Mathew Forstater or Pavlina Tcherneva, have explained that the state has full capacity to give a fixed absolute value or price to its currency through its purchases in the private sector, and therefore in relation to those products, but that all other goods and services exchanged in the market will in turn have certain relative prices that are not controlled by the state, although they will ultimately depend on the fixed and original value of the state currency (Mosler & Forstater, 1989; Mosler, 2023; Tcherneva, 2016). Samuel Levey built a basic model and concluded that "the price level is a function of prices paid by government when it spends", so "'monopoly money' can naturally explain the source of the price level" (Levey, 2021, pp. 1–2). If critics mean that the state cannot determine all prices in the economy, then they agree with the neo-chartalist view using MMT. We will delve more into this in Chapter 6.

We reach the same conclusion if we use the "control space" approach of Garzón et al. (2023b) – presented in Chapter 1: it could be argued that the state's ability to determine the value of its currency is limited to its space of control or influence (the territory over which it exercises its power), so that, if the currency moves through other spaces of control, the exact value will depend on more factors (including the value of other currencies and the productive and export structures of the interacting economies) and will be filtered by the exchange rate between the corresponding currencies. This view would also be compatible with that of the critics just noted, and would not necessarily challenge the essence of the chartalist view: the state cannot set the value of its currency in relation to all goods and services produced in the economy, only to those that move only in its space of control.

Conclusions

MMT relies on the chartalist view of money, which has long held that taxation gives value and acceptability to money, making it a creature of the state and not of the market. In its refined or neo-chartalist view, MMT points out that it is enough for a state to establish a unit of account and to demand taxes on that unit for it to be valued and accepted by the public. The explanation is that households and firms, in order to pay these taxes, have to sell their labour force or sell products in order to acquire the state money, since it is the only money with which they can pay their tax debts. Along the way, the state acquires goods and services with which it can achieve its policy goals. Consequently, the function of taxation is not to finance state spending, but to give value to its currency and allow the centralisation of goods and services from the private to the public sector, which are then redistributed again in a different way – usually more equitable way in democratic and advanced economies. Even so, taxes would also have other functions such as stabilising the currency and the economy, providing incentives and disincentives for certain behaviours, helping certain firms, or allowing the valuation of certain services that are free to the public.

This view has been criticised by many, both orthodox and heterodox (Marxists, post-Keynesians, and circuitists). A common reproach is that MMT considers it a necessary condition for money to exist that a state demands taxes, although this has been countered by some proponents of MMT, who argue that this is not a necessary condition but simply sufficient: money could originate and exist without the need for a state to collect taxes, although they themselves maintain that the historical evidence does not point in that direction.

No doubt because of their overlapping views of money as a commodity, Marxists and orthodox agree that money is not a creature of the state, but arises in the heat of economic transactions in the private sector. Post-Keynesians and circuitists are more refined in this respect, since they consider that money, understood in this case as debt and not as a commodity, is a creation of the banks, so that money exists and is widely used thanks to the role played by banks in economies. However, in many cases they recognise that the state can increase or intensify the acceptability of bank money through taxation, but in any case the origin of money and the cornerstone of it is to be found in the lending operations of banks.

There are other critiques of chartalism that focus on the social convention nature of money. For example, Lawson (2019) points out that any debt could be positioned as money in a society if it makes rights and obligations revolve around it so that neither a state nor its taxes would be necessary for money to exist. There is also Davidson's (1972) view that money is what it is because it is used in contracts and monetary conventions, and even if the state articulates many of these contracts, it would only be one actor among many.

Finally, many of these criticisms, especially those of a Marxist nature, question whether the state can determine the value of the currency it creates. However, this type of criticism does not seem appropriate because the MMT has never asserted such a thing; it has simply limited itself to pointing out that the State can fix the value of its currency in relation to the products it buys directly, not the value of its currency in relation to the rest of the products, whose relative prices would oscillate according to many other factors, even if they were linked to the absolute price fixed by the State with its currency.

Finally, as can be seen, there are many solid approaches that question the chartalist thesis of the MMT. In the opinion of this writer, with the exception of the orthodox and Marxist approaches (for conceiving money as a commodity), all of them have their part of reason. Chartalism makes a fundamental contribution to the existence and acceptability of money, but it does not cover the whole story. First, it seems certain that theoretically there could be a type of money in general use that was neither created by the state nor driven by its taxes, although at present this seems very complicated because of the enormous influence of the state on all economic matters. Secondly, there are other very important elements in explaining the acceptability of money that are not considered by chartalism, such as the number and scope of money contracts as a whole, the social standing of any debt, and the banks' own lending operations (the latter discussed in Chapter 5). Third and finally, taxing in one currency may not result in that currency being widely accepted by the public, as the public may also use a different one that gives them greater stability and confidence. Although we will discuss this in more detail in Chapter 3, I anticipate that this would not necessarily challenge the chartalist thesis, since such state currencies are not usually displaced by private currencies, but by other state currencies issued by states with greater international monetary power and influence. Therefore, taxes would still drive the money, although in this case it would be the taxes of another state.

In any case, even if we do not consider the chartalist thesis to be completely valid, this would not imply rejecting the rest of the teachings of the MMT, especially those of economic policy. And this is even acknowledged by some critics. For example, Lawson notes, referring to his challenge to chartalism, that he is not sure that "the arguments that follow in themselves necessarily undermine any MMT policy stance, at least under current conditions" (Lawson, 2019, p. 109). Eladio Febrero, another critic of chartalism, takes the same view: "actually, we believe that the policy implications that can be drawn from neo-chartalism are essentially correct" (Febrero, 2009, p. 524). Consequently, however stimulating and necessary the theoretical debate on chartalism may be, it is not entirely relevant for those who are more interested in the political implications of MMT.

References

Ake, C. (1981). *A political economy of Africa*. Longman Press.

Aschheim, J., & Tavlas, G. S. (1997). Money. In T. Cate, G. Harcourt, & D. C. Colander (Eds.), *An encyclopedia of Keynesian economics* (pp. 444–450). Edward Elgar Publishing Ltd.

Avi-Yonah, R. (2011). Taxation as regulation: Carbon tax, health care tax, bank tax and other regulatory taxes. *Accounting, Economics, and Law, 1*(1), Article 6.

Baker, A., & Murphy, R. (2020). Modern monetary theory and the changing role of tax in society. *Social Policy & Society, 19*(3), 454–469.

Bell, S. (1998). *Can Taxes and Bonds Finance Government spending?* (Working Paper No. 244). Levy Economics Institute. https://ssrn.com/abstract=115128 or http://dx.doi.org/10.2139/ssrn.115128

Bell, S., Henry, J. F., & Wray, L. R. (2004). A chartalist critique of John Locke's theory of property, accumulation, and money: Or is it moral to trade your nuts for gold? *Review of Social Economy*, *62*(1), 51–65.

Booth, A. (2019, September 6). Marxism vs Modern monetary theory. In *Defense of Marxism*. https://www.marxist.com/marxism-vs-modern-monetary-theory-mmt.htm

Bougrine, H., & Seccareccia, M. (2002). Money, taxes, public spending, and the state within a Circuitist perspective. *International Journal of Political Economy*, *32*(3), 58–79.

Buell, R. L. (1928). *The native problem in Africa* (Vol. 1). Macmillan.

Colander, D. (2019). Are modern monetary theory's lies "plausible lies"? *Real-World Economics Review*, *89*, 62–71.

Davidson, P. (1972). *Money and the real world*. Macmillan.

Ehnts, D. H. (2019). *Knapp's 'state theory of money' and its reception in German academic discourse* (Working Paper No. 115/2019). Berlin Institute for International Political Economy (IPE) Berlin School of Economics and Law.

Epstein, G. A. (2019). What's wrong with modern money theory? A policy critique. *Review of Radical Political Economics*, *51*(2), 262–270.

Fazi, T., & Mitchell, B. (2018). Tax havens must be closed, but not for the reasons you think. *Green European Journal*. https://www.greeneuropeanjournal.eu/tax-havens-must-be-closed-but-not-for-the-reasons-you-think/

Febrero, E. (2009). Three difficulties with neo-chartalism. *Journal of Post Keynesian Economics*, *31*(3), 523–541.

Forstater, M. (2005). Taxation and primitive accumulation: The case of colonial Africa. *Research in Political Economy*, *22*, 51–65.

Forstater, M. (2006). Tax-driven money: Additional evidence from the history of thought, economic history, and economic policy. In J. Setterfield (Ed.), *Complexity, endogenous money, and exogenous interest rates* (pp. 69–86). Edward Elgar.

Forstater, M., & Mosler, W. (2005). The natural rate of interest is zero. *Journal of Economic Issues*, *39*(2), 535–542. https://doi.org/10.1080/00213624.2005.11506832

Friedman, M. (1948). A monetary and fiscal framework for economic stability. *American Economic Review*, *38*(3), 245–264.

Garzón, E., Cruz, E., Medialdea, B., & Sánchez, C. (2023a). Money or crypto-gold? Problematics and possible worlds for cryptocurrencies. *Economia Internazionale/International Economics*, *76*(1), 1–31.

Garzón, E., Cruz, E., Medialdea, B., & Sánchez, C. (2023b). The 'control space' of the state: A key element to address the nature of money. *Review of Radical Political Economics*, *55*(3) 1–24.

Goldberg, D. (2012). The tax-foundation theory of fiat money. *Economic Theory*, *50*(2), 489–497.

Goodhart, C. A. E. (1998). The two concepts of money: Implications for the analysis of optimal currency areas. *European Journal of Political Economy*, *14*(3), 407–432.

Graziani, A. (1990). The theory of the monetary circuit. *Economies et Societes*, *24*(6), 7–36.

Graziani, A. (1997) The Marxist theory of money. *International Journal of Political Economy*, *27*(2), 26–50.

Grishchenko, O. V., Ostapenko, V., Tkachev, V., & Tunev, V. (2021). Modern monetary theory (MMT): New paradigm or a set of recommendations for macroeconomic policy. *Russian Journal of Economics*, *7*(3), 271–296.

Grubb, F. (2015). *Colonial Virginia's paper money regime, 1755–1774: A forensic accounting reconstruction of the data* (NBER Working paper) (pp. 2015–2011).

Henry, J. F. (2004). The social origins of money: The case of Egypt. In Law Review Wray (Ed.), *Credit and state theories of money* (pp. 79–98). Edward Elgar.

Holt, J. P. (2017). Modern money theory and distributive justice. *Journal of Economic Issues*, *51*(4), 1001–1018.

Huber, J. (2014). Modern money theory and new currency theory: A comparative discussion, including an assessment of their relevance to monetary reform. *Real-World Economics Review*, 66, 38–57.

Ingham, G. (1998). On the underdevelopment of the 'sociology of money'. *Acta Sociologica*, *41*(1), 3–18.

Innes, A. M. (1913 [2004]). What is money. In Law Review Wray (Ed.), *Credit and state theories of money* (pp. 14–49). Edward Elgar.

Innes, A. M. (1914 [2004]). The credit theory of money. In Law Review Wray (Ed.), *Credit and* state theories of money (pp. 50–78). Edward Elgar.

Innes, A. M. (1932). *Martyrdom in our times: Two essays on prisons and punishment*. Williams & Norgate, Ltd.

Kauko, K. (2018). Did taxes, decrees or credibility drive money? Early nineteenth century Finland from a chartalist perspective. *Scandinavian Economic History Review, 66*(1), 73–90.

Kelton, S. (2020). *El mito del déficit: La teoría monetaria moderna y el nacimiento de la economía de la gente*. Pengüin Random House.

Keynes, J. M. (1914). What is money? *Economic Journal, 24*(95), 419–421.

Keynes, J. M. (1976 [1930]). *A treatise on money, volumes I and II*. Brace & Co.

Knapp, G. F. (1924 [1905]). *The state theory of money*. MacMillan & Company Limited.

Kregel, J. (2020). External debt matters: What are the limits to monetary sovereignty? *The Japanese Political Economy, 46*(4), 287–299.

Lapavitsas, C. (2016). *Marxist monetary theory: Collected papers*. Brill.

Lapavitsas, C., & Aguila, N. (2020). Modern monetary theory on money, sovereignty, and policy: A Marxist critique with reference to the Eurozone and Greece. *The Japanese Political Economy, 46*(4), 300–326.

Lawson, T. (2019). *The nature of social reality: Issues in social ontology*. Routledge.

Lawson, T. (2022). Social positioning theory. *Cambridge Journal of Economics, 46*(1), 1–39.

Lerner, A. (1946). Money. In *Encyclopedia Britannica*. Encyclopaedia Britannica.

Lerner, A. (1947). Money as a creature of the state. *The American Economic Review, 37*(2), 312–317.

Levey, S. (2021). *Modeling monopoly money: Government as the source of the price level and unemployment* (Working Paper no. 992). Levy Economics Institute.

Louzek, M. (2011). The battle of methods in economics. The classical Methodenstreit – Menger vs. Schmoller. *The American Journal of Economics and Sociology, 70*(2), 439–463.

Lovejoy, P. E. (1974). Interregional monetary flows in the precolonial trade of Nigeria. *Journal of African History, 15*(4), 563–585.

Macleod, H. D. (1969 [1889]). *The theory of credit* (Vol. 1). Edizioni Bizzarri.

Marx, K. (1991 [1894]). *Capital: A critical analysis of capitalist production* (Vol. 3). Penguin Classics.

Mayhew, A. (2019). The sleights of hand of MMT. *Real-World Economics Review, 89*, 1–11.

Mehrling, P. (2000). Modern money: Fiat or credit? *Journal of Post Keynesian Economics, 22*(3), 397–406.

Menger, K. (1892). On the origin of money. *The Economic Journal, 2*(6), 239–255.

Mill, J. S. (1848). *Principles of political economy*. J.W. Parker.

Minsky, H. P. (1986). *Stabilizing an unstable economy*. Yale University Press.

Mitchell, W., Wray, L. R., & Watts, M. (2019). *Macroeconomics*. Red Globe Press.

Mosler, W. (1995). *Soft currency economics* (3rd ed.). http://www.warrenmosler.com

Mosler, W. (2010, August 31). *Mosler economics / modern monetary theory* [Press release]. https://moslereconomics.com/2010/08/31/press-release-2/

Mosler, W. (2023). A framework for the analysis of the price level and inflation. In Law Review Wray (Ed.), *Modern monetary theory* (pp. 87–93). Edward Elgar Publishing.

Murphy, R. (2015). *The joy of tax*. Transworld Publishers.

Murphy, R. (2019). Tax and modern monetary theory. *Real-World Economic Review, 89*, 138–147.

Neovius, E. (1899). *Suomen raha-asian järjestämisestä Porvoon valtiopäiviä lähinnä seuranneina vuosina [Arranging Finnish financial affairs during the years after the Porvoo diet]* (Doctoral dissertation). University of Helsinki, Weilin & Göös, Helsinki.

Palley, T. I. (2012). *Money, fiscal policy, and interest rates: A critique of modern monetary theory*. Mimeograph.

Palley, T. I. (2015a). Money, fiscal policy, and interest rates: A critique of modern monetary theory. *Review of Political Economy, 27*(1), 1–23. https://doi.org/10.1080/09538259.2014.957466

Parguez, A., & Seccareccia, M. (2000). The credit theory of money: The monetary circuit approach. In J. Smithin (Ed.), *What is money?* (pp. 101–123). Routledge.

Pipping, H. (1961). *Paperiruplasta kultamarkkaan: Suomen Pankki 1811–1877 [From paper rouble to gold markka: Bank of Finland 1811–1877].* Bank of Finland.

Polanyi, K. (1977). *The livelihood of Man.* Academic Press.

Prates, D. (2020). Beyond modern money theory: A post-Keynesian approach to the currency hierarchy, monetary sovereignty, and policy space. *Review of Keynesian Economics, 8*(4), 494–511.

Rallo, J. R. (2017). *Contra la Teoría Monetaria Moderna.* Deusto.

Roberts, M. (2019). Modern monetary theory: A Marxist critique. *Class, Race and Corporate Power, 7*(1), Article 1.

Rochon, L. P., & Vernengo, M. (2003). State money and the real world: Or chartalism and its discontents. *Journal of Post Keynesian Economics, 26*(1), 57–68.

Rodney, W. (1972). *How Europe underdeveloped Africa.* Howard University Press.

Roth, S. (2019). *The #MMT case for progressive taxes.* https://www.nakedcapitalism.com/2019/03/the-mmt-case-for-progressive-taxes.html

Ruml, B. (1946). Taxes for revenue are obsolete. *American Affairs, 8*(1), 35–38.

Say, J. B. (1964 [1880]). *A treatise on political economy* (10th ed.). A.M. Kelley.

Schumpeter, J. A. (1954). *Historia del Análisis Económico.* Editorial Ariel.

Semenova, A., & Wray, L. R. (2015). *The rise of money and class society: The contributions of John F. Henry* (Working Paper No. 832). Levy Economics Institute.

Shaikh, A. (2016). *Capitalism: Competition, conflict, crises.* Oxford University Press.

Shubik, M., & Smith, E. (2016). *The guidance of an enterprise economy.* MIT Press.

Smith, A. (1994). *La Riqueza de las Naciones.* Alianza Editorial.

Tcherneva, P. R. (2002, Winter). Monopoly money: The state as a price setter. *Oeconomicus, V,* 124–143.

Tcherneva, P. R. (2006). Chartalism and the tax-driven approach to money. In P. Arestis & M. Sawyer (Eds.), *Handbook of alternative monetary economics* (pp. 69–86). Edward Elgar.

Tcherneva, P. R. (2016). *Money, power and monetary regimes* (Working Paper No. 861). Levy Economics Institute.

Thomas, C. Y. (1984). *The rise of the authoritarian state in peripheral societies.* Monthly Review Press.

Tobin, J., & Golub, S. (1998). *Money, credit, and capital.* Irwin McGraw-Hill.

Tolstoy, L. (1886). *What then must we do?* Green Books.

Tymoigne, E., & Wray, L. R. (2013). *Modern money Theory 101: A reply to critics* (Working Paper Series No. 778). Levy Economics Institute.

Vries, P. H. H. (2002). Governing growth: A comparative analysis of the role of the state in the rise of the West. *Journal of World History, 13*(1), 67–138.

White, J. D. (1996). *Karl Marx and the intellectual origins of dialectical materialism.* Macmillan.

Winczewski, D. (2021). Neo-chartalist or Marxist vision of the modern money? Critical comparison. *International Critical Thought, 11*(3), 408–426.

Wray, L. R. (1998). *Understanding modern money, the key to full employment and price stability.* Edward Elgar Publishing Ltd.

Wray, L. R. (Ed.). (2004). *Credit and state theories of money.* Edward Elgar.

Wray, L. R. (2012). *Modern money theory: A primer on macroeconomics for sovereign monetary.* Palgrave Macmillan.

Wray, L. R. (2014). Outside money: The advantages of owning the magic porridge pot (Working Papers No. 821). Levy Economics Institute of Bard College.

Wray, L. R. (2016). Taxes are for redemption, not spending. *World Economic Review, 7,* 3–11.

3

MODERN MONETARY THEORY'S VIEW OF MONETARY SOVEREIGNTY AND ITS CRITICISMS

Introduction

In the previous chapter we have seen that, for Modern Monetary Theory (MMT), money is a product of the State whose widespread use is achieved through the demand for taxes denominated in that money. We also saw that, precisely because of this, MMT taxes have to be logically prior to public spending, since the State could not collect any money until such money existed, and the only way for it to exist would be through the State, specifically through its public spending: "the state cannot possibly collect currency through taxes before it has provided it through spending" (Tcherneva, 2016, p. 9). However, the latter assertions are not even true in all cases and situations, as it will depend on the specific circumstances surrounding the particular state. This issue leads us to talk about monetary sovereignty, a relatively simple but highly controversial concept, which has been strongly contested by critics of MMT. In this chapter we will present the vision of monetary sovereignty held by the authors of MMT, as well as the limitations encountered by its detractors.

Money issuers and users

The MMT places great emphasis on the distinction between the issuer of money and the users of money. The state that creates the money that is used is the issuer, while the households and firms (as well as other regional governments) that use the money are the users. Issuer states can spend before collecting (in fact, what MMTers argue is that they have to spend before collecting because otherwise the money would not exist), but households and firms cannot do so because they cannot create money. So they have to get money before they can spend it, but issuer states cannot because they create the money that is used by economic agents in their territory. Examples of issuer states are the Sumerian authorities that issued the silas referred to in Chapter 1, the United States that issues dollars or the United Kingdom that issues pounds, but there are many more.

DOI: 10.4324/9781003371809-4

However, although all households and all firms are users of money (although banks play a special role, as we will see in Chapter 5), not all states are issuers of money: some are users, they use money that they do not create. Among these states, there are several types. Some states simply use the currency created by other states, as for example some Latin American countries such as Ecuador, Panama, or El Salvador, which officially use US dollars; or European micro-states, which use euros (or the Swiss franc in the case of Liechtenstein). Obviously these cases do not operate the chartalist implications; the state cannot spend without first having obtained these currencies somehow, as it cannot create them: "relinquishing monetary sovereignty has transformed those countries from 'currency issuers' into 'currency users'" (Tcherneva, 2016, p. 18).

There are other states that use neither their own currency nor the currency of another state, but the common currency shared by several countries. Examples are the Eurozone states in Europe or the Common Monetary Area states in South Africa. Spain, for example, is a state, but uses a currency issued by its monetary union, the euro. Namibia is another state, but uses a currency issued by South Africa, the South African Rand. Spain and Namibia are not money-issuer states, but money-users. Therefore, these states are like households and firms: they also need to raise money before they spend it, through taxation, borrowing, or in some other way. They cannot do like money-issuer states, which spend without needing to get money from anywhere. As a result, their fiscal room for manoeuvre is considerably reduced, as Tcherneva explains in the case of the European Monetary Union: "the only way to fund government programs is by borrowing euros, by raising domestic taxes for revenue, or by cutting those programs. The latter two have contractionary effect, which undermines the governments' ability to pursue its policy agenda further" (Tcherneva, 2016, pp. 18–19). In reality, belonging to a monetary union would be tantamount to using a foreign currency, or becoming a regional public administration, as the state in question cannot create money without permission from the issuer public administration: "member states use a foreign currency, much in the same way as states in the US or Australia do" (Mitchell, 2016a, p. 11).

Indeed, regional governments are not issuers of money either, even if they belong to a state that is. For example, the US State of California is a user of the US dollar. Bern, a canton of the State of Switzerland, is a user of the Swiss franc. So regional administrations also need to raise money before they can spend it, whether by taxation, borrowing, or otherwise. This is what has led some proponents of MMT to suggest a redesign of the countries' fiscal federalism so that it is the money-issuer state administrations that bear the heaviest fiscal burden, thereby relieving the pressure on the non-money-issuer regional administrations (He & Jia, 2020; Liu & Wray, 2016; Wray, 2019).

Consequently, the chartalist thesis that taxes do not finance public spending only applies to currency-issuer states, not to user states or regional governments, which are by definition users of the money. In any case, it is important to note that, according to the MMT, the money used by these user states always comes from an issuing state. They can create money and give it to these user states or regional administrations. And if they were to do so systematically and free of charge or in exchange for very advantageous conditions, these recipient public administrations would not need taxes or debt to finance spending either.

However, the MMT also envisages important differences between money-issuer states. On the one hand, there are states that link the value of their currency to the value of the currency of another state (e.g. Denmark, some countries in the Balkans, the Persian Gulf, and Central Africa, which link their currencies to those of the euro and the dollar). This implies limits on creating their own money, because if they create more than they should, then the value of their currency may fall relative to that of the reference currency, and this is something they want to avoid: "this arrangement severely constrains the ability of the government to spend national currency" (Tcherneva, 2016, p. 9). As a result, these issuer states do not have full monetary sovereignty, because as they have committed their currency to be pegged to others they cannot create as much money as they want; they are dependent on what the states of the currencies they have pegged to do. In this case they might be forced to resort to financing their new spending through taxation or borrowing rather than by creating new money. But the MMT stresses that this is a self-imposed constraint because they are in fact issuers of their own money and could cancel this commitment and have a free hand to create as much money as they need. This is why, according to Tcherneva, when there are severe economic problems, states often break such a peg: "fixed exchange rate regimes are often abandoned in the middle of severe economic and financial crises, freeing additional policy space to conduct independent macroeconomic stabilization monetary or fiscal policy" (Tcherneva, 2016, p. 20).

However, as Tymoigne (2020) points out, some states can peg their currency to a foreign currency and enjoy broad – not full – fiscal flexibility if they hold a lot of international reserves thanks to their favourable external balance, something that may derive from their pattern of economic growth, so abandoning monetary sovereignty would not necessarily be as detrimental to them as to other states with a worse external balance:

> some governments may issue public debt denominated in a foreign currency and/or peg a specific exchange rate, but if their foreign reserves are large, there is no current threat to their ability to service the foreign-denominated public debt or to peg the exchange rate.
>
> *(Tymoigne, 2020, p. 3)*

Linking one's own currency to a foreign currency is equivalent to linking it to gold or any other asset, as was the case during the gold standard system. During that period of time, if these states wanted the value of their currency to be stable, they could not resort as much as they wanted to money creation, so they were forced to finance themselves through taxation and borrowing most of the time (Panic, 1992; Goodhart, 1998). The gold standard monetary system operated from the early nineteenth century until the First World War, and the gold-dollar standard monetary system, in which all currencies were pegged to the dollar and the dollar to gold, from the end of the Second World War until August 1971.

However, although under these monetary systems states committed themselves to create money only if they had gold to back the new money, there is evidence that this commitment was violated on many occasions, especially during wars (Panic, 1992). As Charles Goodhart emphasises, "the countries participating in [gold standard] did so by independent, voluntary choice, each maintaining, and on occasions utilising, the right to withdraw" (Goodhart, 1998, p. 422). This makes sense: when governments saw that their sovereignty was at risk, they created all the money necessary to put the war machine into operation; it would have been absurd to stand idly by and let the enemy conquer them simply because they did not have enough gold. But this resort to creating more money than was committed was not only in wars but also in economic crises. After all, as Glasner (1989, p. 39) emphasises, it can be optimal for a sovereign country to pre-commit to a regime which will ensure price stability so long as that regime continues, but only if it retains the ability to utilise its independent money creation powers in a crisis.

It is a fact that the United States has been in violation of the commitment since 1959 as it began to create far more dollars than it had gold. This gap widened until 1971 when there were already six times more dollars than gold (Viñas, 1976). This is precisely what led the US government to abandon this commitment in August 1971, and since then states can create their money without any limitations because they do not have to tie it to gold or any other asset. For MMT this was a moment of special significance that would have gone largely unnoticed: "most people are not aware that a major historic event occurred in 1971 when President Nixon abandoned gold convertibility and ended the system of fixed exchange rates" (Mitchell, 2016a, p. 10). Since then, this money is commonly referred to as fiat money, from the Latin fiat "let there be", because its value depends on what the state that creates it establishes. Although this concept has a certain similarity with chartalism, it is not the same, because according to the latter the existence and acceptability of money depends on the taxes demanded by the State, while the concept of fiat money focuses only on the legislative and legal aspects.

Finally, there are states which, although they issue their own money and do not tie it to any other currency, have borrowed in a foreign currency. In this case, these states are obliged to pay their debts with a currency that they do not issue, which puts them in a more compromising situation than those who borrow in their own currency because the latter will always be able to pay their debts (by creating money), as we will see in more detail in the next chapter. But these states we are talking about cannot create a foreign currency to pay off their debt. For example, Argentina is a country that, although it issues its own money, Argentine pesos, tends to borrow in a foreign currency, usually the dollar. Again, the MMT stresses that this is a political decision, even though it is traditionally an imposition by international institutions; the key point is that they are not obliged to do so.

Consequently, full monetary sovereignty, that which allows a state to spend without any financial constraint, would only be enjoyed by issuing states that do not tie the value of their currency to any other currency or asset, and that do not borrow in foreign currency: for example, the United States, Japan, Switzerland, or Australia. These states would enjoy maximum fiscal space because they would not need to collect taxes to spend, they would not need to obtain any foreign currency or tie the value of their currency to any asset, so they could spend as much as they wanted and also avoid insolvency or bankruptcy if they wanted to: "a flexible exchange rate frees monetary policy from having to defend a fixed peg to a foreign currency (…). One consequence of this is that governments that issue their own currencies no longer have to 'finance' their spending" (Mitchell, 2016a, p. 10).

However, their spending would have other kinds of limits, such as the availability of real resources (explored in Chapter 6) or political considerations:

> in fully sovereign monetary regimes, however, the economic possibilities before a nation with a freely floating nonconvertible national currency are constrained largely by political considerations and the availability of *real* resources to achieve those priorities, not by the availability of money.
>
> *(Tcherneva, 2016, p. 20)*

In other words, Eric Tymoigne underlines the same point: "a [sovereign] government faces no financial constraint; it cannot involuntarily run out of money. Such a government, however, does face political and potential resource constraints that limit its ability to operate in the domestic economy" (Tymoigne, 2020, p. 20).

The issue of political constraints is not a minor one for MMT: its authors point out that it is possible (and frequent) for a state with full monetary sovereignty to self-impose spending constraints. This is the case, for example, with the United States, which has a debt ceiling, or Australia, which is obliged not to exceed certain deficit or debt levels. In this case, if you do not want to violate the legal provision, you would not be able to spend as much as you want. Of course, the MMT insists that it is important to be clear that these would be voluntary, political restrictions, not technical constraints. MMTer Randall Wray often summarises this as follows: "states with full monetary sovereignty can tie their hands behind their backs if they want to, but there is no good economic reason for them to do so. Politics can cause them to make crazy decisions" (Wray, 2015, p. 138). The MMT Australian economist Bill Mitchell also tells us about this in his book "The Euro Dystopia" which deals precisely with the self-imposed obstacles of the European Monetary Union: "the public debt limits accepted by governments are a classic example of a voluntary restraint that could easily be legislatively rejected if the public really understood how the monetary system works" (Mitchell, 2016a, p. 16).

In short, contrary to the idea that may perhaps be conveyed at first glance,

> MMT does not conceive of monetary sovereignty as a binary state[1]. Ideally, it is imagined as a matter of degree or a spectrum on which we can place different countries according to whether they have more or less of that sovereignty.
>
> *(Kelton, 2020, p. 315)*

Specifically,

> at one end of the spectrum are fully sovereign monetary regimes. These are cases where the state issues non-convertible freely floating national currency (...) At the other end of the spectrum are countries that have completely abdicated monetary sovereignty, thus giving up the right to issue and manage their own national currency.
>
> *(Tcherneva, 2016, pp. 17–18)*

Taking this classification into account is crucial to facilitate policy recommendations (Liu & Wray, 2016).

Political sovereignty

By linking the existence and acceptability of money to taxation, MMT is inevitably also linking money to the concept of political sovereignty. If a society wants to be truly sovereign, it needs to control the currency to be used in its territory, since, among other things, this is what will allow it the possibility of mobilising real resources for its purposes. This is even more important at a time like the present when peoples sharing the same culture and identity are trying to organise themselves through nation-states. The authors of the MMT show some historical examples where peoples could only achieve their full political sovereignty by gaining full monetary sovereignty (remember: issuing the currency they use without linking it to any other currency or asset). For example, following Weintraub and Schuler (2013), Tcherneva notes that India "had been issuing its own notes – rupees – since 1862 (while still under British rule), but for most of that period up until independence the monopoly note issue in India operated like a currency board" (Tcherneva, 2016, p. 11). Another example she adds is that of the Australian colonies, which

> gradually began issuing some notes, but they were all pegged to the pound sterling. The peg continued even after Federation in 1901, up until the time the government assumed control over all currency matters and began issuing the Australian pound in 1910. Full independence required independent monetary sovereignty, which Australia finally achieved in the interwar period.
>
> *(Tcherneva, 2016, p. 11)*

For his part, Charles Goodhart (1998) points to the disintegration in the 1990s of the Soviet Union, Czechoslovakia, and Yugoslavia into several states, each of which created its own currency in order to achieve political sovereignty, and the same happened in Austria and Hungary after the First World War. At the same time, however, he points out that the reverse political process, that of the reunification of states, is also in line with chartalist postulates, and gives the United States, Germany, and Italy as examples. In short, chartalism "predicts that the fragmentation of sovereignty will lead to a fragmentation into separate currencies, and, per contra, that unification into an effective federal state will lead to the unification of previously separate currencies" (Goodhart, 1998, p. 423). He finds only a few exceptions to this rule, such as tiny states, which use foreign currencies, but precisely because they are politically weak and dependent on others, so they would not have true political sovereignty, but also monetary unions such as the European one, with which he is very critical (as we have already mentioned), for detaching the sovereignty of the nation-state from the control of the currency used: "this divorce between monetary (federal) centralisation and governmental decentralisation at the level of the nation state, especially with the main fiscal functions remaining at that lower, national level is the source of potential tensions" (Goodhart, 1998, p. 424).

Following Tcherneva (2016), so important is the control of money to a state's political sovereignty that states have always tried to prevent other agents from eroding or taking away that control, one of those possible ways being the counterfeiting of money. This is why such an act has always been severely prosecuted by the authorities and penalised with severe sanctions. But it is not only that States have persecuted and prohibited counterfeiting to protect one of their main tools for exercising power, but they have also promoted it in the case of the currencies of their enemies or adversaries, precisely as a weapon of war. There would be many historical examples:

> Counterfeiting as an act of war has been used in other cases. Such are the cases of government-sponsored counterfeiting of German reichsmarks by the British during WWI (Cooley, 2008), of US dollars by Stalin in the interwar period (Krivitsky, 2011), of British notes by Hitler during WWII (operation Bernhard), and of Vietnamese and Cuban currency by the US during the Vietnam War (Asselin, 2013, p. 189) and the failed Bay of Pigs invasion (Cooley, 2008), respectively.
>
> *(Tcherneva, 2016, p. 13)*

Another documented historical example would be that of the British colonies in North America: when the war of independence began, the British Empire and supporters of the crown in the Americas flooded the colonies with counterfeit banknotes to erode their stability and thus weaken the independence movement. Indeed, "on the eve of the Revolution, American counterfeiting had surpassed British imperialism as the No. 1 threat to Colonial currency" (Rhodes, 2012, p. 35).

In any case, counterfeiting would be an even older phenomenon. Numismatic studies reveal that even the earliest coins minted in Lydia during the seventh century BC were imitated or manipulated in various ways, all of which were punishable by death (Tcherneva, 2016, p. 14). Counterfeiting has hardly received any attention from orthodox economic theory (the few studies on it refer only to a question of "efficiency" (Kultti, 1996)), as it considers money as a mere veil of commercial transactions, but historical evidence would reveal that it has always existed, which would be in line with the chartalist thesis: "a history of counterfeiting, as well as that of independence from colonial and economic rule, is another way of telling the history of 'money as a creature of the state'" (Tcherneva, 2016, p. 1).

Because of all this, MMT relies on the close link between money and political sovereignty to argue for each nation-state to have its own currency, as they believe it would be the most democratic and also the most politically powerful option, emphasising that nation-states have enough political tools to impose their sovereignty even in a globalised and financialised world (Fazi & Mitchell, 2017). Hence, neo-chartalists and supporters of MMT have always been so critical of the European Monetary Union in which many nation-states share their own currency (Goodhart, 1998; Kelton & Wray, 2009; Kelton, 2011; Papadimitriou & Wray, 2012; Ehnts, 2016), going so far as to propose its simple dissolution (Mitchell, 2016a) or the introduction of a parallel currency to the euro in order to gain monetary sovereignty (Andresen, 2019). This is in contradiction with more cosmopolitan views that advocate supranational forms of macroeconomic governance to overcome the obstacles and constraints faced by smaller economies (including by issuing their own currency), although there are those who consider that "neo-chartalism and cosmopolitanism can fruitfully correct and enrich each other" (Kotilainen, 2022). This MMT vision is also opposite to those who consider that the money created by nation-states has become subordinate to the money created by banks, which would totally dominate the current system: "the minor extent to which nation-states still may have monetary sovereignty is open to question. For the most part today, monetary sovereignty is something that has to be recaptured from the banking industry" (Huber, 2014, p. 51).

In the following section we will analyse the most important criticisms of this MMT concept of monetary and political sovereignty.

Criticisms

The MMT concept of monetary sovereignty has been widely questioned. From an orthodox point of view, the critique is as simple as it is poor: since money is a creature of the market and not of the state, the state does not have monetary sovereignty but depends on the private sector to be able to make any expenditure, by raising money first, by borrowing, or by obtaining it in some other way. If the private sector loses confidence in the state for whatever reason – usually financial irresponsibility for spending too much or creating too much money – then the state's currency would be less valued and used. As economist Robert Murphy summarises, "in short, the reason most governments (including state governments in the US) in the world aren't 'monetary sovereigns' is that members of the financial community are worried that they would abuse a printing press" (Murphy, 2020, pp. 239–240). From this point of view, it is the loss of confidence in the state currency by economic agents that leads states to abandon their monetary sovereignty (using a foreign currency, pegging or borrowing in it): "a government that engaged too recklessly in monetary inflation – thus leading investors to shun that particular 'sovereign' currency – would be forced to pursue one or more of these concessions in order to remain part of the global financial community" (Murphy, 2020, p. 240).

And this loss of confidence in the state currency by private agents could affect even the most developed economies issuing their own currency. For example, Omran and Zelmer (2021) point out that even the Canadian state could suffer a significant devaluation of its currency (leading to import-led inflation and less fiscal space) if financial investors lose confidence in the stability of its public finances: "to the extent that investors believe future resources might need to be directed to servicing the additional debt (…) this would likely be accompanied by an exchange-rate depreciation in real terms" (Omran & Zelmer, 2021, p. 8). The key would be that investors, in a context of international capital freedom, would be able to withdraw their funds quickly and easily from any country about which they had the slightest doubts regarding the stability of public accounts. Therefore, they criticise MMT on the grounds that it "overstates the degree of monetary sovereignty that governments enjoy in a world where both domestic and foreign investors can deploy their funds wherever they see fit with the click of a mouse" (Omran & Zelmer, 2021, p. 3).

As can be seen, orthodox critics consider that the monetary sovereignty of countries depends on the mood and actions of private agents, especially financial ones (we will discuss this further in the next chapter). In contrast, the criticisms coming from the heterodox world are much more complex, realistic, and constructive.

The main criticism of the MMT concept of monetary sovereignty from a heterodox point of view is that it is only valid for a very few national economies, most notably the United States. After all, most economies use a foreign currency or link it to another currency, if they do not borrow in foreign currency, so that the concept of full monetary sovereignty would only apply to a few of the more than 200 states in the world. Hence, the usefulness of the concept of monetary sovereignty and MMT itself is questioned from the beginning; they would only apply to those few economies, not the rest: "although MMT advocates claim that its macroeconomic framework applies to all countries with 'sovereign currencies', there is significant evidence that it does not apply to the vast majority of developing countries that are integrated into global financial markets" (Epstein, 2019). This is why MMT is often criticised for suffering from a view that focuses only on developed economies and does not contribute much to developing economies (Cesaratto, 2020; Vergnhanini & de Conti, 2018; Bonizzi et al., 2019; Epstein, 2019; Edwards, 2019).

In any case, the central issue is not that most states do not currently have monetary sovereignty, which is not in dispute, but whether they can ever have it. MMT does not ignore the current situation of most countries, it simply points out that, as long as they do not have full monetary sovereignty, they will have less fiscal space than economies that do, and obviously its policy recommendation for these countries is not to use foreign currencies, to establish a flexible exchange rate so as not to tie themselves to any other currency or asset, and not to borrow in foreign currency (Mitchell, 2016b; Kelton, 2020, p. 31). The point made by most critics is that these economies, even if they wanted to, cannot do such a thing. Why? Basically because of the implications of the so-called "external constraint" once introduced and developed by the economist Thirlwall (1979).

The issue is basically that most economies (if not all) need to continually import many products from other countries, for which they need foreign currencies, not their own. This continued trade and current account deficit leads to a constant need for foreign currencies which, if not secured, causes a significant depreciation of their domestic currency (something that makes imports more expensive, which could lead to imported inflation if passed on to other domestic products). Moreover, given the dependence of these economies on financial flows to obtain the foreign currencies they need, any significant withdrawal of financial investment by foreign economic agents could depress the value of the national currency and lead to imported inflation. Finally, many of these economies tend to allow fluctuations in the local currency and use a foreign currency (usually the US dollar) to protect themselves from the inflation they have historically suffered.

This delicate macroeconomic context would force these economies to abandon their full monetary sovereignty through two different channels: on the one hand, to avoid investment flight by foreign agents, they tend to adopt a fixed exchange rate that sends signals that the currency will remain stable; on the other hand, to obtain the foreign currencies they may need in crisis situations, these economies tend to resort to foreign borrowing (usually US dollars). As a result, these economies would be setting aside full monetary sovereignty – as defined by the MMT – practically out of obligation, in order to avoid financial investment flight and a high depreciation of their currency that would only lead to imported inflation. As Rodrigo Vergnhanini and Bruno De Conti summarise:

> in the context of financial globalization, are not fully sovereign in determining its own macroeconomic policy (…) the exchange rate is potentially under the pressure of this capital flows movements. Finally, monetary, fiscal and exchange policies in peripheral countries have constrains that are not considered by MMT.
>
> *(Vergnhanini & De Conti, 2018, p. 16)*

This is why only a few national economies, whose currencies enjoy a certain stability, could afford to meet the criteria for full monetary sovereignty even if they were to run continued current account deficits. And one of the most important factors that would make currencies stable is that they are in demand internationally because they are used in trade, financial transactions, or simply as a store of value. Hence, some like Epstein point out that "only countries that issue their own internationally accepted currency ('hard currency') could have the policy space to pursue MMT policies" (Epstein, 2019). Some critics have emphasised that this comes about because of the economic, political, and financial strength of the country in question:

> not all national currencies are on the same plane. There are currencies that by virtue of the economic and political soundness and financial solvency of the issuing country (which for example has no history of financial failure) are commonly accepted in international payments.
>
> *(Cesaratto, 2020)*

This approach reverses the causality between monetary sovereignty and exchange rate flexibility posited by MMT: instead of the flexible exchange rate granting monetary sovereignty, it is precisely monetary sovereignty that grants the possibility of establishing a flexible exchange rate (Bonizzi et al., 2019).

Some go further and indicate that, in reality, only the United States has complete monetary sovereignty because its currency is the only hegemonic one at the international level, used also massively as an international reserve – it is estimated that 90% of world trade is conducted in dollars (Reinbold & Wen, 2019) and that approximately 60% of international reserves are denominated in dollars (FED, 2021) –, which de Gaulle's Finance Minister Giscard D'Estaing called an "exorbitant privilege": "there is only one country in the world that could possibly follow MMT's policy prescriptions without necessarily triggering inflationary pressures in the short run: the United States. This is simply because the dollar is a global currency" (Ocampo, 2021, p. 49).

It has also been pointed out that it is not necessary for the currency to be used internationally to enjoy monetary sovereignty, it can also routinely run current account surpluses, which is just what gives them enough foreign currencies and international reserves to control the stability of their own currency: "only the currencies of mercantilists countries – that is, those with persistent current account surpluses – and the United States of America may have unlimited acceptance. Non-mercantilist countries do need to implement exchange rate management in order to obtain external equilibrium" (Vergnhanini & de Conti, 2018, p. 23). As mentioned above, this is something that the MMT also contemplates: countries that maintain a sustained current account surplus "have a steady inflow of foreign currency reserves, they are able to maintain an exchange rate peg even while pursuing domestic policy independence and (if they desire) free capital flows" (Wray, 2012, p. 139). This recognition does not run counter to the MMT postulates of monetary sovereignty: the fact that having a flexible exchange rate always provides more fiscal space does not mean that it is not possible to have ample fiscal space with a fixed exchange rate, even if this requires running current account surpluses. If this were no longer the case, the state would lose that greater degree of fiscal space. By contrast, this would never happen if the flexible exchange rate is maintained; so for the MMT the latter is a preferable option for fiscal space, especially given that, by accounting identity, it is not possible for every economy in the world to run current account surpluses (something we discuss in more detail in Chapter 5).

From a Marxist point of view, it is emphasised that it is not only the economic or commercial power of these developed economies that explains why their currencies are used in the global monetary system but also their political and military power:

> those superpowers like the United States can afford a significant surplus of imports over exports because the strength of their monetary domination is based on their political and military power, which keeps the demand for their currency. (…) However, the economic capacity of individual states is reduced by neo-chartalists to strictly accounting issues, while the political dimension seems neutral.
>
> *(Winczewski, 2021, p. 12)*

This idea is shared by analysts of development economics and international political economy (notably Helleiner, 1994; Strange, 1988; Kaltenbrunner & Paanceira, 2018). This would have been the case throughout history, as Kirshner (1995) explains: central or hegemonic states manipulated international money markets, controlling exchange rates or disrupting the functioning of financial markets, in order to subjugate weaker countries in the periphery. As Lapavitsas and Aguila develop,

> international monetary payments to have an obligatory rather than a voluntary character, that is, nations are obliged to deliver the prevailing form of world money. (…) Lack of

monetary sovereignty is the result of international structural constraints, rather than policy choices.

(Lapavitsas & Aguila, 2020, p. 14)

From a Keynesian point of view, Prates (2020) combines this factor of the political position of currency at the international level with the concept of monetary sovereignty (understood as the ability to issue the currency being used) to explain the degree of policy space available to different countries. Therefore, from this point of view, simply having monetary sovereignty does not confer the greatest degree of fiscal manoeuvre, but it is also important to consider the position of the currency in the international hierarchy of currencies. This hierarchy would be explained by the liquidity of currencies, which in turn, following Davidson (1972), would depend on the number of contracts signed and which would be related to their capacity to perform the three functions of money at the global level. Thus, at the top of the pyramid would be the most liquid and used currency of all, the US dollar, which would act as the centrepiece around which the other, less liquid and used currencies would be organised; it would be followed by the euro as an important international reserve currency; then the currencies of the other central economies; and finally the currencies of the peripheral economies:

> the monetary asymmetry is a consequence of the CH, that is, of the hierarchical structure of an IMFS organized around a national currency that becomes its so-called key currency (Keynes, 1930, 1944). Currencies are hierarchically positioned according to their degree of liquidity (l), which relates to their ability to perform the three functions of money internationally.

(Prates, 2020, p. 503)

According to this classification, the state with the highest degree of fiscal space would be the United States, followed by the rest of the central economies with their own currency, which would be placed before the Eurozone states as they do not have monetary sovereignty. Next Eurozone, it would be the developing economy states that have monetary sovereignty, then those that have partial monetary sovereignty because they do not manage to have their currency fully used in their own territory, and finally those that do not issue their own currency. As can be seen, this is a more complex and detailed classification than the one made by the MMT and it reaches different conclusions, since, for example, it places the Eurozone with a higher degree of fiscal space than other states with monetary sovereignty: "if we consider the actual monetary, financial, and macroeconomic asymmetries of the current IMFS, we come to very different conclusions from Wray's (2015) one regarding the relationship between policy space and exchange-rate regimes in emerging-market economies" (Prates, 2020, p. 505).

On the other hand, there are critics who consider that even countries whose currency is used internationally do not have full monetary sovereignty, basically because such a phenomenon might cease to occur and thus the privilege might end:

> even for those countries that issue their own international currencies, the sustainability and "exploitability" of international paper is not absolute. Historical and empirical evidence suggests that even considerable forces for the persistence of key currency positions can weaken over time, perhaps even fall rapidly and dramatically.

(Epstein, 2019)

Moreover, some critics believe that even today the United States is not safe from losing its full sovereign status, something that recent history would have already demonstrated:

> the reality that the United States is, in principle, potentially subject to the same kind of constraints as other governments is evidenced by the economic history of the 1970s. That era was a period of dollar weakness, and shows that the US can also be subject to strong financial constraints.
>
> *(Palley, 2020)*

Response to criticisms

Many supporters of MMT recognise that the United States is in an extraordinary position because of its "exorbitant privilege": "the United States is special in the sense that the US dollar (USD) plays a central role in the international monetary system" (Tymoigne, 2020, p. 13). They also recognise that something similar is true of the major developed economies: "countries such as Japan, the United Kingdom and Australia also have a high degree of monetary sovereignty. Even China, which administers and decrees the value of the yuan, enjoys considerable monetary sovereignty" (Kelton, 2020, p. 315). Although there are other MMT authors, such as Fazi and Mitchell, who have rejected the idea that there is a hierarchy of currencies dominated by the dollar: "the core MMT developers do not consider a 'hierarchy of currencies' with the US dollar at the top, nor do they assume that non-dollar currencies have only limited currency sovereignty. All currency-issuing governments enjoy monetary sovereignty, as outlined above" (Fazi & Mitchell, 2019).

The main point, in any case, is that all MMT authors consider that any country can have full monetary sovereignty, even less developed economies. The idea is not that an economy, simply by achieving monetary sovereignty, will reach a certain level of development or that it will be free of problems; the idea is that it will thus be able to freely mobilise all idle real resources that are sold in the currency issued by the sovereign state:

> of course, issuing one's own currency doesn't make a nation 'rich'. A nation with limited access to real resources will remain materially poor. Sovereignty, though, means that it can use its currency capacity to ensure that all available resources are always fully employed.
>
> *(Fazi & Mitchell, 2019)*

In this sense, proponents of MMT reject "external constraint" altogether and replace it with "real resource constraint", which would be very different (Mitchell, 2016c), and which may greatly limit the potential of poorer economies, but which would in any case present fewer limits than if the state were to abandon its monetary sovereignty:

> while there are some general statements that can be made with respect to MMT that apply to any nation where the government issues its own currency, floats its exchange rate, and does not incur foreign currency-denominated debt, we also have to acknowledge special cases that need special policy attention. In the latter case, the specific problems facing a nation cannot be easily overcome *just* by increasing fiscal deficits.
>
> *(Mitchell, 2016c)*

There are several arguments used by MMT proponents to deny the external constraint. The first is that running continuing current account deficits does not necessarily imply currency devaluation: "while the usual assumption is that current account deficits lead more-or-less directly to currency depreciation, the evidence for this effect is nor clear-cut" (Wray, 2012, p. 139). They have often presented some real examples to empirically support such an assertion, such as in the case of Australia: "why hasn't the growing current account deficit over the last 40 years or more precipitated a balance of payments crisis?" (Mitchel, 2016b). This has been answered by Cesaratto pointing out that the case of the Australian currency is special and not extrapolable to the rest of national economies, for reasons of international positioning of the currency, but also for reasons of real wealth and stabilisation in external debt over GDP:

> Commonwealth WASP countries seem to enjoy this privilege (...) The economic, social and institutional stability of these countries has probably favoured this privilege, as has their immense natural wealth. Moreover, being constantly indebted to other countries counts for little if the economy develops and the debt-to-GDP ratio is stable.
>
> *(Cesaratto, 2020)*

The second argument of MMT to deny the importance of the external constraint is that any misalignment that the current account deficit may produce will sooner or later be corrected by the exchange rate since depreciation cannot happen forever: either the depreciation itself makes exports so cheap that its momentum stabilises the exchange rate, or external agents stop saving in local currency so that the current account deficit would disappear, and therefore so would the depreciation. As Mitchell notes: "for a flexible exchange rate economy, the exchange rate does the adjustment. There is no balance of payments constraint facing a nation in this regard" (Mitchell, 2016c). Moreover, the risk that such currency depreciation could lead to import-led inflation appears to be minimised: "these exchange rate movements will tend to be once off adjustments anyway to the higher growth path and need not be a source of on-going inflationary pressure" (Mitchell, 2016b).

Consequently, while MMT recognises the complicated situation of many developing economies, they still maintain that all of them can achieve full monetary sovereignty to mobilise whatever real resources they have, however many or few, so their approach would not be invalidated: "if MMT cannot find a simple solution to the complex problems facing developing nations, then somehow MMT is wrong. It is a most bizarre claim" (Wray, 2014). They recognise that if the economy has few real resources, then it will have more trouble increasing economic development and social welfare: "I suspect that for many of the world's poorest countries, the exchange rate regime is not the central issue – and they are probably screwed whether they fix or they float" (Wray, 2014). In any case, MMTers believe that enjoying full monetary sovereignty gives these countries more fiscal space to achieve their objectives, so they should ideally use the monetary sovereignty they have achieved to develop and diversify their productive structure and their energy and food self-sufficiency, so that they are not so dependent on imports and not so sensitive to currency depreciations (Kaboub, 2013, 2019a, 2019b; Mitchell, 2016b, 2016c). However, they also point out that they may need to implement some additional measures to protect themselves from the risks of sharp devaluation, such as, for example, capital or import controls:

> The MMT principles apply to all sovereign countries. Yes, they can have full employment at home. Yes, that could lead to trade deficits. Yes that could (possibly) lead to currency

depreciation. Yes that could lead to inflation pass-through. But they have lots of policy options available if they do not like those results. Import controls and capital controls are examples of policy options. Directed employment, directed investment, and targeted development are also policy options.

(Wray, 2014)

Capital controls are thus understood as a last resort that certain economies should use to, above all, protect themselves from speculative movements in finance: "nations should consider imposing capital controls where they can be beneficial bulwarks against the destructive forces of speculative financial capitalism" (Mitchell, 2016c), forces that, according to Mitchell, would be desirable to prohibit and abolish: "a further progressive policy intervention, which, ideally, should be agreed to at the international level should be to declare illegal speculative financial flows that have no necessary relationship with improving the operation of the real economy" (Mitchell, 2016c). Another possibility mentioned to prevent government spending being transformed into imports and putting pressure on currency devaluation is to make in-kind payments: "payments in kind may also be necessary (to make sure to create a demand for the domestic production and to avoid imports of foreign products that are similar)" (Tymoigne & Wray, 2013).

They also incorporate a class view to point out that it is, after all, a choice between different scenarios in which there are different winners and losers: either full employment and some depreciation and inflation, which they believe would benefit the poorer population and hurt the better-off; or unemployment and low inflation and a stable currency value, which would benefit those at the top to the detriment of those at the bottom. It would therefore be a purely ideological and political question. On the one hand, maintaining a fixed exchange rate would particularly benefit the wealthy:

> what I observe out in the real world is that pegged exchange rates in developing countries are usually in the interests of the elites – who like their luxury imports and vacations in NYC and Disneyworld. Typically somewhere around half the population is either unemployed or "casually" employed (washing windshields of the luxury imports at stoplights). Seems like a bad trade-off to me.
>
> *(Wray, 2014)*

On the other hand, currency depreciation – the result of letting the currency float freely – could especially benefit the unemployed, who are most in need, and hurt the better-off: "lower currency parities can stimulate local employment (via the terms of trade effect) and tend to damage the middle and higher classes more than the poorer groups because luxury imported goods (ski holidays, BMW cars) become more expensive" (Mitchell, 2016c).

In any case, several proponents of MMT have pointed out that the serious problems faced by less developed economies should not be solved by themselves in isolation but should be addressed internationally in a way that developed economies really do their part. One possibility mentioned by Mitchell is to create an international institution that would provide sufficient real (non-monetary) resources to the neediest economies:

> a new multilateral institution should be created to replace both the World Bank and the IMF, which is charged with the responsibility to ensure that these highly disadvantaged nations

can access essential real resources such as food and not be priced out of international markets due to exchange rate fluctuations that arise from trade deficits.

(Mitchell, 2016c)

Alternatively, Kelton suggests that the United States could use its exorbitant privilege of creating dollars with stable value to mobilise the idle resources of all the world's economies to achieve full employment with price stability:

The US government can supply all the dollars our domestic private sector needs to achieve full employment, just as it can supply all the dollars the rest of the world needs to accumulate its own reserves and protect its trade flows. Instead of using its monetary hegemony to mobilise global resources in its own limited self-interest, the United States could thus lead a campaign to mobilise resources for an international Green New Deal that would keep interest rates low and stable to promote global economic calm.

(Kelton, 2020, p. 181)

A proposal that, it seems, some critics might accept:

even if the role of the dollar continues indefinitely to create space to implement MMT macro policies, that does not mean that the US should do so. MMT's proposed policy amounts to a "US first" macroeconomic policy. Presumably a progressive approach to policy would adopt a more internationalist perspective.

(Epstein, 2019)

Conclusions

The concept of monetary sovereignty used by the MMT is extremely useful analytically despite its simplicity, and it is surprising that it has hardly been considered in academia when analysing the different macroeconomic situations of countries. However, despite its enormous usefulness, the criticisms it has received have shown it to be an incomplete concept. Some of these criticisms are correct in pointing out that full monetary sovereignty approaches are not equally applicable to all economies around the world, and that many developing economies face significant constraints in achieving and enjoying full monetary sovereignty. While I believe that the proponents of MMT are right to point out that any developing economy could enjoy full monetary sovereignty (own currency, flexible exchange rate, and own currency debt) and thus mobilise all the real resources at its disposal (whether many or few), I also believe that they underplay the economic problems that many developing economies would face if they tried to do so.

In particular, I have not found much mention of the problem of imported inflation by supporters of MMT. Even if we agree with them that currency depreciation cannot last forever and that it might even benefit the poorest and hurt the richest, the real problem is that during this time the rise in import prices can raise the prices of domestic products significantly, dealing a heavy blow to economic activity and the population as a whole. However, this problem is hardly considered by supporters of the MMT, and when they do address it, they minimise its importance. And it is not merely a question of a lack of real resources, it is a specifically monetary issue that could make things very difficult for the economy concerned beyond its material wealth: even with full employment, if inflation is out of control, the situation may be worse for the whole population, not just for the wealthiest. But, in any case, I agree that this is a political and ideological question: it depends on whether one wants to give more weight to full employment or to price stability. Still, in my view, the best possible solution to this complex problem must come from the developed economies as some advocates of MMT have proposed, not from the developing economies individually.

I also believe that part of this incomplete analysis of monetary sovereignty is due to a strictly economic definition of monetary sovereignty, when in fact, as many critics point out, monetary sovereignty is not only an economic concept but also a political one. Proponents of MMT speak of monetary sovereignty as a gradient of situations in which only the institutional details (currency issuance, exchange rate, and debt issuance) matter, but they forget that the position of each of these states on the geopolitical chessboard is fundamental. And this omission prevents them from providing convincing explanations for some situations. For example, the MMT concept of monetary sovereignty alone cannot explain why the United States has a currency that is much more widely used than others, nor can the chartalist view: the world's hegemonic currency is not so because its state collects more taxes than anyone else; it is so for another reason. Another example, the MMT concept of monetary sovereignty cannot explain why Eurozone states, even if they cannot issue the currency they use, are better off than many developing economy states that can issue the currency they use. The last example: the concept of monetary sovereignty cannot explain why there are states that, even though they have full monetary sovereignty, do not manage to have their currency used in their own territory and why part of the transactions are carried out in foreign currencies (usually the US dollar). On the other hand, all these cases can be better explained if the political issue is included: the US dollar is hegemonic because its State is the world's number one economic, military, cultural, and technological power; the euro is more stable than the currencies of developing economies because of the Eurozone's significant political weight on the planet; there are countries in which economic agents use currencies other than those issued by their State because their political power is weakened or in question.

Nor do I think that this implies a challenge to the concept of monetary sovereignty used by MMT; rather, I see the incorporation of the political question as enriching the analysis without overthrowing the concept. After all, the institutional details of the monetary sphere raised by MMT are crucial for analysing countries' fiscal room for manoeuvre, and this is a very valuable contribution. As Kelton comments,

> MMT helps us see why countries that peg their currency to a stronger currency, as Argentina did until 2001, or that incur debt denominated in a foreign currency, as Venezuela has done, weaken their monetary sovereignty and subject themselves to the kinds of restrictions that other currency users are subject to, as is the case for Italy, Greece and other euro area states.
>
> *(Kelton, 2020, p. 31)*

The only thing is that, although it makes an important contribution, the concept of monetary sovereignty falls short of accurately explaining the reality.

Moreover, the incorporation of the political question into the analysis need not be understood as an element alien to the postulates of MMT but can be understood precisely as a derivative of the very analysis that links money to the concept of political sovereignty mentioned above. Money is a tool of state power and, as such, is linked to the degree of power exercised by the state.

In other words, the value of a state's currency will depend on the degree of political sovereignty it achieves, and not only on the degree of taxation it manages to impose. This issue enriches the central postulate of chartalism whereby the value of money depends on taxation; in this case, it would depend on the degree of political sovereignty or power exercised by the state, which is a concept that encompasses taxation but goes much further. This idea is precisely the one defended in Garzón et al. (2023) using the concept of "influential space" derived from the chartalist thesis: the state not only exercises its power through taxation but also through its military power, its diplomatic, technological, productive, commercial, and cultural influence, which can precisely affect beyond its borders, allowing its money to be used there as well. And the opposite is true: a state with little political power and weakened by war, political or economic conflicts will not be able to exert full influence over its territory and will not be able to have its currency fully used in that area. Again, this is not a challenge to the MMT thesis, but a complement that enhances it.

Moreover, just such a view can be inferred from the writings of the neo-Chartalist Goodhart (1998):

> One implication of the C[hartalist] form theory is that the value of fiat currency will depend on expectations of the future existence of the current government and the prospective treatment of that currency by a successor government. This suggests that the valuation of a currency should be affected by both war "news" and news about the treatment of a defeated country after the war, regardless of the past and future rate of expansion of that money supply.
>
> *Goodhart (1998)*

Although he referred to wartime conflicts, relying also on the American and Vietnamese wars of independence – following Mitchell (1903) and Dacy (1984), respectively – such an analysis can clearly be extrapolated to a government undergoing political conflicts that threaten its survival or, at least, its credibility (as might be the case in Venezuela or Argentina recently). Moreover, Goodhart explicitly referred to what would happen if a state turned out to be too weak to fully enforce the use of its currency:

> Under the C[hartalist] view of money creation, the collapse of strong government would lead to the cessation, or downgrading of the quality, of minting and a reversion towards barter. In more recent centuries, however, the alternative, chosen by the private sector has been, instead, to switch from using the inflationary currency of the domestic government to the more stable currency of some other government, see Bernholz, 1989. The existence of such substitute currencies places some high upper limit on the potential ravages of the inflation tax.
>
> *Goodhart (1998)*

The flight to barter or to rudimentary trading systems has been observed in countries such as Russia just after the disintegration of the Soviet Union (Palazuelos & Fernández, 2002), and the flight to currencies of other states is what happens systematically in many Latin American countries, which, due to the enormous influence exerted by the neighbouring United States, tend to rely heavily on dollars for a large part of their transactions.

But there are other analysts who have also used the chartalist approach to analyse state power and its application in the global sphere. For example, Fields and Vernengo (2013) point out the following:

"If money of account derives its existence from the political power that establishes it, so does the international unit of account" (…). "the dollar is the key currency because the United States can impose that key products be traded in its own currency, and agents must trade in dollars to settle transactions with US corporations. The dollar's role in international markets and the advantages it brings are the spoils of hegemonic power (…) it is the power to coerce other countries that is central to monetary hegemony".

(Fields & Vernengo, 2013, pp. 7, 14)

Consequently, it is in the original postulates of chartalism that we can find the ingredient that MMT needs to complete and enrich its concept of monetary sovereignty: the link between money and political sovereignty.

Note

1 There is only one proponent of MMT, precisely its founder, Warren Mosler, who opposes the multi-faceted concept of monetary sovereignty because he considers that it increases confusion and makes it susceptible to a multitude of criticisms. For him, the important thing is to know whether the state is the sole issuer of the currency or not; "but it is not necessary to be sovereign to be the sole issuer" (Medina 2021).

References

Andresen, T. (2019). Initiating a parallel electronic currency in a eurocrisis country – why it would work. *Real-World Economics Review*, issue no. 89, 23–31.

Asselin, P. (2013). *Hanoi's Road to the Vietnam War: 1954–1965*. University of California Press.

Bernholz, P. (1989). Currency competition, inflation, Gresham's law and exchange rate. *Journal of Institutional and Theoretical Economics, Zeitschrift fur die gesamte Staatswissenschaft, 145,* 465–488.

Bonizzi, B., Kaltenbrunner, A., & Michel, J. (2019). Monetary sovereignty is a spectrum: Modern monetary theory and developing countries. *Real-World Economics Review, 89*, 46–61.

Cesaratto, S. (2020). Money and the external constraint: Heterodox challenges in economics. In S. Cesaratto (Ed.) Heterodox *challenges* in *economics* (pp. 123–159). Springer.

Cooley, J. (2008). *Currency wars: How forged money is the new weapon of mass destruction*. Skyhorse Publishing.

Dacy, D. (1984). The effect of confidence on income velocity in a politically unstable environment: Wartime South Vietnam. *Kyklos, 17*(3), 414–423.

Davidson, P. (1972). *Money and the real world*. Macmillan.

Edwards, S. (2019). Modern monetary theory: Cautionary tales from Latin America. *Cato Journal, 39*(3), 472–493. https://doi.org/10.36009/CJ.39.3.3

Ehnts, D. H. (2016). *Modern monetary theory and European macroeconomics*. Routledge.

Epstein, G. A. (2019). *What's wrong with modern money theory? A policy critique*. Palgrave Macmillan.

Fazi, T., & Mitchell, W. (2017). *Reclaiming the state: A progressive vision of sovereignty for a post-neoliberal world*. Pluto Press.

Fazi, T., & Mitchell, W. (2019, June, 5). For MMT. *Tribune*. https://tribunemag.co.uk/2019/06/for-mmt

Federal Reserve. (2021, October 6). The international role of the U. S. Dollar. *FEDS Notes*. https://www.federalreserve.gov/econres/notes/feds-notes/the-international-role-of-the-u-s-dollar-20211006.html

Fields, D., & Vernengo, M. (2013). Hegemonic currencies during the crisis: The dollar versus the euro in a Cartalist perspective. *Review of International Political Economy, 20*(4), 740–759. https://doi.org/10.1080/09692290.2012.698997

Garzón, E., Cruz, E., Medialdea, B., & Sánchez, C. (2023). The 'control space' of the state: A key element to address the nature of money. *Review of Radical Political Economics*, *55*(3), 448–465.

Glasner, D. (1989). *Free banking and monetary reform*. Cambridge University Press.

Goodhart, C. A. E. (1998). The two concepts of money: Implications for the analysis of optimal currency areas. *European Journal of Political Economy*, *14*(3), 407–432.

He, Z., & Jia, G. (2020). Rethinking China's local government debts in the frame of modern money theory. *Journal of Post Keynesian Economics*, *43*(2), 210–230. https://doi.org/10.1080/01603477.2020 .1734468

Helleiner, E. (1994). *States and the reemergence of global finance, from Bretton woods to the 1990s*. Cornell University Press.

Huber, J. (2014). Modern money theory and new currency theory: A comparative discussion, including an assessment of their relevance to monetary reform. *Real-World Economics Review*, 66, 38–57.

Kaboub, F. (2013). The low cost of full employment in the United States. In M. Murray & M. Forstater (Eds.), *The job guarantee: Toward true full employment*, pp. 59–71. Palgrave Macmillan.

Kaboub, F. (2019a). *Monetary sovereignty, colonialism and independence. The MMT podcast*. https:// archive.org/details/4hhpu7px3eabrdor3sviotkmr0lrbhkfx28ewxen

Kaboub, F. (2019b). This is how MMT applies to emerging markets. *Bloomberg Podcast*. https://www .bloomberg.com/news/audio/2019-04-05/this-is-how-mmt-applies-to-emerging-markets-podcast

Kaltenbrunner, A., & Painceira, J. P. (2018). Subordinated financial integration and financialisation in emerging capitalist economies: The Brazilian experience. *New Political Economy*, *23*(3), 290–313. https://doi.org/10.1080/13563467.2017.1349089

Kelton, S. (2011). Limitations of the government budget constraint: Users vs. issuers of the currency. *Panoeconomicus*, *58*(1), 57–66.

Kelton, S. (2020). *El mito del déficit: La teoría monetaria moderna y el nacimiento de la economía de la gente*. Pengüin Random House.

Kelton, S., & Wray, R. (2009). Can Euroland survive? The Levy Economics Institute of Bard College Public Policy Brief No. 106.

Keynes, J. M. (1976 [1930]). *A treatise on money, volumes I and II*. Harcourt, Brace & Co.

Kirshner, J. (1995). *Moneda y coerción*. University Princeton Press.

Kotilainen, K. (2022). A cosmopolitan reading of modern monetary theory. *Global Society*, *36*(1), 89–112. https://doi.org/10.1080/13600826.2021.1898343

Krivitsky, W. G. (2011). *In Stalin's secret service*. Enigma Books.

Kultti, K. (1996). A monetary economy with counterfeiting. *Journal of Economics*, *63*(2), 175–186.

Lapavitsas, C., & Aguila, N. (2020). Modern monetary theory on money, sovereignty, and policy: A Marxist critique with reference to the Eurozone and Greece. *The Japanese Political Economy*, *46*(4), 300–326.

Liu, X., & Wray, L. R. (2016). A sovereign currency approach to China's policy options. *The Chinese Economy*, *49*(3), 173–198. https://doi.org/10.1080/10971475.2016.1159905

Medina, S. (2021). Encuentro en Mallorca: Una larga entrevista con Warren Mosler. RedMMT. https:// redmmt.es/encuentro-en-mallorca-una-larga-entrevista-con-warren-mosler-parte-3-3/

Mitchell, B. (2016a). *La distopía del euro: pensamiento gregario y negación de la realidad*. Lola Books.

Mitchell, B. (2016b, February 11). *Ultimately, real resources availability constrains prosperity*. Retrieved February 20, 2020, from http://bilbo.economicoutlook.net/blog/?p=32938

Mitchell, B. (2016c, February 10). *Balance of payments constraint*. Retrieved February 20, 2020, from http://bilbo.economicoutlook.net/blog/?p=32931

Mitchell, W. C. (1903). *A history of the greenbacks*. University of Chicago Press.

Murphy, R. (2020). Book review: "The deficit myth: modern monetary theory and the birth of the People's economy". *LSE Blog*. https://blogs.lse.ac.uk/lsereviewofbooks/2020/06/22/book-review-the -deficit-myth-modern-monetary-theory-and-the-birth-of-the-peoples-economy-by-stephanie-kelton/

Ocampo, E. (2021). MMT: Modern monetary theory or magical monetary thinking? *Revista de Instituciones, Ideas y Mercados*, 72, 34–83.

Omran, F., & Zelmer, M. (2021). Deficits do matter: A review of modern monetary theory. *C.D. Howe Institute Commentary, 593*. https://ssrn.com/abstract=4094414

Palazuelos, E., & Fernández, R. (2002). *La decadencia económica de Rusia*. Debate.

Palley, T. (2020). What's wrong with modern money theory: Macro and political economic restraints on deficit-financed fiscal policy. *Review of Keynesian Economics, 8*(4), 472–493.

Panic, M. (1992). *European monetary union: Lessons from the gold standard*. Macmillan.

Papadimitriou, D. B., & Wray, L. R. (2012). *Euroland's original sin*. Levy Economic Institute Policy Note 2012/8.

Prates, D. (2020). Beyond modern money theory: A post-Keynesian approach to the currency hierarchy, monetary sovereignty, and policy space. *Review of Keynesian Economics, 8*(4), 494–511.

Reinbold, B., & Wen, Y. (2019). *Historical U.S. trade deficits* (No. 13). Federal Reserve Bank of St. Louis Economic Synopsis. https://doi.org/10.20955/es.2019.13

Rhodes, K. (2012). The counterfeiting weapon. *Federal Reserve Bank of Richmond, Econ Focus, First Quarter, 16*(1), 34–37.

Strange, S. (1988). *States and markets*. Continuum Bloomsbury Publishing

Tcherneva, P. (2016). *Money, power and monetary regimes* (Working Paper No. 861). Levy Economics Institute.

Thirlwall, A. P. (1979). The balance of payments constraint as an explanation of international growth rate differences. *Banca Nazionale del Lavoro Quarterly Review, 128*, 45–53.

Tymoigne, E. (2020). Monetary sovereignty: Nature, implementation, and implications. *Public Budgeting & Finance, 40*(3), 49–71. https://doi.org/10.1111/pbaf.12265

Tymoigne, E., & Wray, L. R. (2013). *Modern money Theory 101: A reply to critics* (Working Papers Series No. 778). Levy Economics Institute. https://ssrn.com/abstract=2348704 or http://dx.doi.org/10.2139/ssrn.2348704

Vergnhanini, R., & De Conti, B. (2018). Modern monetary theory: A criticism from the periphery. *Brazilian Keynesian Review, 3*(2), 16–31. https://doi.org/10.33834/bkr.v3i2.115

Viñas, A. (1976). *El oro español en la Guerra Civil* (p. 37). Instituto de Estudios Fiscales.

Weintraub, C., & Schuler, K. (2013, December 9). India's paper currency department (1862–1935) as a quasi currency board. *Studies in Applied Economics*, 1–27. http://krieger.jhu.edu/iae/economics/Indias_Paper_Currency_DepartmentWorkingPaper.pdf

Winczewski, D. (2021). Neo-chartalist or Marxist vision of the modern money? Critical comparison. *International Critical Thought, 11*(3), 408–426. https://doi.org/10.1080/21598282.2021.1966641

Wray, L. R. (2012). *Modern money theory: A primer on macroeconomics for sovereign monetary*. Palgrave Macmillan.

Wray, L. R. (2014, de febrero 25). *MMT and external constraints. Nakedcapitalism*. https://www.nakedcapitalism.com/2014/02/randy-wray-mmt-external-constraints.html

Wray, L. R. (2015). *Teoría Monetaria Moderna: Manual de macroeconomía para los sistemas monetarios modernos*. Lola Books.

Wray, L. R. (2019). *Fiscal reform to benefit state and local governments: The modern money theory approach* (Working Paper No. 936). Levy Economics Institute. https://ssrn.com/abstract=3448084 or http://dx.doi.org/10.2139/ssrn.3448084

4

MODERN MONETARY THEORY'S VIEW OF THE DEFICITS AND PUBLIC DEBT AND ITS CRITICISMS

Introduction

Adopting a chartalist view has many theoretical implications that lead to very different positions from conventional ones. We have already seen that one of these implications is the concept of monetary sovereignty: a State that fully enjoys this status can fully deploy its capacity to mobilise the real resources of its territory. But there is another equally important and controversial implication, as it is in direct opposition to many orthodox approaches: the concept of public accounts. For the Modern Monetary Theory (MMT), public deficits and public debt are fiscal situations that are understood practically the opposite of how they are understood by mainstream economic theory. In this chapter, we will identify these differences, delve into the implications of the MMT view of public deficits and public debt, and conclude by pointing out the most important criticisms that have been made on this particular point. Finally, we will draw our conclusions.

Different views on public deficits

Classical economists had a distinctly negative view of the public deficit and fiscal policy in general. This was because they considered that public spending and income policies did not affect the aggregate level of output and employment. Specifically, it was assumed that each monetary unit spent by the State was a monetary unit that the private sector stopped spending so that the total volume of expenditure and income remained unchanged. Underlying the idea that the natural state of the economy was full employment and full utilisation of the productive capacity, no fiscal stimulus could increase the product additionally since there would be no unemployed people to use or resources to increase production. Public sector spending could only be materialised as a substitute for private spending that, in the absence of the first, would have been carried out anyway (Blinder & Solow, 1973 p. 1). Consequently, the public deficit would crowd out private sector spending and reduce its potential for growth, something that was considered essential for economic development in a capitalist economy.

DOI: 10.4324/9781003371809-5

However, after the detailed exposition that John Maynard Keynes made – in an article in *The Times* in 1934 and later in *The General Theory* – it began to gain momentum the idea that a monetary unit additionally spent could raise the national income. Keynes was able to make this novel interpretation because he started from a different premise: contrary to the general belief that in an economy all resources are always used, the British economist emphasised that such a state was only one of many possible, being in fact more common that resources (labour among them) were idle (Keynes, 1964 [1936], p. 3). Indeed, in an economy in which there were unemployed people and machines in disuse, increases in public spending or tax cuts would allow unemployed people to get going to use these machines, thus raising the product (Keynes, 1964 [1936], p. 210; Samuelson, 1948; Seidman, 2012, p. 88). This was one of the main contributions of Keynes: the development of the concept of "effective demand" (as he called it in Chapter 3 of *The General Theory*).

The logical corollary of all this reasoning is the invitation to use expansive fiscal policy (increased spending or tax reduction), normally registering public deficit, during periods of economic crisis or recession – and, conversely, to relax this policy during periods of expansion. Accordingly, Keynes proposed the use of fiscal policy to stimulate output, especially through greater tax pressure on all forms of income disproportionately received by the wealthiest (Keynes, 1964 [1936], p. 95). But Keynes not only pointed out that an additional increase in spending could raise the national product in equal amount but also that it could be extended thanks to what he came to call "fiscal multipliers", the impact that a change in public spending or revenue could have on the output. Consequently, expansionary fiscal policies, which would normally lead to public deficits, could be very positive in times of recession or economic crisis; although they would have to be relaxed in times of economic upswing.

However, this Keynesian fiscal view was soon challenged by the "neoclassical" approach led by Lucas (1972, 1973) and Sargent and Wallace (1975). In order to achieve this goal, they based on the distinction between transitory and permanent impacts of that fiscal policy, although this distinction had already been made clear by Friedman (1957) and Modigliani and Brumberg (1954), among others. According to these ideas, even if a shock of public spending – that could record a public deficit – could increase the product in the short term, it would also generate a series of conditions that would end up impairing the economic activity, thereby neutralising the initial positive effects. There are two types of reasoning that would explain this effect: one associated with the demand for credit and another with the wealth effect.

The first one is known as the crowding-out effect of public spending. Some authors have referred to this term as the phenomenon of displacement of real resources that classical economists had in mind and that has already been mentioned: public spending is done at the expense of private spending (Blinder & Solow, 1973, p. 3). But, in this case, it is a different effect: the positive economic impact of any public expenditure shock financed with debt would end up being neutralised by the fall in other components of aggregate demand. It is important to note that this type of "financial" crowding-out is independent of the "real" crowding-out mentioned above: taking into account the different degrees of productive-capacity utilisation that an economy has, the "real" crowding-out could only occur when the economy is at full capacity; in contrast, "financial" crowding-out could occur both in a full-employment economy and without it (Friedman, 1978, p. 4).

The reasoning for this crowding-out effect is as follows. Obtaining financing to cover the increase in public spending would decrease the amount of loanable funds, causing an increase in their cost. On the one hand, the increased cost of financing private economic agents harms consumption and investment; on the other hand, national financial assets become more attractive than foreign assets, leading to an influx of capital that appreciates the currency, boosting imports, and harming exports. Consequently, the drop in investment, consumption, and net exports would displace the initial positive effect caused by the public expenditure shock. The result would be, therefore, neutral or even negative (Van der Ploeg, 2005). This is the result of empirical studies like those of Coenen and Straub (2005) and Cwik and Wieland (2009), which conclude that the public deficit financed with debt provokes a crowding-out effect on private consumption and, above all, investment.

This approach has been widely contested in the literature. Some have pointed out that this crowding-out effect can occur regardless of how the increase in public spending is financed so that the public deficit would not be the cause of this effect but in any case only public spending (Baxter & King, 1993; Ludvigson, 1996; Bom & Ligthart, 2014). Other authors have pointed out that this negative effect does not occur – or its effect is reduced – if the indebtedness is external since the crowding-out effect is transferred abroad (Shen & Yang, 2012; Farhi & Werning, 2017; Priftis & Zimic, 2018; Broner et al., 2018). Other analysts show that the crowding-out effect does not exist on consumption, and only in a reduced way on investment (Fatás & Mihov, 2001; Burnside et al., 1999; Basu & Kimball, 2004; Gali et al., 2007) or on wages (Linnemann, 2009; Ravn et al., 2006). Finally, other works reveal that the public deficit has more positive effects precisely when it is financed with debt. For example, Jong et al. (2017) point out that public investment financed with debt leads to more productivity gains than if it were financed by spending cuts, while Mountford and Uligh (2009) point out that, to finance a tax expansion with debt, it is better to do so with tax cuts and not with increases in spending.

The second explanation given – on why public deficit does not stimulate economic activity in the medium term – revives an argument used by David Ricardo called "Ricardian equivalence hypothesis": economic agents increase their savings in exactly the same amount in which the public deficit raises, completely erasing its positive effect. The basis for this reasoning is the following: consumers would understand that the increase in the public deficit would have to be compensated in the future with tax increases, so in order to face these future expenses, they would increase their savings, which would harm consumption and investment. Result: the public deficit would have no impact on economic activity (Barro, 1974; Buiter, 1977). Empirical evidence of this type of neoclassical effect is provided in Feldstein (1982), Christiano and Eichenbaum (1992), Aiyagari et al. (1992), and Baxter and King (1993).

From this neoclassical approach, reductions in public deficit could be expansive if they were interpreted as an indicator of future tax reductions, which would encourage current spending. This is just known as non-Keynesian expansive effects, studied through different methodologies and definitions of fiscal contraction. For example, Perotti (1999), Van Riet (2018), and Afonso (2010) find that expansive fiscal consolidation is more likely when public debt levels are high. Some authors, such as Feldstein (1982), Giavazzi and Pagano (1990, 1996), and Giavazzi et al. (2000), point out the importance of the fiscal consolidation dimension, while others such as Alesina and Ardagna (1998), Alesina et al. (2002), Giudice et al. (2003), and Forni et al. (2009) highlight the importance of its composition. For McDermott and Westcott (1996), both factors have the same level of importance.

On the other hand, some authors, relying on the idea that multipliers of expenditure are higher than those of income, propose a type of fiscal consolidation that aims to be as efficient and less harmful as possible: budget-balanced expansion. It consists in increasing income and expenses simultaneously to clean up the public accounts while stimulating economic activity. Concrete developments of this proposal can be found in Wren-Lewis (2011), Mulheirn (2012), Ragan (2013), Karagounis et al. (2015), Uxó and Álvarez (2017), and Uxó et al. (2018).

In short, as can be seen, and regardless of the nuances that exist between them, all these latter visions pursue the reduction of the public deficit to a target level, thus considering that it is negative that it remains high (if not directly that it exists). Keynesian views are more flexible in this respect: it may be positive to raise the public deficit in periods of crisis, but not in periods of economic boom. In contrast, the MMT takes a radically different view, which not only sees positive effects in keeping the public deficit permanently high but even considers it necessary for the economy to function.

MMT's view of the public deficit

Due to its chartalist view of money, MMT conceives public accounts in a completely different way from the ones we have dealt with in the previous section, but only if it is a State that is the issuer of its money (in this case it does not need to have full monetary sovereignty, it is enough that it can issue the money it uses). These states are the only ones that can create such money, hence public spending is equivalent to money creation: "the government spends simply by writing Treasury cheques or by crediting private bank accounts" (Tcherneva, 2006, p. 78). Conversely, tax collection is equivalent to money destruction: "Treasury spending always involves monetary creation as private bank accounts are credited, while taxation involves monetary destruction" (Tymoigne & Wray, 2013, p. 30).

Consequently, the government deficit would be nothing more than the amount of new money that the state has injected into the economy and has not destroyed. Conversely, the government surplus would be nothing more than the amount of money that the state has withdrawn from the economy, money that it would of course have had to create first:

> [The MMT/neo-Chartal] approach recognises that most HPM enters the economy as a result of fiscal policy. Whenever the government spends, it "emits" HPM [while]... payment of taxes drains HPM from the economy... Thus, government budget deficits mean that there has been a net creation of HPM, while surpluses drain HPM from the economy.
>
> *(Wray, 2000, p. 14)*

Precisely because the public deficit is a residual balance of the public accounts, something that is ascertained once it is counted how much money has been spent/created and how much has been raised/destroyed, it would make no sense to talk about its financing: "while both taxation and bond sales drain reserves from the banking system, neither provides the government with money with which to finance its spending. Indeed, both taxation and bond sales lead (ultimately) to the destruction of high-powered money" (Bell, 2000, p. 616). The issuing state has no need at all to get the money from anywhere in order to spend it; it does not need to raise it, nor does it need to borrow it. In fact, it could do neither if it had not previously created the money through public spending. Moreover, from this point of view, it makes no sense at all for a sovereign state to borrow money that it can always create and which, in fact, it has only been able to create itself at some point in the past.

This conception of the public deficit as a residual value is not only typical of Modern Monetary Theory but is also shared by the Theory of the Monetary Circuit, whose main exponent is the

Italian Augusto Graziani and which was officially presented in 1989. For example, in the words of Alain Parguez and Mario Seccareccia, economists belonging to this current:

> since it is an ex post value, the deficit is by its very nature already financed. When mainstream economists speak of "deficit financing" or the "monetization of the deficit", they display a profound misunderstanding of the nature of monetary circulation.
>
> *(Parguez and Seccareccia, 2000, p. 111)*

This analytical coincidence is acknowledged by MMT authors such as Scott Fullwiler: "there's very little difference between the entire paradigm put forth by chartalists and circuitistes/horizontalists like Marc Lavoie and Mario Seccareccia" (Fullwiler, 2010a).

With this conception of the public deficit, the theoretical phenomena used by neoclassical theory to disavow the fiscal balance, namely the crowding-out effect and Ricardian equivalence, are completely contested. Since the sovereign state does not have to (or even can) finance this deficit, it does not have to borrow money from anyone, so it does not reduce private sector savings and there is no crowding-out effect. And since it also does not need to raise taxes to cover the deficit, there is no Ricardian equivalence either.

Hence, from the point of view of Modern Monetary Theory, the public deficit does not reduce private saving, as the dominant view claims, but precisely the opposite occurs: the public deficit increases private saving. Because with the public deficit the issuing state is creating more money than it is destroying, ergo there will be more money in the economy, more money coming in for families and firms. This assertion is supported by the macroeconomic accounting identity that equates expenditure to income. If one economic agent spends a monetary unit, another economic agent receives it. Similarly, if we divide the whole economy into the public sector and the private sector, if the former has a deficit of one monetary unit, the latter necessarily has a surplus of one monetary unit. Consequently, the public deficit, far from reducing private sector saving, increases it. This is why Randall Wray comments: "government spending greater than taxing should not be called a 'deficit,' rather, it is government's contribution to our saving" (Wray, 2012, p. 18). Or in words of James Juniper and Bill Mitchell: "at the aggregate level, a government deficit is offset by (and identically equal to) a nongovernment surplus" (Juniper & Mitchell, 2008, p. 19). Again, this is shared by Monetary Circuit Theory: "the presence of deficit spending reduces the bank debt of firms and may allow firms to accumulate liquid holdings" (Graziani, 2003, p. 153). Conversely, when a state is running public surpluses, it is destroying private sector savings: "the systematic pursuit of government budget surpluses must be manifested as systematic declines in private sector savings" (Mitchell & Mosler, 2002, p. 248).

But probably the most interesting point that MMT makes on this issue is that, based on the premise that the private sector usually wants to save money to deal with unforeseen events in the future, public deficits are normal and usual: "persistent deficits are the expected norm (...) normally, taxes in aggregate will have to be lower than total public spending because of public preferences for holding some fiat money reserves" (Wray, 1998, pp. 81, 123). This is an assertion that completely breaks with conventional approaches. Modern Monetary Theory, far from understanding public deficits as something to be avoided or minimised, understands them as necessary and usual for households and firms to hold money and save. Moreover, MMT points to another reason for concluding that it is normal to run a government deficit rather than a surplus, and this has to do with the timing of operations:

note that it would be logically impossible for the government to collect more than it spends (or run a budget surplus), unless it had already previously spent more than it collected (past budget deficits). Thus the normal budgetary stance to be expected under these institutional arrangements is a budget deficit.

(Mosler & Forstater, 2004, p. 7)

And, indeed, this assertion corresponds to the empirical evidence: almost all states tend to run public deficits (Garzón, 2021).

It is important to note that, according to the MMT, the latter conclusions would not only be valid for money issuers, but for all states, including those that are users of money (although there is some difference). States or public administrations that do not issue the money they use do need to obtain money before they can spend it. Let us suppose that a non-issuing state collects 1,000 monetary units through taxes but spends 1,100, obtaining the missing 100 through borrowing. A private investor lends this money to the state, in exchange for repayment in one year plus interest for the risk incurred. The amount of savings of this investor has not diminished, the only thing that has happened is that it has changed form: before he had 100 liquid monetary units and now he has a financial asset (a public bond) that gives him the right to see back his 100 monetary units plus interest. In fact, at the end of the year, he will have more money than at the beginning thanks to this interest.

On the other hand, the money borrowed by the State is to cover some public expenditure, be it a salary, a public benefit, or a purchase of a product. Therefore, these 100 monetary units will end up increasing the income of a private sector agent, be it a public employee, a beneficiary of the benefit, or a firm awarded a contract. Consequently, as the investor who has lent the money maintains his level of savings, and as the State has spent 100 more monetary units in the private sector, the result is that the private sector has seen its savings increase by 100 monetary units, the same as the increase in the public deficit. As can be seen, in the short term this would be the same result as in the case of the issuing state: one currency unit of public deficit would increase private saving by one currency unit.

In the long run it would be different, but even better for the private sector because due to interest payments the investor will end up with more money, ergo one currency unit of public deficit would increase private savings by one currency unit and a little more. This is also pointed out by the father of the Monetary Circuit Theory Augusto Graziani: "a deficit financed by issuing government bonds increases the amount of interest payments and therefore the money incomes of savers" (Graziani, 2003, p. 140).

Public debt

The conventional view presents public debt as the amount of money that the state needs to borrow to meet its deficits. This money would come from the pockets of private firms or households and would have to be repaid over time with interests. This, according to the dominant view, would be negative per se, fundamentally for the same reasons mentioned in the case of public deficits, the displacement effect and Ricardian equivalence, since if they are negative for the economy when there are deficits, they are also negative for the economy when there is public debt, since this is an accumulation of deficits.

But in addition to these two reasons, there is another new one: interest payments. This is the reasoning used: as long as there is a public deficit, the state would have to pay the interest again by borrowing more, but this time by a larger amount, so it would also pay more interest. As the credit market is drained of funds and public debt increases, investors will no longer be so confident that the state can pay back the money, so they will lend the new money at higher interest rates to compensate for the risk. In this way, the state would have to pay more and more interest on its debts, and a snowball effect would occur, which would only increase public debt until it reached a point where no investor would lend it money for fear of not getting it back, leading to bankruptcy or insolvency because the state would not be able to meet its payment commitments.

In conceiving public debt as detrimental, the proposals of the dominant view are always along the lines of reducing or eliminating the amount of public debt. Many studies have tried to identify the optimal levels of public debt that a state should not exceed if it does not want to face bankruptcy and damage the economy (Woodford, 1990; Aiyagari & McGrattan, 1998; Collard et al., 2015). Probably the most famous study of all is that of Carmen Reinhart and Kennett Rogoff (2010), which established that from a public debt of 90% of GDP onwards, economic problems begin to skyrocket. However, it is also true that these economists were found to have made significant errors in their spreadsheets, so that, if corrected, no evidence was found that exceeding 90% debt to GDP was problematic (Krugman, 2013).

Modern Monetary Theory takes a radically different view. For a start, if the state is the issuer of its money, it would not need to borrow at all, it would create all the money it needs to cover its deficits. Moreover, if it did not create the money first, it would not be able to borrow it, because it would not yet exist. If it borrowed money, in reality the money it would be borrowing would be the money it created long ago: "of course, governments believe that they must sell bonds to borrow the funds necessary to financing spending. However, this is an illusion, as the spending must come first" (Wray, 1998, p. 78).

Consequently, from this point of view, what is called public debt would not really be debt, but simply the accumulated record of all the money created and spent in the economy, so it would not cause a crowding-out effect (because it would not absorb private resources), there would be no Ricardian equivalence because it would not be the prelude to new taxes (since it would not need them to cover its deficit), and it would not have to worry about interest payments (because it could create money to pay them). Therefore, what is called public debt would not be a negative thing per se, since it would be nothing more than the amount of money that the state has injected into the economy through public deficits, and therefore, the amount of private savings that has been created. Hence, economist Randall Wray points out that "calls to cut the government's debt are, equivalently by identity, calls to cut our net financial wealth. Fiscal Austerians are, by definition, wealth destroyers" (Wray, 2012, p. 19).

By accounting identity, increasing public debt would be tantamount to creating money and thus increasing the financial wealth of the private sector. However, this does not mean that it is a good thing to increase public debt and people's financial wealth as much as one wants, because doing so can lead to macroeconomic imbalances such as inflation. This would lead us to ask how much money a sovereign state can create through its public debt without causing macroeconomic imbalances such as inflation, but, as we will see in Chapter 6, this is a problem of a very different nature than finding a certain level of public debt that should not be exceeded, which is the typical one and the one that usually constrains countries' public policies (Garzón, 2021).

In practice, however, states, including the issuers of their money, often issue government bonds, thus borrowing money from investors. Why do they do this if it would not be necessary?

The answer given by MMT is because it is a way of controlling the interbank interest rate. The reasoning is given below.

The very recording of government deficits would increase private sector income, and thus the volume of bank reserves in the banking system: "government taxing and security sales drain (subtract) reserves from the banking system. When the government realizes a budget deficit, there is a net reserve add to the banking system" (Mosler and Forstater, 2004, p. 9). Again, this approach is not specific to MMT either, but is shared by Monetary Circuit Theory: "the higher the state deficit, the greater is the net increase in commercial bank reserves" (Parguez and Secareccia, 2000, p. 112).

Banks seek to make their reserves as profitable as possible, for example, by lending them to other banks, but as there are more of them in the system due to the government deficit, their attractiveness decreases and therefore so does the interest rate at which they can place them. Consequently, the public deficit pushes down the interbank interest rate (Mosler, 1994, p. 12). To prevent this from happening (as it might not be the objective of the monetary authorities), government bonds could be issued that offer a higher yield than bank reserves yield when borrowed. In this way, banks would prefer to use bank reserves to buy government bonds, so that their attractiveness on the interbank market would not fall, and therefore neither would their interest rate. The result is that the state, by issuing government bonds, would succeed in stabilising the interbank interest rate: "bond sales (whether by the Treasury or by the central bank) function to drain excess reserves; they cannot finance or fund deficit spending" (Wray, 1998, p. 85). Consequently, government bonds, like taxes, would not serve to finance government spending, but to serve another purpose: "taxes can be viewed as a means of creating and maintaining a demand for the government's money, while bonds, (…) are a tool that allows positive overnight lending rates to be maintained" (Bell, 2000, p. 614). But bond issuance would not be the only way to achieve the same result; the return on idle bank reserves could also be raised, since banks would also have no incentive to lend them in the interbank market, and their interbank interest rate would not fall:

> Treasury debt could be eliminated entirely if the central bank were to simply pay interest on reserves, or if the Fed were to adopt zero as its overnight interest rate target. In either case … there would be no need for sales of sovereign debt.
>
> *(Wray, 2003, p. 95)*

All this holds true for the reverse process: in the event that the interbank rate tended to be higher than the monetary authorities wanted, government bonds could be bought to add to bank reserves and thus bring the rate down. Eric Tymoigne sums it up as follows: "the central bank must intervene by buying an equal amount of treasuries from banks to avoid a rise in the OLR [overnight interbank lending rate]" (Tymoigne, 2016b, p. 1323).

Again, this approach is not unique to MMT; circuitists and post-Keynesians see this issue in the same way. For example, Eladio Febrero (2009) explains it as follows:

> the central bank, being the monopoly supplier of bank reserves, has the ability to control the base interest rate through the provision of reserves to the banking system, acting as a price maker and a quantity taker in the corresponding market.
>
> *(Febrero, 2009, p. 527)*

The authors of the MMT make a strong point that government bonds are just another bank account at the central bank, only this one would yield more interest than bank reserves. The issuance of public debt would be nothing more than a change in an accounting entry: "when the government does what we call 'borrowing', all that happens is that funds are moved from current accounts (bank reserves) at the central bank to savings accounts (public bonds) at that same central bank" (Mosler, 2014, p. 41).

So that would be the role of government bonds in money-issuing states: not to finance public expenditures, but to control market interest rates. In other words, government bonds would be a monetary policy tool, not a fiscal policy tool as traditionally conceived.

It is interesting to note that this is the opposite of conventional reasoning. As we have seen, mainstream economic theory tells us, based on the crowding-out effect, that public deficits tend to raise interest rates because they make private sector savings scarcer. However, from the MMT point of view, the government deficit tends to lower interest rates because of the effect on the interbank market of the higher volume of bank reserves. And this downward effect also occurs on government bond interest rates because the higher demand for government bonds pushes up their price and pushes down their interest rates. This approach, again, is not unique to MMT but is also shared by other post-Keynesian authors such as Marc Lavoie (1999, 2003) and the Monetary Circuit Theory: "[with public deficits] if reserves are excessive, banks will actually try to purchase new bonds, whose effect would be to push up bond prices and thus bring about a collapse in interest rates" (Parguez & Seccareccia, 2000, p. 119). Consequently, the public deficit, far from raising interest rates and the risk premium, would be doing precisely the opposite. And, of course, from this point of view, the interest rates on public debt do not depend on the "market watchers", as is implied by the view of financial displacement, but would depend solely on the decisions of the monetary authorities: "what monetary sovereignty implies is that the government, not bond vigilantes, has control over the cost of its public debt" (Tymoigne, 2020, p. 21). Hongkil Kim's study (2021) provides empirical evidence to support this approach, as it shows that the government bond risk premium is only a problem for non-monetarily sovereign nations: "a monetarily sovereign government, as a monopoly issuer of currency, can influence the prices of their liabilities to a significant extent, somewhat independent of existing public debt and market sentiment" (Kim, 2021, p. 577).

Moreover, from the Modern Monetary Theory approach, since public deficits are the normal and usual situation, interest rates will normally tend to the minimum unless the authorities act by selling government bonds or raising the yield on bank reserves. Therefore, in response to the academic debate on what is the "natural" interest rate in the economy, Modern Monetary Theory answers that, if such a level exists, it is 0%, the minimum possible (Mosler & Forstater, 2004).

Now, if there are other possibilities to control the exchange rate than issuing bonds, why do many sovereign states continue to do so? According to Bill Mitchell, this is simply reminiscent of the years before 1971, when there was still a gold standard and when states had to limit their money creation:

> during the breakdown of the gold standard system in 1971 and the rise of monetarism, governments came under intense pressure to maintain the behaviours and institutional structures that constrained their spending capabilities. Governments therefore continued to issue debt, even though financially this was no longer necessary.
>
> *(Mitchell, 2016, p. 22)*

In any case, such a procedure of issuing government bonds would not be problematic for a state with full monetary sovereignty (it issues the money it uses and does not tie it to any foreign currency or borrow in it), because it could avoid bankruptcy whenever it wanted by simply creating new money to pay the maturities of government bonds: "sovereign government is not constrained financially, which means it can never face a solvency issue" (Nersisyan & Wray, 2010, p. 19).

This, which may sound strange or naïve from a conventional point of view, has actually been recognised even by many important economic personalities and institutions. For example, Nobel laureate Joseph Stiglitz has remarked more than once in his television appearances:

> does anyone believe that the United States can go bankrupt? The US government can create money, and you can bet on what the level of inflation will be, but betting on the government going bankrupt is literally absurd (...) The US debt is a promise to pay US dollars, but the fact is that we create US dollars, so we will pay them. There is zero chance of default.
>
> *(Wonkmonk, 2012)*

Alan Greenspan, former chairman of the US Federal Reserve, said the same:

> that all of these claims on government are readily accepted reflects the fact that a government cannot become insolvent with respect to obligations in its own currency. A fiat money system, like the one we have today, can produce such claims without limit.
>
> *(Greenspan, 1997, p. 2)*

Also the famous billionaire Warren Buffet has also pointed this out many times, for example in an interview in 2011 when asked about the bankruptcy of the United States after seeing the problems faced by Greece: "we have the right to create our own money, that's the key. Greece lost the power to create its money. If they could create drachmas they would have other problems, but not a debt problem" (Wonkmonk, 2014).

In the same vein, the former president of the European Central Bank, Mario Draghi, was speechless when asked whether the institution he presided over, which is the sole issuer of the euro, could run out of euros: "well, technically no, we cannot run out of money. We have ample resources to deal with all emergencies. That's the only answer I can give you" (Medin, 2017). Even the former US President Donald Trump commented in a radio interview: "this is the US government. First of all: you never have to go bankrupt because you create the dollars, I hate to tell you, okay? So there will be no bankruptcy" (Nevertrump, 2016). Also the current president of the European Central Bank, Christine Lagarde, has recently reminded us that "the European Central Bank cannot go bankrupt even if it makes a loss" (Reuters, 2020). The Bank of England, which is the issuer of pounds, also points out in a report: "fundamentally as the creator of its domestic currency, a central bank will always be able to meet its liabilities in that currency" (Rule, 2015, p. 24). So did the president of the St Louis Federal Reserve: "as the sole manufacturer of dollars, whose debt is denominated in dollars, the U.S. government can never become insolvent" (Fawley & Juvenal, 2011).

As can be seen, the central idea is that the issuer of money, when it has full monetary sovereignty, can avoid bankruptcy whenever it wants. It does not need to issue government bonds to obtain financing, but should it decide to do so, the central bank, as the sole issuer of money, can always keep interest rates under control.

However, this is quite different in the case of states or public administrations that are users of money and not issuers, since they operate in a very similar way to firms and households: if they have a deficit, they have to borrow money, because they cannot create it. That is why these public entities could go bankrupt if they do not get enough money to pay off their debt. And it is the same for states that borrow in a foreign currency because to meet their payments they have to obtain a currency they do not create; it is also the same for states that link their currency to gold or some other asset because they cannot create it unlimitedly, or those that commit to linking their currency to another, because if they want to keep the commitment they cannot create as much money as they want.

To recapitulate, Modern Monetary Theory understands public debt as the total net financial wealth injected by the state through its public deficits, both in the case of an issuing and a user state. Issuer states do not need to issue public bonds to finance their expenditures; they do so to control interest rates. On the other hand, such public debt is not a problem for a state with full monetary sovereignty, but it can be a problem for a state without full monetary sovereignty.

Criticisms

Criticisms of the MMT concepts of public deficit and public debt coming from more orthodox sides are basically based on the financial crowding-out effect: as public deficit crowds out private savings, it is a negative phenomenon that should be avoided to a greater or lesser extent (Newman, 2020; Omran & Zelmer, 2021). This criticism has even been used by economists in the Keynesian tradition. For example, according to Paul Krugman "budget deficits do crowd out private spending, because tax cuts or spending increases will lead to higher interest rates" (Krugman, 2019). Another example: Thomas Palley comments that "both money- and bond financed fiscal policy are effective in Keynesian theory, and money-financed deficits are more expansionary because they deter any proclivity to interest rate crowding-out from increased bond supplies" (Palley, 2020, p. 474).

In contrast, more heterodox criticisms focus on the theoretical consolidation of the state and the central bank by MMT, as it tends to make no distinction between these entities, implying an unrealistic merger of fiscal and monetary policy. However, this criticism is not exclusive to heterodoxy. For example, according to Coats, "the relevant question is whether this way of thinking about and characterizing monetary and fiscal policy produces a more insightful and useful approach to formulating fiscal/monetary policy" (Coats, 2019, p. 573). Another example is Meyer: "the Fed doesn't do a stealth "reserve add" whenever the Treasury wants to spend money" (Meyer, 2020, p. 19). Interestingly, however, some of these critics have come to recognise that the theoretical consolidation between Treasury and Central Bank is appropriate:

> consolidating public finance, whether it's held on a balance sheet of the Fed or held on the balance sheet of the fiscal authority, is the appropriate strategy to understand debt burdens and debt sustainability even as the independence of the Fed relative to its role in the fiscal space is a legitimate topic of discussion.
>
> *(Mann, 2020, p. 21)*

However, as discussed above, most of the criticisms of MMT coming from such authors focus on other aspects.

Heterodox critics argue that the central bank is an institution with a different functioning and dynamics than the state: "irrespective of the country, we believe that the treasury and the central bank are different institutions that perform very different functions" (Gnos & Rochon,

2002, p. 49). For his part, Palley emphasises that the institutions of treasuries and central banks are very different from country to country: "the important point is institutional arrangements vary across countries owing to differences in country choices" (Palley, 2015a, p. 5). This is why they consider the theoretical consolidation of the state and the central bank to be "fictional" (Schlotmann, 2021) and unrealistic: "Neochartalists insist on presenting their counter-intuitive stories, based on an abstract consolidation and an abstract sequential logic, deprived of operational and legal realism" (Lavoie, 2013, p. 17).

To be precise, Lavoie does not find theoretical consolidation in itself illegitimate, but considers that it is not appropriate for some questions of public spending, revenues, and deficits: "such a consolidation, in itself, is not illegitimate. (…) But such integration may not be appropriate for the purpose at hand, as it confuses the readers" (Lavoie, 2013, p. 9). This is shared by Fiebiger: "conflating the central bank and the Treasury into an ambiguous 'authorities' (…) is inappropriate when the analyst is seeking to illuminate: (1) the processes of money creation; and, (2) the roles of fiscal and monetary policy" (Fiebiger, 2012b, p. 28). In the view of Lavoie (2019), it is one thing to believe that such consolidation may be preferable in order to achieve certain economic outcomes, and quite another that consolidation accurately describes reality:

> it would be best for MMT to abandon the story based on the general case, or else to present the consolidation of the central bank and the government into a single entity as an objective to be achieved through institutional change, (…) instead of an actual feature of economies upon which policy advice could be offered.
>
> *(Lavoie, 2019, p. 99)*

In fact, critics do not often doubt that such consolidation can be realised in practice; not even the critics furthest from MMT postulates, such as Coats: "if it were desirable to remove the existing barriers to central bank monetary financing of the government, it could be done" (Coats, 2019, p. 573). Although some critics such as Palley do not even believe that full consolidation is desirable: "my own preference is for greater consolidation and less central bank independence, but I would stop short of full consolidation" (Palley, 2015a, p. 5).

Proponents of MMT offer several justifications for such consolidation. First, they point out that Treasury and Central Bank consolidation is not an exercise unique to MMT, but has been applied by authors such as Marc Lavoie, Wynne Godley or Basseto and Messer (Tymoigne & Wray, 2013, p. 14). This is also acknowledged by some critics. For example, Marc Lavoie notes that: "other authors, including Wynne Godley (1999B), have occasionally consolidated the central bank with the government" (Lavoie, 2013, p. 9). For his part, Thomas Palley acknowledges that "old Keynesian analysis of stabilization policy (see Haliassos & Tobin, 1990, and references therein) also used the consolidated entity assumption" (Palley, 2015b, pp. 46–47). However, as we have already advanced, these critics do not agree with the consolidation assumption for the case at hand.

Another justification MMTers put forward for consolidation is that the central bank is simply an artificial and unnecessary institution whose existence is a convention, and that, even if there are institutional designs that differentiate one part from the other, for economic reasons they necessarily have to coordinate their actions: "the consolidation hypothesis does not aim at describing current institutional arrangements, rather, it is a theoretical simplification to get to the bottom of the causalities at play in the current monetary system" (Tymoigne & Wray, 2013, p. 13).

For this reason, they believe that consolidating the central bank and the Treasury into a single institution greatly simplifies the analysis and description of reality without affecting economic outcomes. For them, this theoretical simplification would also reveal the "natural" state in which the central bank and the state should be: any separation between these institutions would be an artificial and dysfunctional political decision, since, in order to pursue the best possible economic outcomes, the central bank is obliged to operate in harmony with the state. As James Juniper, Timothy Sharpe, and Martin Watts point out:

> no single model can capture the different institutional arrangements prevailing in these economies. But, the relevant question to ask is whether the MMT depiction of the operation of fiscal policy misrepresents the intrinsic features of a modern monetary system within a sovereign economy.
>
> *(Juniper et al., 2014, p. 292)*

In relation to US institutions, Dan Kervick notes the following:

> the central bank is itself an arm of the US government and thus liabilities of the Fed held as assets by the Treasury are just amounts owed by one government account to another government account. That the US government chooses to operate in such a way that payments from one arm of the government are processed on the books of another arm of the government is an administrative and policy choice, not a deep feature of the monetary system.
>
> *(Kervick, 2019)*

But the consolidation hypothesis would not be based solely on US institutions but would be valid for any other sovereign state: "that logic was reached after an extensive analysis of the institutional framework of monetarily sovereign governments; it does not result from ivory tower thinking" (Tymoigne and Wray, 2013, p. 14). Turning to the British case, Pantelopoulos and Watts point out that "even though the Central Bank and Treasury are separate entities, the consolidation of the two is not an abstraction which is divorced from the operational reality" (Pantelopoulos & Watts, 2021, p. 241).

MMTers insist that the central bank is obliged to coordinate with the Treasury if it wants to respect its own monetary policy of setting interest rates. Since the government deficit increases bank reserves and these push down the interbank interest rate, if the central bank does not want the interbank rate to move away from its target, it will or will not have to issue government bonds to drain excess reserves:

> the central bank will need to offset Treasury's fiscal operations unless it targets a FFR of zero percent (in which case it can leave excess reserves in the system) or gives up FFR targeting (and accepts potentially highly unstable overnight interest rates). Both the Treasury and the central bank are involved in these reserve management operations to maintain interest-rate stability.
>
> *(Tymoigne & Wray, 2013, p. 25)*

This argument is a torpedo in the waterline of central bank independence: "independence of the central bank is rather limited and it must ultimately financially support the Treasury in one way or another" (Tymoigne & Wray, 2013, p. 26). In support of their thesis, at least for the

United States, Tymoigne and Wray (2013) use the words of MacLaury of the Federal Reserve Bank of Minneapolis:

> The central bank is in constant contact with the Treasury Department which, among other things, is responsible for the management of the public debt and its various cash accounts. Prior to the existence of the Federal Reserve System, the Treasury actually carried out many monetary functions. And even since, the Treasury has often been deeply involved in monetary functions, especially during the earlier years. (…) Following the 1951 accord between the Treasury and the Federal Reserve System, the central bank was no longer required to support the securities market at any particular level. In effect, the accord established that the central bank would act independently and exercise its own judgment as to the most appropriate monetary policy. But it would also work closely with the Treasury and would be fully informed of and sympathetic to the Treasury's needs in managing and financing the public debt. (…) The Treasury and the central bank also work closely in the Treasury's management of its substantial cash payments and withdrawals of Treasury Tax and Loan account balances deposited in commercial banks, since these cash flows affect bank reserves.
>
> *(MacLaury, 1977, quoted in Tymoigne & Wray, 2013, pp. 26–27)*

Also in support of this particular thesis, Sergio Cesaratto recovers statements by Eccles Marriner Eccles, chair of the Fed from 1934 to 1948.

> In a testimony before the Congress, Eccles defended a bill that would reinstate the possibility for the Treasury to borrow directly from the Fed. This possibility had been abolished in 1935, although exemptions remained in place until 1981 (Garbade, 2014; Tymoigne, 2014, pp. 13–14). In brief, Eccles maintains that, although that possibility was removed to prevent the government from increasing the public debt by letting it perceive market discipline, this objective was deemed to fail since it was the Fed (and not the market) that determined interest rates.
>
> *(Cesaratto, 2016, p. 62)*

Kelton clarifies that this necessary cooperation between institutions

> it doesn't mean that the Fed has no authority to set monetary policy. What the Fed will not do is to refuse to clear a payment that has been authorized by Congress. As the Treasury's fiscal agent, the Fed will never bounce a Treasury check due to "insufficient funds". What this means in practice is that fiscal and monetary policies are operationally linked.
>
> *(Kelton, 2020 quoted in Meyer, 2020, p. 19)*

But proponents of MMT point out that this necessary coordination is not only the case in US institutions but also in many other countries, and for this they offer a varied literature (Allen, 2019; Silva & Richard, 2010; Sundararararajan et al., 1997; Vajs, 2014; Pantelopoulos & Watts, 2021). In the words of Tymoigne (2020), "the central bank is involved routinely in fiscal operations and the treasury is involved routinely in monetary operations" (Tymoigne, 2020, p. 3).

However, some critics have pointed out that the mere fact that the two institutions coordinate their operations does not imply that it is accurate to assume that they are a single institution. For example, Cesaratto notes that "cooperation between the Treasury and the CB is not proof of the consolidation" (Cesaratto, 2016, p. 51). For his part, Lavoie notes that "collaboration and information exchanges between two parties do not mean that they act as a single consolidated institution" (Lavoie, 2019, p. 104). For their part, Drumetz and Pitzer, while acknowledging that it is correct that "there is thus a need for some 'coordination', of a purely technical nature (provision of information), between the central bank and the Treasury" (Drumetz & Pitzer, 2021, p. 7), criticise that "MMT never explains what this 'coordination' consists in, instead letting the reader assume that the central bank would receive instructions from the Treasury that dictate the amount of liquidity to be provided or withdrawn" (Drumetz & Pitzer, 2021, p. 7).

MMT proponent Bill Mitchell adds to the debate that such an artificial separation between central bank and state is ideologically driven:

> elaborate voluntary constraints on their operational freedom to obscure the intrinsic capacities that the monopoly issuer of the fiat currency possessed (…) These accounting frameworks and fiscal rules are designed to give the (false) impression that the government is financially constrained like a household.
>
> *(Mitchell, 2016)*

This aspect seduces some critics such as Lavoie (2019, p. 105), and seems to convince other critics such as Cesaratto: "MMTers are right to argue that institutional complications can obscure simpler facts. After all, these technical problems have been cleverly introduced to hide the plain truth that the central bank finances public spending" (Cesaratto, 2016, p. 61). Precisely Pilkington (2011) highlights the value of MMT's attempt to ignore the ideological and "weak and fairly inconsequential" constraints that separate the central bank from the treasury, as it draws a simple discursive framework that helps a lot to disseminate the theoretical postulates, just as neoliberalism did.

The theoretical consolidation of the treasury and the central bank has several implications that critics find jarring, one of them being the equating of government deficit and money creation. Many of these critics argue that the state, before spending, first needs to obtain financing, either through the central bank (which they consider another institution), or from private investors:

> the "Treasury spending equals money creation" storyline requires highly-implausible assumptions (…) Any plausible description of deficit-spending must begin with a bond auction (act of procuring finance) followed by the expenditure (act of executing finance) and include the on-sale of the bond by private banks. After all, the Treasury must obtain "money" before spending.
>
> *(Fiebiger, 2012a, pp. 1, 6)*

Even if the money comes from the creation of the central bank, the central bank has to credit the treasury account, which would be a fundamental step and prior to deficit public spending: "far from paying for goods and services with its debt, which then the public would accept because it needs to pay taxes, the treasury thus borrows from the central bank and uses central bank money" (Gnos & Rochon, 2002, p. 50).

Proponents of MMT insist that this may be the specific case for a state because of the institutional design with which it has chosen to wrap its operations in practice, which would be a self-imposed constraint, not an economic inevitability. They argue that there is a "general case" for all sovereign states for which, once institutional specificities and voluntary constraints are removed, public deficits logically precede taxes and bond sales (Fullwiler, 2010b; Fullwiler et al., 2012).

Critics do not usually deny that they are self-imposed restrictions, nor that they are negative, but simply that their existence requires a different analysis:

> there is no debate that all of the policy constraints imposed on the Treasury's activities are arbitrary and should be abolished; however, it is no minor issue that the existence of these constraints invalidates the MMT description of how the State spends (e.g. Fiebiger, 2012a). MMTers acknowledge that such constraints complicate matters but believe that these constraints do not change their analysis.
>
> *(Fiebiger, 2012b, p. 28)*

Nor do they deny that in the "general case" things work the way MMT does; what they deny is that results drawn from the general case can be extrapolated smoothly to the specific case: "there are no logical arguments explaining how the 'results' of the 'general' case (...) apply to the 'specific' case" (Fiebiger, 2012b, p. 29). In Van Lear's view, the case referred to in the MMT "requires a very different institutional structure than what currently prevails" (Van Lear, 2002, p. 257). For his part, Marc Lavoie considers that the specific case captures "exactly the right story" and with which he "fully agrees", while he is uncomfortable with the general case (Lavoie, 2019, p. 98).

In this respect, Wray argues that, even in the specific case of the United States, the state can spend even if it does not yet have the funds provided by the central bank, since in that case the central bank provides overdrafts (Wray, 1998, pp. 115–118). This, by the way, is also shared by some non-MMT authors: "the fact that the central bank (e.g., the Fed) is not allowed to monetize public debt does not mean that it cannot let the Treasury draw checks on its account at the central bank" (Febrero, 2009, p. 528). According to Fullwiler, "there is no economically meaningful difference from the Treasury's perspective between the government enabling itself to obtain an overdraft and the government forbidding itself from doing so" (Fullwiler, 2010a, p. 5). This has been countered by Van Lear (2002) by pointing out that the fact that the central bank may offer overdrafts at some point "does not prove that state spending is independent of Fed policy or financing needs. The Fed will not approve of overdrafts continuously, and to do so would undercut its monetary authority" (Van Lear, 2002, p. 255).

On the other hand, proponents of MMT point out that the different chronological order involved in consolidation does not affect the economic analysis at all because actions involving only the central bank and the treasury do not change the situation in the private sector:

> a central bank could buy treasury debt and credit the treasury's deposit to the central bank, but this has no impact on the reserves of the banking system until the treasury uses its deposits (...) Thus, strictly domestic actions involving only the central bank and the treasury, which is the main justification for consolidating its accounts, should be ignored.
>
> *(Wray, 2003, p. 92)*

However, this is somewhat countered by pointing out that the central bank not only serves to finance the state but directly supports the operations of private banks, so that state money would not be equivalent to central bank money, hence consolidation makes no sense:

vis-à-vis the treasury, as well as vis-à-vis private banks, the latter's role is to convert money between themselves and thus enable banks to meet their reciprocal obligations. So central bank money and state money are different, not the same thing.

(Gnos & Rochon, 2002)

The question of bank money will be dealt with in the next chapter, but suffice it here to point out that for MMT all state money has its origin in the central bank, even if it has been injected by commercial banks from credits, since in that case it would be a kind of "leverage" on the money created by the central bank. This excerpt summarises this approach:

> The question becomes how the Treasury acquired the deposits it has in its account at the central bank. In the current institutional framework, the apparent answer is through taxation and bond offerings. While usually economists stop here, MMT goes one step further and wonders where the receipts of taxation and bond purchases came from; the answer is from the central bank. This must be the case because taxes and bond offerings drain CB currency so the central bank had to provide the funds (as it is the only source). The logical conclusion is then that CB currency injection has to come before taxes and bond offerings.
>
> *(Tymoigne & Wray, 2013, p. 30)*

Cesaratto, after studying the debate between MMT and its critics on this point, ends up agreeing with the MMTers: "'where do the funds for taxation and bond purchases come from,' and the answer cannot but be 'from the Federal Reserve' so that government spending 'is done through monetary creation ex-nihilo'" (Tymoigne, 2014, p. 11) (Cesaratto, 2016, p. 68). Cesaratto stresses that the logic of MMTers is acceptable from a Keynesian point of view and that it would be correct to consider that first goes the financing of public spending (in its totality, not only the deficit) by the central bank, and then the financing by taxes and savings: "the CB 'finances' government spending (initial finance) while taxes and saving 'fund' it (final finance). The consolidation hypothesis perfectly fits the Keynesian logic of this scheme" (Cesaratto, 2016, p. 66). This is exactly what Tymoigne (2016) argues: that the post-Keynesian endogenous money thesis itself leads to an understanding of the need for the central bank to cooperate with the state: "the traditional endogenous money approach can be generalised substantially by including the insights of Modern Money Theory regarding the necessary coordination of fiscal and monetary policies" (Tymoigne, 2016a, p. 1317).

However, this chronological order of monetary flows becomes more questionable when considering a state belonging to a monetary union, such as the Eurozone. In this case, the central bank is prohibited from financing the public spending of national states, so that critics point out that the source of financing here is indeed in the private sector:

> the euro system is not allowed to purchase government debt directly or indirectly. Thus, public spending now relies on bank credit (newly created money) or the sale of bonds in financial markets or through banking intermediation (hoarded money). In this institutional framework, all deficit-spending units, including national treasuries, make payments using money created by private banks.
>
> *(Febrero, 2009, p. 530)*

Other critics, such as Cesaratto, agree that in this case the story may be different: "I believe that further research on the actual institutional mechanism through which 'the state spends first' is still necessary, in particular in the Eurosystem" (Cesaratto, 2016, p. 66).

Finally, another conclusion that the theoretical consolidation of treasury and central banking leads to that also grates on critics is that public deficits are necessary for the private sector to be able to save. Economists such as Palley point out that there is another way for money to reach households and firms; the central bank through its operations in relation to the private sector:

> the central bank is the source of state money (so-called outside or high-powered money). It can inject outside money into the system by buying existing government bonds, buying private sector assets, or by lending to private banks. Moreover, under the current system, the central bank will increase the outside money stock by paying interest on existing money balances. That means government spending is not the only way to get state money to pay taxes into the system.
>
> *(Palley, 2020, p. 478)*

The same is argued by Marc Lavoie: "even if the government kept running balanced budgets, central bank money could be provided whenever the central bank makes advances to the private sector" (Lavoie, 2013, p. 9). Furthermore, Lavoie (2013, p. 9) notes that this is acknowledged by Wray himself when he states that "a surplus on the Treasury's account is possible as long as the central bank injects reserves through purchases of assets or through loans of reserves" (Wray, 1998, pp. 79–80). Tymoigne and Wray acknowledge that this is true but point out that such a phenomenon is only temporary:

> advances have to be repaid so the gain in government currency is only temporary. Only a government deficit induced by fiscal policy leads to net saving. Monetary policy can change the composition of net saving by substituting currency for other assets, but it cannot change the size of net saving, i.e. the net accumulation of financial assets.
>
> *(Tymoigne & Wray, 2013, p. 21)*

In any case, Wray also notes that this amount of money injected by the central bank is a minority:

> while it is true that central bank net purchases (or lending) also supplies reserves (thus fiat money), this is small relative to [federal] government spending and taxing and is taken as a defensive action to add/drain reserves on a short term basis (…) Thus it is fiscal policy [i.e. expenditure decisions] that determines the amount of new money directly created by the federal government.
>
> *(Wray, 1998, pp. 81, 97)*

The idea that the public deficit is greater than central bank advances by increasing the net financial assets of the private sector is criticised by Sergio Cesaratto because he does not consider the former to be more expansionary than the latter. While he acknowledges that deficit spending would increase private sector net wealth, he understands that from the point of view of the economy as a whole there would be no net wealth creation: "in case of productive-capacity underutilization, an increase of public deficit spending or of autonomous private spending (investment and autonomous consumption financed out of credit) has the same effectiveness in raising the degree of capacity utilization" (Cesaratto, 2016, p. 64).

In summary, following Wray and Tymoigne there are basically three reasons that MMT uses to justify its theoretical consolidation of the state and the central bank:

> First, the balance sheet outcome is the same regardless of the institutional framework. Second, the impact of Treasury spending, taxing, and bond offering on interest rates and aggregate income is the same with or without consolidation. Third, ultimately, the central bank and the Treasury work together to ensure that the Treasury can always meet its obligations, and that the central bank can smooth interest rates. The central bank is involved in fiscal policy and the Treasury is involved in monetary policy.
>
> *(Tymoigne & Wray, 2013, pp. 13–14)*

Conclusions

The MMT conception of public deficit and public debt is very different from the conventional one, no doubt due to the money-debt and chartalist money view as opposed to the money-market view. Public spending is equivalent to money creation and tax collection is equivalent to money destruction, so the public deficit is an *expost* indicator that simply shows the amount of money injected into the economy, hence it does not even make sense to talk about its financing. This conception of the public deficit invalidates the displacement and Ricardian equivalence effects that are used by economic orthodoxy to deny the public deficit. In contrast, for MMT the public deficit is not only a frequent outcome that is not negative or unsustainable in itself, but is even necessary for the private sector to be able to save and the economy to function. Public debt is not an amount of money borrowed from the private sector, but simply the cumulative record of all the money injected by the state through the public deficit. The issuer state does not need to borrow money because it is the only economic agent that creates that money; indeed, the borrowed money is money that it once had to create. This is precisely why a state with monetary sovereignty could avoid insolvency whenever it wanted to; simply by creating money to pay its obligations. From this point of view, the issuance of government bonds does not finance government expenditures but serves to stabilise interest rates and achieve monetary policy objectives. Consequently, fiscal policy and monetary policy are closely linked, which is why MMT consolidates the treasury and the central bank into a single institution when describing economic reality (and recommending economic policies, as we will see in Chapter 7).

The MMT conception of public accounts has hardly been criticised from heterodox approaches. The only point of contention has to do with the limits of government deficit (and debt) before it leads to inflation, which is something we will discuss in Chapter 6. In their view, not only is the treasury a very different institution from the central bank, but each country has very different institutional arrangements that make it impossible for the MMT simplification to fit all of them adequately. Moreover, some criticise that MMT is confusing the institutional design they would like to have with the institutional design that prevails in real economies. The rejection of such consolidation leads critics to question whether government deficit is equivalent to money creation and whether government expenditure is chronologically prior to government revenue, as MMT argues. For their part, MMTers justify the theoretical simplification by claiming that the institutional and operational separation between central bank and treasury is artificial, voluntary, and ideologically motivated, which only serves to hide the fact that sovereign states have full financing capacity. Moreover, according to them, treasuries in all states are obliged to coordinate their activities with their central bank, hence consolidation makes sense because it simplifies the analysis without changing the results.

From the point of view of this writer, it is very difficult to state categorically, as the MMT does, that the theoretical consolidation between central bank and state does not distort the practical analysis in all countries of the world, since there is a wide variety of institutional arrangements and it would be necessary to know all of them in detail. In any case, this does not seem to me to be a relevant issue. Instead, the important question would be whether such a consolidation is feasible in any country and whether it is much more reasonable and appropriate than the clearly ideological separation between the two institutions. And my answer is clearly affirmative; the theoretical consolidation of the treasury and the central bank seems to me appropriate and useful because it allows us to talk about a scenario that, although it does not currently exist in any country, can be achieved if there is political will. Focusing the analysis on an institutional arrangement that is artificial and circumstantial, however real it may be in many countries, only obscures the analysis and prevents us from understanding the potential of sovereign states. In other words, while it may not make sense under the current institutional arrangement in a particular country to say that public spending comes before public revenue, or that public deficits are equivalent to creating money, that does not mean that this could not be the case if the institutional design were simply slightly modified. And, since the ultimate purpose of MMT is to recommend economic policies that will lead to full employment with price stability (and not so much to describe reality as it is), it seems to me that such a theoretical consolidation is appropriate and relevant.

References

Afonso, A. (2010). Expansionary fiscal consolidation in Europe: New evidence. *Applied Economics Letters, 17*(2), 105–109.

Aiyagari, S. R., Christiano, L., & Eichenbaum, M. (1992). The output, employment, and interest rate effects of government consumption. *Journal of Monetary Economics, 30*(1), 73–86.

Aiyagari, S. R., & McGrattan, E. R. (1998). The optimum quantity of debt. *Journal of Monetary Economics, 42*(3), 447–469.

Alesina, A., & Ardagna, S. (1998). Tales of fiscal adjustments. *Economic Policy, 27*, 489–545.

Alesina, A., Ardagna, S., Perotti, R., & Schiantarelli, F. (2002). Fiscal policy, profits, and investment. *American Economic Review, 92*(3), 571–589.

Allen, W. A. (2019). *The bank of England and the government debt: Operations in the gilt-edged market, 1928–1972.* Cambridge University Press.

Barro, R. J. (1974). Are government bonds net wealth? *Journal of Political Economy, 82*(6), 1095–1117.

Basu, S., & Kimball, M. (2004). *Investment planning costs and the effects of fiscal and monetary policy.* University of Michigan.

Baxter, M., & King, R. (1993). Fiscal policy in general equilibrium. *American Economic Review, 83*, 315–334.

Bell, S. (2000). Do taxes and bonds finance government spending? *Journal of Economic Issues, 34*(3), 603–620.

Blinder, A., & Solow, R. M. (1973). Does fiscal policy matter? *Journal of Public Economics, 2*(4), 319–337.

Bom, P. R. D., & Ligthart, J. E. (2014). Public infrastructure investment, output dynamics, and balanced budget fiscal rules. *Journal of Economic Dynamics & Control, 40*, 334–354.

Broner, F., Clancy, D., Erce, A., & Martin, A. (2018). *Fiscal multipliers and foreign holdings of public debt* (Working Papers, 30). European Stability Mechanism.

Buiter, W. H. (1977). Crowding out and the effectiveness of fiscal policy. *Journal of Public Economics, 7*(3), 309–328.

Burnside, C., Eichenbaum, M., & Fisher, J. D. M. (1999). *Assessing the effects of fiscal shocks* (NBER Working Paper, 7459).

Cesaratto, S. (2016). The state spends first: Logic, facts, fictions, open questions. *Journal of Post Keynesian Economics*, *39*(1), 44–71.

Christiano, L. J., & Eichenbaum, M. (1992). Current real business cycle theories and aggregate labor market fluctuations. *American Economic Review*, *82*, 430–450.

Coats, W. L. (2019). Modern monetary theory: A critique. *CATO Journal*, *39*(3), 563–576.

Coenen, G., & Straub, R. (2005). Does Government spending crowd in private consumption? Theory and empirical evidence for the euro area. *International Finance*, *8*(3), 435–470.

Collard, F., Habib, M., & Rochet, J.-C. (2015). Sovereign debt sustainability in advanced economies. *Journal of the European Economic Association*, *13*(3), 381–420.

Cwik, T., & Wieland, V. (2009). *Keynesian government spending multipliers and spillovers in the Euro Area* (Discussion Paper Series No. 7389). CEPR.

Drumetz, F., & Pfister, C. (2021). De quoi la MMT est-elle le nom? *Revue française d'économie*, *XXXVI*, 3–46.

Farhi, E., & Werning, I. (2017). Fiscal multipliers: Liquidity traps and currency unions. *Handbook of Macroeconomics*, *2*, 2417–2492.

Fatás, A., & Mihov, I. (2001). *The effects of fiscal policy on consumption and employment: Theory and evidence* (CEPR Discussion Paper No. 2760).

Fawley, B., & Juvenal, L. (2011). *Why health care matters and the current debt does not*. Federal Reserve Bank of St. Louis.

Febrero, E. (2009). Three difficulties with neo-chartalism. *Journal of Post Keynesian Economics*, *31*(3), 523–541.

Feldstein, M. (1982). Government deficits and aggregate demand. *Journal of Monetary Economics*, *9*(1), 1–20.

Fiebiger, B. (2012a). *A rejoinder to "modern money theory: A response to critics"*. Political Economy Research Institute.

Fiebiger, B. (2012b). *Modern money theory and the 'real-world' accounting of 1–1<0*. Political Economy Research Institute.

Forni, L., Monteforte, L., & Sessa, L. (2009). The general equilibrium effects of fiscal policy: Estimates for the euro area. *Journal of Public Economics*, *93*(3–4), 559–585.

Friedman, B. M. (1957). *A theory of the consumption function*. Princeton University Press.

Friedman, B. M. (1978). Crowding out or crowding in? The economic consequences of financing government deficits. *Brookings Papers on Economic Activity*, *3*, 593–654.

Fullwiler, S. (2010a, July 8). Re-viewing chartalism/neo-chartalism, comment. *Reviewing Economics*.

Fullwiler, S. (2010b). *Modern monetary theory – A primer on the operational realities of the monetary system*. Social Science Research Network Paper.

Fullwiler, S., Kelton, S., & Wray, L. R. (2012). *Modern money theory: A response to critics*. Political Economy Research Institute.

Gali, J., López, D., & Vallés, J. (2007). Understanding the effects of government spending on consumption. *Journal of the European Economic Association*, *5*(1), 227–270.

Garbade, K. D. (2014). Direct purchases of U.S. treasury securities by federal reserve banks. 2014, FRB of New York Staff Report no. 684.

Garzón, E. (2021). *Vínculo entre saldo fiscal y endeudamiento privado. Propuesta analítica y estudio empírico* (PhD Thesis). Autónoma University of Madrid, Madrid.

Giavazzi, F., Jappelli, T., & Pagano, M. (2000). Searching for non-linear effects of fiscal policy: Evidence from industrial and developing countries. *European Economic Review*, *44*(7), 1259–1289.

Giavazzi, F., & Pagano, M. (1990). Can severe fiscal contractions be expansionary? Tales of two small European countries. *NBER Macroeconomics Annual*, *5*, 75–111.

Giavazzi, F., & Pagano, M. (1996). Non-Keynesian effects of fiscal policy changes: International evidence and the Swedish experience. *Swedish Economic Policy Review*,*3*, 75–111.

Giudice, G., Turrini, A., & In't Veld, J. (2003). *Can fiscal consolidations be expansionary in the EU? Ex-post evidence and ex-ante analysis* (European Commission Economic Papers No. 195). European Commission.

Gnos, C., & Rochon, L. P. (2002). Money creation and the state: A critical assessment of chartalism. *International Journal of Political Economy, 32*(3), 41–57.

Godley, W. (1999b). Money and credit in a Keynesian model of income determination. *Cambridge Journal of Economics, 23*(4), 393–411.

Graziani, A. (2003). *The monetary theory of production.* Cambridge University Press.

Greenspan, A. (1997). Opening remarks. In *Managing financial stability in a global economy.* Federal Reserve Bank of Kansas City. https://fraser.stlouisfed.org/title/statements-speeches-alan-greenspan-452/opening-remarks-maintaining-financial-stability-a-global-economy-8607/fulltext

Haliassos, M., & Tobin, J. (1990). The macroeconomics of government finance. In B. Friedman & F. Hahn (Eds.), *Handbook of monetary economics* (Vol. 2). North-Holland.

Jong, J., Ferdinandusse, M., Funda, J., & Vetlov, I. (2017). *The effect of public investment in Europe: A model-based assessment* (Working Paper Series No. 2021). European Central Bank.

Juniper, J., & Mitchell, W. (2008). *There is no financial crisis so deep that cannot be dealt with by public spending* (Working Paper No. 08-10). Centre of Full Employment and Equity.

Juniper, J., Sharpe, T. P., & Watts, M. J. (2014). Modern monetary theory: Contributions and critics. *Journal of Post Keynesian Economics, 37*(2), 281–307.

Karagounis, K., Syrrakos, D., & Simister, J. (2015). The stability and growth pact, and balanced budget fiscal stimulus: Evidence from Germany and Italy. *Intereconomics: Review of European Economic Policy, 50*(1), 32–39.

Kervick, D. (2019, June 6). Do banks create money from thin air? *Naked Capitalism.* https://www.nakedcapitalism.com/2013/06/dan-kervick-do-banks-create-money-from-thin-air.html

Keynes, J. M. (1964). *The general theory of employment, interest and money.* Harcourt Brace Jovanovich.

Kim, H. (2021). Sovereign currency and long-term interest rates. *International Review of Applied Economics, 35*(3–4), 577–596. https://doi.org/10.1080/02692171.2021.1908237

Krugman, P. (2013, April 21). La depresión del Excel. *El País.* https://elpais.com/economia/2013/04/19/actualidad/1366398440_370422.html

Krugman, P. (2019, February 2). What's wrong with functional finance? (Wonkish). *The New York Times.* https://www.nytimes.com/2019/02/12/opinion/whats-wrong-with-functional-finance-wonkish.html

Lavoie, M. (1999). Understanding modern money: The key to full employment and price stability. *Eastern Economic Journal, 25*(3), 370–372.

Lavoie, M. (2003). A primer on endogenous credit-money. In L. P. Rochon & S. Rossi (Eds.), *Modern theories of money: The nature and role of money in capitalist economies* (pp. 506–543). Edward Elgar Publishing.

Lavoie, M. (2013). The monetary and fiscal nexus of neo-chartalism: A friendly critique. *Journal of Economic Issues, 47*(1), 1–32.

Lavoie, M. (2019). Modern monetary theory and post-Keynesian economics. *Real-World Economics Review, 89*, 97–108.

Linnemann, L. (2009). Macroeconomic effects of shocks to public employment. *Journal of Macroeconomics, 31*(2), 252–267.

Lucas, R. E. (1972). Expectations and the neutrality of money. *Journal of Economic Theory, 4*(2), 103–124.

Lucas, R. E. (1973). Some international evidence on output-inflation tradeoffs. *American Economic Review, 63*, 326–334.

Ludvigson, S. (1996). The macroeconomic effects of government debt in a stochastic growth model. *Journal of Monetary Economics, 38*(1), 25–45.

Maclaury, B. (1977). Perspectives on Federal Reserve independence - A changing structure for changing times (1976 annual report). Federal Reserve Bank of Minneapolis.

Mann, C. L. (2020). Some observations on MMT: What's right, not right, and what's too simplistic. *Business Economics, 55*(1), 21–22.

McDermott, C. J., & Westcott, R. F. (1996). An empirical analysis of fiscal adjustment. *IMF Staff Papers*, *43*(4), 725–753.

Medin. (2017). *Video of Mario Draghi's statements*. https://www.youtube.com/watch?v=_fF3pNTtmfc

Meyer, L. (2020). MMT: Assume a can opener. *Business Economics*, *55*(1), 18–20.

Mitchell, B. (2016). *Modern monetary theory – What is new about it? Bill Mitchell – Modern monetary theory.*

Mitchell, W., & Mosler, W. (2002). Fiscal policy and the job guarantee. *Australian Journal of Labour Economics*, *5*(2), 243–259.

Modigliani, F., & Brumberg, R. (1954). Utility analysis and the consumption function: An interpretation of cross-section data. In K. K. Kurihara (Ed.), *Post Keynesian economics*. Rutgers University Press.

Mosler, W. (1994). Soft currency economics. Social Science Research Network.

Mosler, W. (2014). *Los siete fraudes inocentes capitales de la política económica*. ATTAC España.

Mosler, W., & Forstater, M. (2004). *The natural rate of interest is zero* (Working Paper No. 37). https://www.pragcap.com/wp-content/uploads/2011/02/WP37-MoslerForstater.pdf

Mountford, A., & Uhlig, H. (2009). What are the effects of fiscal policy shocks? *Journal of Applied Econometrics*, *24*(6), 960–992.

Mulheirn, I. (2012). *Osborne's choice: Combining fiscal credibility and growth*. Social Market Foundation.

Nersisyan, Y., & Wray, L. R. (2010). *Does excessive sovereign debt really hurt growth? A critique of this time is different, by Reinhart and Rogoff* (Working Paper No. 603). Levy Economics Institute of Bard College.

Nevertrump. (2016). *Video of Donald Trump's statements*. https://twitter.com/NeverTrumpPAC/status/729659605937205248?lang=es

Newman, P. (2020). Modern monetary theory: An Austrian interpretation of recrudescent Keynesianism. *Atlantic Economics Journal, 48*, 23–31. https://doi.org/10.1007/s11293-020-09653-7

Omran, F., & Zelmer, M. (2021, March 11). Deficits do matter: A review of modern monetary theory. *C.D. Howe Institute Commentary 593*. https://ssrn.com/abstract=4094414 or http://dx.doi.org/10.2139/ssrn.4094414

Palley, T. I. (2015a). Money, fiscal policy, and interest rates: A critique of modern monetary theory. *Review of Political Economy*, *27*(1), 1–23.

Palley, T. I. (2015b). The critics of modern money theory (MMT) are right. *Review of Political Economy*, *27*(1), 45–61.

Palley, T. I. (2020). What's wrong with modern money theory: Macro and political economic restraints on deficit-financed fiscal policy. *Review of Keynesian Economics*, *8*(4), 472–493.

Pantelopoulos, G., & Watts, M. (2021). Voluntary and involuntary constraints on the conduct of macroeconomic policy: An application to the UK. *Journal of Economic Issues*, *55*(1), 225–245.

Parguez, A., & Seccareccia, M. (2000). The credit theory of money: The monetary circuit approach. In J. Smithin (Ed.), *What is money?* (pp. 101–123). Routledge.

Perotti, R. (1999). Fiscal policy in good times and bad. *Quarterly Journal of Economics*, *114*(4), 1399–1436.

Pilkington, P. (2011). Philip Pilkington: A scribbler's response to Marc Lavoie on MMT. Nakedcapitalism, December, 12. https://www.nakedcapitalism.com/2011/12/philip-pilkington-a-scribbler%E2%80%99s-response-to-marc-lavoie-on-mmt.html

Priftis, R., & Zimic, S. (2018). *Sources of borrowing and fiscal multipliers* (Working Paper Series No. 2209). European Central Bank.

Ragan, C. T. S. (2013). *Economics*. Pearson.

Ravn, M., Schmitt-Grohé, S., & Uribe, M. (2006). Deep habits. *Review of Economic Studies*, *73*(1), 195–218.

Reinhart, C., & Rogoff, K. (2010). *Growth in a time of debt* (National Bureau of Economic Research Working Paper No. 15639).

Reuters. (2020). *Christine Lagarde's statements*. https://www.reuters.com/article/us-ecb-policy-bonds/ecb-cant-go-bankrupt-even-it-suffers-losses-idUSKBN27Z12S

Rule, G. (2015). *Understanding the central balance sheet.* Bank of England.

Samuelson, P. (1948). *Economics: An introductory analysis.* McGraw-Hill.

Sargent, T. J., & Wallace, N. (1975). Rational expectations, the optimal money instrument, and the optimal money supply rule. *Journal of Political Economy, 83*(2), 241–254.

Schlotmann, O. (2021). Is now the time for modern monetary theory or permanent monetary finance? Credit and capital markets. *Kredit und Kapital, 54*(1), 17–36.

Seidman, L. (2012). Keynesian stimulus versus classical austerity. *Review of Keynesian Economics, Inaugural Issue, 0*(1), 77–92.

Shen, W., & Yang, S. C. (2012). *The effects of government spending under limited capital mobility* (IMF Working Papers No. 129). International Monetary Fund.

Silva, A. C., & Richard, B. J. P. G. (2010). *Primary dealer systems: Draft background note.* World Bank Group.

Sundararajan, V., Dattels, P., & Bloomstein, H. J. (Eds.). (1997). *Coordinating public debt and monetary management: Institutional and operational arrangements.* International Monetary Fund.

Tcherneva, P. R. (2006). Chartalism and the tax-driven approach to money. *Journal of Post Keynesian Economics, 29*(3), 371–390.

Tymoigne, E. (2014). Modern money theory and interrelations between the treasury and the central. Bank: The Case of the United States. Levy Economics Institute of Bard College, Working Paper no. 788.

Tymoigne, E. (2016a). *Money and Banking – Part 2: Central Bank balance sheet and immediate implications.*New Economic Perspectives, January 16. https://neweconomicperspectives.org/2016/01 /money-banking-part-2.html

Tymoigne, E. (2016b). Government monetary and fiscal operations: Generalising the endogenous money approach. *Cambridge Journal of Economics, 40*(5), 1317–1332.

Tymoigne, E. (2020). Monetary sovereignty: Nature, implementation, and implications. *Public Budgeting and Finance, 40*(1), 49–71.

Tymoigne, E., & Wray, L. R. (2013). *Modern money theory 101: A reply to critics (November 1)* (Working Papers Series No. 778). Levy Economics Institute. https://ssrn.com/abstract=2348704 or http://dx.doi .org/10.2139/ssrn.2348704

Uxó, J., & Álvarez, I. (2017). Is the end of fiscal austerity feasible in Spain? An alternative plan to the current stability programme (2015–2018). *Cambridge Journal of Economics, 41*(4), 999–1020.

Uxó, J., Álvarez, I., & Febrero, E. (2018). Fiscal space on the Eurozone periphery and the use of the (partially) balanced-budget multiplier: The case of Spain. *Journal of Post Keynesian Economics, 41*(1), 26–49.

Vajs, S. (2014). Government debt issuance: Issues for central banks. In B. I. S. Paper (Ed.), *The role of central banks in macroeconomic and financial stability* (BIS Paper No. 76) (pp. 1–20). Bank for International Settlements.

van der Ploeg, F. (2005). Back to Keynes? *CESifo Economic Studies, 51*(4), 777–822.

Van Lear, W. (2002). Implications arising from the theory on the Treasury's bank reserve effects. *Journal of Post Keynesian Economics, 25*(2), 251–261. https://doi.org/10.1080/01603477.2002 .11051358

van Riet, A. (Ed.). (2018). *Euro area fiscal policies and the crisis* (ECB Occasional Paper No. 109).

Wonkmonk. (2012). *YouTube. Video interview with Joseph Stiglitz.* https://www.youtube.com/watch?v =HYXASbjErx0.

Wonkmonk. (2014). *YouTube. Video interview with Warren Buffet.* https://www.youtube.com/watch?v =Q2om5yvXgLE.

Woodford, M. (1990). Public debt as private liquidity. *American Economic Review, 80,* 382–388.

Wray, R. (1998). *Understanding modern money, the key to full employment and price stability.* Edward Elgar Publishing Ltd.

Wray, R. (2000). *The neo-chartalist approach to money* (CFEPS Working Paper No. 10). University of Missouri at Kansas City.

Wray, R. (2003). Seigniorage or sovereignty? In L. P. Rochon & S. Rossi (Eds.), *Modern theories of money* (pp. 84–101). Edward Elgar Publishing.

Wray, R. (2012). *A meme for money* (Working Paper No. 736). Levy Economics Institute of Bard College.

Wren-Lewis, S. (2011). Lessons from failure: Fiscal policy, indulgence and ideology. *National Institute Economic Review, 217*(1), 31–46.

5

MODERN MONETARY THEORY'S VIEW OF THE BANK AND ENDOGENOUS MONEY AND ITS CRITICISMS

Introduction

Conventional economic theory usually describes banks as simple savings intermediaries, connecting those who have money to spare at a given moment with those who need it at that moment. In this view, customer deposits would be used to extend bank credit. Again, this conception derives from the commodity view of money: money would be a kind of commodity that needs to be obtained first in order to be used later. On the other hand, the MMT, based on a money-credit or money-debt view, conceives banks as economic agents that create money by granting credits. From this point of view, bank credits create deposits, and not the other way around. MMT shares the post-Keynesian view of endogenous money: the demand for credit increases the volume of money. However, in contrast to the post-Keynesian authors, MMT sees the money created by banks as a kind of leverage on state money, all allowed and consented to by the authorities. This is precisely the point most questioned by some heterodox authors.

Debt pyramid

According to the money-debt or money-credit view – shared by the MMT –, any economic agent has the capacity to issue his own promissory notes; he can commit to deliver value in the future in exchange for receiving something of value in the present. Whether the counterparty accepts the proposal will depend fundamentally on the confidence in the issuer of the promissory note. After all, if the commitment is not honoured, there will no longer be any incentive to accept promissory notes from the defaulting party. This is none other than the keystone of Mitchell Innes' credit theory: the necessary condition for any debt to have value is that the debtor must fulfil his promise, or else the promise becomes meaningless (Innes, 1913, p. 53). Therefore, although everyone can issue promissory notes, the ability to get them used is limited to a very specific space: to those economic agents who accept the promise. This is what the economist Hyman Minsky referred to when he stated that "anyone can create money, the problem lies in getting it accepted" (Minsky, 1986, p. 228). However, as Stephanie Kelton reminds

DOI: 10.4324/9781003371809-6

us, because these commitments necessarily involve two parties (the one who makes the commitment and the one who accepts it) it makes no sense to speak of their existence before the deal takes place. Therefore, it would be more accurate to say that "anyone can make promises or offer to go into debt but the 'problem' is to find someone who is willing to become a creditor (i.e., to hold that promise or debt)" (Bell, 2001, p. 151). Or, to put it another way, "money is created privately when one party is willing to go into debt and another is willing to hold that debt" (Wray, 1990, p. 14).

Some promissory notes or IOU ("I owe you") are widely accepted while others are only accepted in a minority. According to this degree of acceptability all promissory notes can be classified, thus forming what Hyman Minsky called a "hierarchy of money" (1986, p. 228) or Foley a "debt pyramid" (Foley, 1987). In Randall Wray's words, "there is a hierarchical arrangement whereby liabilities issued by those higher in the pyramid are generally more acceptable" (Wray, 2012, p. 86).

At the top of this pyramid or hierarchy would be the IOUs issued by the state, as they would be the most widely accepted by the public, which, according to the chartalist view discussed in Chapter 2, is because taxpayers are obliged to use them to settle their tax debts: "the legal obligation to pay taxes and the state's proclamation that it will accept its own currency at state pay-offices elevate the state's liabilities to the top of the pyramid, rendering them the promises with the highest degree of acceptability" (Bell, 2001, p. 160). These state IOUs are also called high-powered money or base money and have both a physical and an electronic form. The physical form is cash, coins, and banknotes (the latter accounting for approximately 95% of the entire value of physical IOUs). The electronic form is the IOUs held in the central bank's electronic accounts, called bank reserves, which account for up to 5 times more than cash (McLeay et al., 2014).

Since in modern economies government spending and revenue collection are done through the banking system, government spending increases the balance of the beneficiary's bank account, and thus also the bank reserves of the bank concerned. Conversely, tax collection reduces the balance on the taxpayer's bank account, and thus also the bank reserves of the bank concerned. This positioning of government IOUs within the banking system is considered by many to be one of the main contributions of MMT, for example Marc Lavoie: "their main contribution, both to monetary theory at large and to post-Keynesian economics in particular: to show and analyze the links between the central bank and the government within the context of the payment system" (Lavoie, 2019, p. 97). Consequently, as we saw in the previous chapter, government deficits increase bank reserves and government surpluses reduce them: "government spending and lending adds reserves to the banking system. Government taxing and security sales drain (subtract) reserves from the banking system" (Forstater & Mosler, 2005, p. 156). And all this is without intervention by commercial banks or the central bank. Although, as we already advanced in the previous chapter, this approach is not specific to MMT either, but is shared by the Monetary Circuit Theory: "the higher the state deficit, the greater is the net increase in commercial bank reserves" (Parguez & Secareccia, 2000, p. 112).

Precisely because all private sector economic agents are obliged to use government IOUs to pay taxes, private sector IOUs are also denominated in the government unit of account, as this would facilitate their acceptability. Thus, there is only one unit of account, not as many as there are economic agents issuing IOUs: "the unit in which state money is denominated and in which taxes are due determines the unit of account for all money in the hierarchy" (Bell, 2001, p. 158).

In this pyramid or hierarchy of money, just below state IOUs would be bank IOUs, because they are also widely accepted by the whole population even though they are not compulsory. There are two interrelated reasons for this. The first one would be that the state allows these IOUs to be used to pay taxes, thus conferring on them virtually the same chartalist status as government IOUs: "the government will also accept some kinds of bank liabilities in payment of taxes" (Mitchell et al., 2019, p. 155). The early chartalists already explained this ability of the state to determine that something is considered to be money in general use. For example, in Knapp's words:

> all means by which a payment can be made to the state are part of the monetary system. On this basis it is not the problem, but the acceptance, as we call it, that is decisive. State acceptance delimits the monetary system.
>
> *(Knapp, 1924, p. 95)*

Lerner was also quite clear on this, stating that the modern state can, by accepting it in its offices of payment, "make anything it chooses generally acceptable as money" (1947, p. 313). Finally, James Tobin himself, who did not recognise himself as a chartalist but who studied money and the banking system in depth, also came to the same conclusion:

> by its willingness to accept a designated asset in settlement of taxes and other obligations, the government makes that asset acceptable to any who have such obligations, and in turn to others who have obligations to them, and so on.
>
> *(Tobin, 1998, p. 27)*

The second reason that would explain why bank IOUs are so widely accepted, and which is interrelated to the first, is that they would be easily convertible into government IOUs. No one would pay taxes directly with bank IOUs, but, in doing so, banks would be responsible for converting them into government IOUs, so it would be with them that taxes would actually be paid:

> in the modern economy, it appears that taxes are paid using bank money, but analysis of reserve accounting shows that tax payments always lead to a reserve drain (that is, reduce central bank liabilities), so that in reality only the government's money is definitive (finally discharging the tax liability).
>
> *(Wray, 1998, p. 37)*

Consequently, private banks act as intermediaries between taxpayers and the government, making cash payments (reserves) on behalf of taxpayers. Therefore, however much banks act as intermediaries, taxes could only be paid with state IOUs, hence it could be argued that "in reality only the government's money is definitive (finally discharging the tax liability)" (Bell, 2001, p. 160).

The key to this whole issue would be that banks have a lot of facilities to convert their IOUs into government IOUs, equating the former with the latter, and so the taxpayer would not normally be aware that the bank is acting as an intermediary between him and the state. And this would not be because banks have little leverage or create few bank IOUs; because in fact they do the opposite to maximise their profitability: "banks *leverage* their currency reserves, holding a very tiny fraction of their assets in the form of reserves against their deposit liabilities"

(Wray, 2012, p. 78). What would happen is that the state would make it very easy for such a conversion to take place because it would guarantee a healthy and stable banking system: "in modern financial systems, central banks stand behind the liabilities of the banking sector to maintain a sound payments system and accept bank liabilities for payments of taxes, thereby making them as equally acceptable as state-issued liabilities" (Tcherneva, 2016). If it were not for the state's guarantee of bank deposits, bank IOUs would not be so widely accepted:

> we accept bank IOUs as nearly equivalent to those of the state because banks promise to convert their liabilities into the state's at par. But such a promise would not be sufficiently credible without backing from the government through deposit insurance.
>
> *(Nersisyan & Wray, 2016, p. 1302)*

In any case, it is important to note that both motives would be important. If bank promissory notes were easily convertible into other types of promissory notes, and not into ones that would settle the tax debt, then they would not be so widely used:

> because the central bank guarantees that demand deposits will trade at par with government currency and because they are accepted in payment of taxes, bank promises (demand deposits) are nearly as liquid as state money and therefore occupy the second tier in the pyramid.
>
> *(Bell, 2001, p. 160)*

In short, bank promissory notes would be almost as widely accepted as government promissory notes because the state would be concerned that they should be readily convertible into the latter, which is what would be needed to pay taxes. Hence, bank IOUs are a step below government IOUs, even though the public cannot easily distinguish between them: "there is one big difference between governments and banks, however. Banks normally do promise to convert their liabilities to something" (Wray, 2012, p. 78). That "something" is precisely the government promissory note. And conversion does not only work for paying taxes but for anything else. For example, when a bank customer converts his balance into cash, the bank has to give him coins and notes, which are state promissory notes: "when cash is withdrawn from the bank, its reserves at the central bank are debited" (Wray, 2012, p. 79).

Finally, below the IOUs of the state and banks, there are the IOUs of the other private economic agents (households and non-financial firms): "the debts of firms and households occupy the third and fourth tiers, respectively. This is because there is at least some chance that they will not trade at par with government money (which is needed to pay taxes)" (Bell, 2001, p. 159). The IOUs that any family or business might create would have very low acceptability because no one would be obliged to use them (as they are not used to pay taxes), so only those with a close link to their issuers (e.g. a family member or a customer) would be willing to accept them. However, the acceptability of corporate promissory notes would normally be higher than household promissory notes, partly because firms tend to have greater economic weight and deeper markets: "firms' promises are more readily convertible into the medium of exchange (i.e. are more liquid) than household's promises because better secondary markets exist for their resale" (Bell, 2001, p. 159).

Economic agents would promise to convert their own IOUs into IOUs higher up in this hierarchy of money; a household can promise to pay with a share in a company, a company with a bank balance, and a bank with coins and notes: "each economic unit, except the government, has to deliver a third party's IOU (that sits somewhere higher in the pyramid) to settle its debt obligations" (Tcherneva, 2016, p. 16). The key is that there would be nothing above the state money at the top of the pyramid; the state would be the only economic agent that does not deliver anything in exchange for its IOUs: "the notes should actually say 'I promise to accept this note in payment of taxes'. We know that the UK Treasury will actually pay nothing (apart from another note) when the five-pound paper money is presented" (Wray, 2012, p. 49). Therefore, government IOUs would form the core of the debt pyramid: "the whole pyramid is based on leveraging of (a relatively smaller number of) government IOUs" (Wray, 2012, p. 87). Government IOUs, because they should be used to settle tax debts and because they would not be convertible into anything, would form the type of money that would shape the rest of the IOUs, the most important money of all:

> fiat money issued by the state is thus the money used as the link between the public and the private pay communities. It is the money that sits at the top of the debt pyramid (or hierarchy), or the "definitive" and "valuta money".
>
> *(Wray, 1998, p. 77)*

Bank money

The promissory notes of banks would be issued when they grant credits: "banks create bank money at the stroke of a pen via the process of lending" (Tcherneva, 2016, p. 15). When a bank grants a loan to an economic agent, it is not handing over anything, it is only committing to pay a certain amount of promissory notes from the state. If a family requests a credit of a certain number of monetary units, the bank would credit its bank account so that it would increase by that amount, which would be reflecting the amount of government promissory notes it has committed to deliver when it requests it. This is what was called stylograph money by James Tobin (1963), referring to the fact that the money given on credit was simply what was written (or typed in modern times) by the bank worker. Some economists at the Bank of England have recognised that money creation works in this way and have explained it in detail: "whenever a bank makes a loan, it simultaneously creates a matching deposit in the borrower's bank account, thereby creating new money" (McLeay et al., 2014, p. 14). This was, after all, something even Schumpeter noted: "the banker plays the role of the 'ephor of capitalism ... the creation of new purchasing power out of nothing – out of nothing" (Schumpeter, 1912, pp. 72–73).

The bank's promissory note would be extinguished when the customer withdrew his entire balance in cash – since it is a government note in physical form; or when the customer made, for the full value of his balance, a transfer to another bank or an electronic payment to someone with an account at a different bank – so that the original bank's note would be converted into a receiving bank's note (Wray, 2012, pp. 84–85). If these transactions were made in an amount less than the total balance, then the promissory note would not be extinguished, but would simply be smaller in magnitude. In Randall Wray's words:

> when the recipient "cashes" a Treasury cheque, a bank will convert reserves to currency – which is always supplied on demand by the Fed, which acts as the Treasury's "bank," converting one kind of Treasury liability (a cheque written to the public) to another kind (coins or an IOU to the Fed, offset by Fed issuance of paper notes).
>
> *(Wray, 1998, pp. 77–78)*

MMT argues that this conception of bank money helps explain many typical phenomena in the banking system, such as liquidity failures: banks would issue more of their own IOUs than they hold in government notes, so that if they were forced to extinguish more of their own IOUs than they had in government notes, they would be forced to fail (unless the government provided them with more state notes): "without guarantees of access to the central bank (to make their liabilities more liquid) and to government insurante (to reduce default risk on their liabilities), banks could not operate with such high leverage ratios" (Wray, 2012, p. 280).

The banks' objective in issuing IOUs would be to make a profit through the interest collected. When a customer repays a loan, the bank would no longer have a commitment to deliver state-issued promissory notes on demand, so it would simply extinguish its own promissory note. But the interest on the loan would be paid with state promissory notes, and that is where we would have to find the source of the banks' enrichment. In short, the banks would be constantly creating and deleting IOUs for the sole purpose of charging interest on them, which is what they primarily profit from (they would also do so with commissions and other transactions). As Wray explains, "[banks] are true 'intermediaries', making profits not out of commodity production but rather by providing the liquid 'money' needed for commodity production – creating their IOUs to purchase the IOUs of others, and reaping profits from the interest rate differential" (Wray, 2012, p. 280).

As bank credits are simply a commitment by the bank to deliver state promissory notes, an amount that would be typed into the bank account, one would think that banks can extend credit endlessly, because the typing or the ink on the stylographs does not run out. But in reality the ability to commit to something would be limited. As we have already seen, according to Innes' theory of credit, the necessary condition for any debt to have value is that the debtor must fulfil his promise, otherwise the promise would become meaningless. Banks would not escape this maxim: if they issue too many of their own IOUs promising to deliver government IOUs, it could happen that at some point they would not have as many as they have promised to deliver, thus losing people's confidence and their deposits, and possibly going bankrupt due to lack of liquidity.

However, banks would have several ways to obtain government notes. One way would be through the bank's founding capital. The founders would set up the bank using government IOUs, with the intention that the banking business would multiply their amount in the future. Another way would be through external financing from economic agents who would invest in the company through shares, bonds, or loans. All of this would obviously be done with government promissory notes. Another, the fundamental one, and as we have already pointed out, would be through the banking business itself: with interest, commissions, and other services, as clients would pay with state promissory notes. And finally, there would be the channel of obtaining government IOUs from the central bank. This channel would normally be available because it would not be in the interest of states for their banks to fail and leave customers without their savings. Post-Keynesian economists James Culham and John King explain: "the central bank's primary responsibility is to ensure that there is enough liquidity in the banking system to facilitate bank transfers" (Culham & King, 2013, p. 395). And, as economist Thomas Palley reminds us, failure to do so could cause banks to fail: "if central banks do not accommodate the increase in deposits that follows the increase in lending, the banking system, which will have become insolvent, will collapse" (Palley, 2006, p. 71).

What would happen is that, as a rule, the central bank would grant them these government notes at a higher cost than normal, so that banks would resort to this route only if they had no other choice; this is why the central bank is known as a lender of last resort: "in a crisis, an important role played by the central banks is to operate as a 'lender of last resort', providing reserves on demand to financial institutions" (Wray, 2012, p. 89).

Endogenous money

The conventional view of how the central bank supplies state money to banks is known as the monetary multiplier, which was explained in some detail by Paul Samuelson and is the one that appears in mainstream economics textbooks (Friedman, 1960; Mathews, 1961; Samuelson et al., 2003): first, the central bank would create a quantity of high-powered money, the monetary base (which would be the equivalent of the state money we have been talking about), and then the private banks would create bank money from that quantity, thus obtaining the money supply, the total quantity of money. This quantity would be a multiplication of that first monetary base. Consequently, the monetary authorities, through the central bank, would be controlling the amount of money that is put into circulation through the private banks. If they wanted more money in circulation, they would create more high-powered money because banks could multiply it; if they wanted less, they would create little high-powered money because banks would be forced to create less bank money.

But this view has been strongly criticised by both post-Keynesian economists and central bankers (Goodhart, 1984). In the aforementioned bulletin of the Bank of England itself, one can read: "neither step in that story represents an accurate description of the relationship between money and monetary policy in the modern economy" (McLeay et al., 2014, p. 21). For his part, economist Thomas Palley reminds us that "modern central banks abandoned in the 1980s their attempt to control the total amount of money created from the monetary base" (Palley, 2006, p. 71). Even former Federal Reserve Chairman Ben Bernanke explained in a lecture that the money multiplier is not a faithful explanation of reality (Bernanke, 2007).

An alternative view is that of endogenous money: first, banks would extend credit to customers they believe to be creditworthy, which would create bank deposits, and then, only in case they needed government IOUs to meet their obligations or legal requirements, would they take care to obtain them by borrowing them from other banks or, in the last case, directly from the central bank: "banks make loans independent of reserve positions, then during the next accounting period borrow any needed reserves" (Mosler, 1995, p. 5). This is something that even a vice-president of the New York Federal Reserve, Alan Holmes, acknowledged a long time ago: "in the real world, banks extend credit, creating deposits in the process, and look for the reserves later" (Holmes, 1969, p. 73). The name "endogenous" money refers to the fact that money would be created endogenously to economic activity (i.e. money would originate with economic activity, just when bank credit is granted because it is requested by someone to buy or invest), not exogenously or outside of it as the conventional view, which states that the central bank creates money independently of the purchases or investments taking place in the economy (Pollin, 1991).

Therefore, the monetary authorities would not control the quantity of bank money, because it would not be limited by the state money created. On the contrary, banks would grant credit on their own, thus creating bank money, and then central banks would create state money to adapt it to the banks' needs: "the imperatives of the accounting system require the Fed to lend the banks whatever they need. … A central bank can only be the follower, not the leader when it adjusts reserve balances in the banking system" (Mosler, 1995, p. 5). It is the banks that would determine the total amount of money that will be available through the granting of credit, which, in turn, would depend on how much credit households and firms demand, and this in turn would depend on the economic cycle; in times of economic growth more credit would be demanded, and in times of crisis less would be demanded: "as the endogenous money approach stresses, loans create deposits, which in the aggregate create purchasing power from private credit" (Tcherneva, 2016). The central bank would not determine the quantity of money; it would only adapt to what is happening in the economy; it is the inverse view of the monetary multiplier: "the money multiplier is backwards. Changes in the money supply cause changes in bank reserves and the monetary base, not vice versa" (Mosler, 1995, p. 3). According to one of the most important proponents of the endogenous money view, Basil Moore (1988), the endogenous money approach should not be understood as a framework that presents the central bank as an agent that has no influence whatsoever on the quantity of money, but rather that this influence would be through prices rather than quantity, which would significantly change the analysis.

Whether banks need these bank reserves and ask the central bank for them or not will depend mainly on two factors: (1) on what their customers do – because if they withdraw the money in cash or if they pay people whose bank is different, the banks will have to extinguish their IOUs and will have to deliver state IOUs – and (2) on banking regulations – such as the statutory cash ratio or credit provisions, which establish a minimum of state IOUs for each amount of bank IOU issued. Should they eventually need these bank reserves, then they would obtain them through the various avenues mentioned above, with the central bank as a last resort. Only when the bank was in a very weak situation, close to insolvency, would it not be able to obtain sufficient bank reserves. But if the bank was of considerable size and could destabilise the economy with its failure, the authorities would most likely do what was necessary for it to obtain bank reserves, either through bailouts, nationalisations, or mechanisms for it to be absorbed by another healthier bank.

This view of endogenous money was pointed out long ago by some economists of the British School of Banking in the mid-nineteenth century and used by economists such as John Maynard Keynes, Michael Kalecki, and Joan Robinson, although it was not explicitly and directly addressed until the late 1960s by the economist Nicholas Kaldor (1960). According to Wray (2015), Hyman Minsky also based his work in those years on the endogeneity view of bank money, something also discussed by Lavoie (1997). Years later, the economist Basil Moore developed this endogenous money view in detail and updated it to modern monetary systems, forming one of the best-known explanations to date (Moore, 1988). Thereafter, the founders of MMT adopted the endogenous view of money (Wray, 1990, 1992a, 1992b).

In short, what MMT does is to combine the endogenous money approach with the chartalist state money approach to provide a theoretical framework that, according to them, better describes the reality of modern monetary systems: "MMT-by providing a more complete picture of how money is created in modern capitalist economies that is grounded in historical and institutional analysis-extends endogenous money theory, integrating it with the state money approach" (Nersisyan & Wray, 2016, p. 1299). This is highlighted by Tymoigne in the very title of one of his articles: "Government monetary and fiscal operations: generalising the endogenous money approach" (Tymoigne, 2016).

Criticisms

The main heterodox criticism of the MMT conception of bank money and endogenous money comes from post-Keynesian economists – the first to develop the endogeneity of money approach:

"Wray's account of the money-creation process is at odds with the post-Keynesian approach" (Gnos & Rochon, 2002, p. 45). These authors question the idea that the money created by banks is a leveraging of state money, and they do so basically for two reasons: (1) private banks would have historically created their own IOUs without the need for state money and, therefore, without leveraging on it, and (2) bank money would be created from the demand for credit from the private sector, ergo the state would play no role in this process. In the words of Eladio Febrero:

> we find the term "leverage," relating bank money to state money, a rather troublesome term from a historical perspective (private money predates state money) and because of the logic of endogenous money (banks create deposits when they accept demands for credit and reserves are obtained later).
>
> *(Febrero, 2009, p. 524)*

On the first point, Perry Mehrling notes that "private finance is a better logical place to start when trying to understand modern money" (Mehrling, 2000, p. 402), and Rochon and Vernengo point out that "it is the fact that bank loans must be repaid that ensures the utilization of bank money, and money becomes a creature of banks rather than a creature of the state" (Rochon & Vernengo, 2003, p. 61). On the other hand, as we saw in Chapters 1 and 2, the MMTers place the origin of state money much earlier than bank money, so that the latter would not only be later, but also dependent on the former:

> states (and their predecessors) managed without banks for thousands of years and today the central banks and private banks operate within state money systems – with the state choosing the money of account and with currency and reserves occupying the top spot in the money hierarchy. (...) state money comes before bank money.
>
> *(Nersisyan & Wray, 2016, p. 1304)*

Parguez and Secareccia (2000) attempt to bridge the gap between the two views with the following approach. On the one hand, they agree with the MMTers that bank money could not exist without the state: "we have argued that credit money could not exist without the state, and that all credit-driven money is by its very nature a fiat money, irrespective of whether it takes the form of a commercial bank or central bank liability" (Parguez & Secareccia, 2000, p. 107). But, on the other hand, they also believe that bank money is essential for state money to operate properly: "state power alone cannot guarantee the existence and survival of a viable monetary system" (Parguez & Secareccia, 2000, p. 107). This would be so because what would give value to any kind of money, including state money, would be the future production that is financed by bank money:

> money is at all times the liabilities issued by banking institutions which have been endorsed by the state primarily for the purpose of financing the formation of future real wealth. This money has a real extrinsic value because every holder of these liabilities has acquired a claim on the future physical wealth that results from the initial bank credit advances.
>
> *(Parguez & Secareccia, 2000, p. 107)*

As in Chapter 4, the experience of the European Economic Union is used by some authors to position themselves in this debate, in this case by differentiating between state money and central bank money. Due to the prohibition by the European Central Bank to directly finance member states, the key and original money of the economic process would be bank money, which would challenge the chartalist view:

> it is the cancellation of bank debt and not tax settlement that moves all agents in the European economy (national states included), in the last instance, to accept money which, in turn, is the logical consequence of (private) bank credit.
>
> *(Febrero, 2009, p. 530)*

Some MMTers such as Ehnts (2014) have tried to respond to these criticisms by using the institutional design of the European Economic Union, but in general this matter has not been addressed as the European case is only a specific one deriving from a general case that would be more interesting to describe and analyse.

With respect to the second point made, that bank money is endogenous and therefore cannot be a leverage of state money, Marc Lavoie considers that "if bank reserves are endogenous to required level, then the expression 'leverage' does not seem appropriate" (Lavoie, 1999, p. 371). Parguez and Secareccia deduce that if, as the MMT says, bank money is leveraged over state money, then the former cannot be endogenous: "this presupposition signifies that state money is endogenous but bank money is not since, in the final analysis, it is constrained by the variation of the former" (Parguez & Secareccia, 2000, p. 120). However, this seems a wrong deduction since the MMTers do not say that bank money is constrained by state money: it would be one thing for banks to create IOUs referenced to state IOUs, which is what would explain the use of the word "leverage", but it would be another thing that banks cannot create bank IOUs until they have state IOUs. As we have already pointed out, MMT considers that the bank first creates the credit, and only after that does it worry about getting the bank reserves it needs. Some MMTers charge that their critics have a misconception of the term "leverage":

> in the world of finance, "to leverage" signifies being able to take a position in an asset without having to provide all or any funds for the position. Banks necessarily leverage CB currency, because they acquire asset position by issuing financial instruments that promise to deliver CB currency on demand or on some contingency at a later date.
>
> *(Tymoigne & Wray, 2013, p. 37)*

They insist that this is not the same as multiplying central bank-provided money, as some critics have said:

> statements like: "For chartalists, state money is exogenous, and credit money is a multiple of the former" (Rochon & Vernengo, 2003, p. 61) is not correct and simply reflects a misunderstanding of the way that terms like "leverage" are used by financial markets participants.
>
> *(Tymoigne & Wray, 2013, p. 37)*

It seems that some critics such as Cesaratto agree with the MMTers on this point: "clearly, Wray's meaning of 'leveraging' must be understood in a broad sense, stressing the hierarchical primacy of the state in producing HPM" (Cesaratto, 2016, p. 63).

For their part, Gnos and Rochon point out that the high-powered money used by the central bank to balance transactions in the interbank market is not the same as the money used by the state for its fiscal operations, which brings us back to the debate addressed in Chapter 4 on the relevance of consolidating the central bank and the treasury:

> there is actually no doubt that state expenses and receipts affect the amount of high-powered money at the disposal of commercial banks (...) What is questionable, as we shall discuss in the next section, is the identification of high-powered money with state money.
>
> *(Gnos & Rochon, 2002, p. 46)*

Based on Graziani's approach, the function of central bank high-powered money would be merely to compensate bank debts: "the role of the Central Bank is in fact of acting as a third party between single banks so far as their reciprocal payments are concerned" (Graziani, 1990, p. 18). Or, in the words of Rochon and Rossi, "transactions in the interbank market can only be settled using central bank money" (Rochon & Rossi, 2004). For them, there is a crucial difference between central bank money and state-created money – the former would be endogenous in nature while the latter would not:

> if banks cannot borrow from other banks or sell assets to the central bank, then it can borrow high-powered money from the central bank as lender of last resort. In this sense, the supply of high-powered money is always endogenous, a result of the demand for it.
>
> *(Gnos & Rochon, 2002, p. 45)*

In contrast, and as we discussed in Chapter 4, for MMT, state and central bank money are fully comparable: "it should be obvious, but it usually does not appear to be so ... that central bank liabilities do not differ in any significant degree from treasury liabilities—in other words, we can treat both as essentially 'high powered money' or liabilities of the state" (Wray, 2003, p. 87).

On the other hand, critics question whether bank money is widely used by the public because it is used to pay taxes as MMT claims: "it is one thing that the state encourages the acceptance of money, even that the 'which thing' should be accepted, but it is quite another thing that the acceptance of money depends on the means to pay taxes" (Febrero, 2009, p. 537). Parguez and Secareccia point out that if banks' promissory notes are denominated in the unit of account of the state, it is basically to facilitate their circulation: "the debts banks issue on themselves are denominated in the unit of account because it is the means of acquisition that ensures a viable circulation process upon which the creation of real wealth is based" (Parguez & Secareccia, 2000, p. 105). In fact, they understand the process in the opposite way to MMT: first, there is the creation of bank money – which has extrinsic value because it finances the production of future wealth –, then the state supports this process with its authority, and finally the state can create its own IOUs in an unlimited way because it makes them convertible into bank money:

> the state's power to create money at will is the logical consequence of its role in the endorsement of bank activity. Having the legal authority to bestow on bank debt the characteristic feature of money, the state has also the power to issue debt on itself that will be money, freely convertible into bank liability.
>
> *(Parguez & Secareccia, 2000, p. 106)*

MMTers have responded to this type of criticism by pointing out that central banks must exogenously accommodate the number of bank reserves (government IOUs) that can be produced endogenously to economic activity:

it is an exogenous fluctuation (or a "vertical" injection of base) for the domestic non-federal sector even though it may be endogenous to the state of the economy (...) All this of course does not mean that MMT is throwing away the endogenous component of variations in L1.

(Tymoigne & Wray, 2013, p. 24)

That is, despite much bank reserves change as a result of private economic activity, the central bank is obliged to accommodate them in detail:

any central bank that administers an overnight interest rate target must supply reserves on demand – for otherwise it would lose control of the interest rate. In the PK literature, it is said that CB policy always "accommodates" the demand for reserves. Given that this demand is highly interest-inelastic, there is little room for "error" by the central bank. It must accommodate more-or-less exactly the demand.

(Fullwiler et al., 2012, p. 18)

In other words, MMT considers the exogeneity of government IOUs injected through fiscal policy to be compatible with the endogeneity of government IOUs injected through the central bank in response to the evolution of bank IOUs:

one can conceive of a vertical component of the money supply process that consists of the government supply of fiat money; money drops vertically to the private sector from government. ... On the other hand, the bankmoney-supply process is horizontal; it can be thought of as a type of "leveraging" of the hoarded vertical fiat money.

(Wray, 1998, p. 111)

Also in the words of Mosler and Forstater: "[h]orizontal activity represents leveraged activity of a vertical component. ... The creation of bank loans and their corresponding deposits is a leveraging of the currency" (Mosler & Forstater, 1999, p. 168). For this very reason, MMTers argue that "the endogenous money theory and the state theory of money are not contradictory, but rather complement one another to build an understanding of our modern monetary system" (Nersisyan & Wray, 2016, p. 1299). Moreover, they also consider that the MMT view is more complete than the endogenous money view, since it not only serves to analyse bank IOUs, but also government IOUs and those of any other economic agent: "it presents a more complete picture of how money enters the economy, compared with endogenous money theory, since it applies to not only bank IOUs, but also other privately created IOUs, as well as those of the public sector" (Nersisyan & Wray, 2016, p. 1301).

Nesiba (2013) and Febrero (2009) point out that MMT's interpretation of the link between banks and the central bank implies that banks would have no limits, apart from the demand for credit, in creating IOUs of their own: "Wray (1998, pp. 111–115, 2004, p. 259) addresses the question of how state and bank money are related, but his discussion does not, at least in these two places, elucidate definitive financial limits to bank money creation" (Nesiba, 2013, p. 52). From an institutionalist approach, MMT has been criticised for not attaching sufficient importance to the endogeneity of money and relying heavily on the exogenous capacity of the state to control the amount of money needed by the economy. Some like Mayhew (2019) have gone so far as to say that MMT does not really believe in the endogenous money approach, even though they claim otherwise: "MMT advocates, by adopting a state money story, and by using sleight of hand to convert money into a physical thing, convert MMT into a form of monetarism while still allowing its advocates to play lip service to endogeneity" (Mayhew, 2019, p. 131).

On this point Marxist authors are even more critical. Although they consider money to be distinct from credit (since they adopt a money-commodity view), they confer on the latter a behaviour entirely endogenous to economic activity: "Marxists generally agree that credit mechanism has endogenous character" (Winczewski, 2021, p. 10). Concretely, endogeneity would be explained by the dynamics of the capitalist system itself, which would give rise to the creation of credit without the need for the participation of any public authority:

> credit relations emerge spontaneously in capitalist production and circulation, giving rise to an integral financial system. They also give rise to credit money, the dominant form of money in capitalism, the creation and circulation of which are very different from commodity and simple fiat money. The capitalist economy does not need the state to supply it with money – it can create credit money privately and endogenously.
>
> *(Lapavitsas & Aguila, 2020, p. 8)*

Consequently, Marxists also chastise MMT for claiming to be proponents of the endogenous theory of money because, in reality, they would focus all their attention on the state being able to control the amount of money circulating in the economy: "MMT claims that it has an endogenous theory of money, but in reality it has an exogenous one, based on state issuance of money" (Roberts, 2019, p. 13).

Other authors, such as Etzrod (2018), share a similar critique. He believes it is incompatible to talk about endogeneity of money at the same time as MMT claims that the state has to spend or lend its money before the private sector can have it, which reminds him more of the monetary multiplier:

> MMT cannot be applied in an economy that allows endogenous money creation, because the state has no monopoly over the money supply. Unfortunately, it can also not be applied to an economy that gives the private banks the permission to multiple state money.
>
> *(Etzrod, 2018, p. 128)*

Conclusions

The MMTers adopt the post-Keynesian view of the endogeneity of money, but they incorporate nuances and elements to adapt it to their own chartalist view so that they end up drawing a holistic view of state money and bank money. In this way, bank money would be a promissory note that banks create autonomously when they grant credit, hence its origin and quantity depend endogenously on economic activity. The coincidences with the conventional view finish here. The novelty is that for the MMTers these promissory notes are quantified in the unit of account of the state and are commitments to deliver state promissory notes in the future, hence they are considered as a leveraging of state money. Bank promissory notes would be widely used because they are convertible into state promissory notes (the only ones that serve to settle tax debts, which is what would give them value) and because the state manoeuvres so that this conversion is always – or almost always – possible due to its interest in maintaining the health of the banking system. In short, banks have the autonomy to increase the amount of money used in the economy, but their own operations and survival ultimately depend on the state.

This holistic view of bank money and state money has been heavily criticised in heterodoxy, especially by post-Keynesian authors and, to a lesser extent, by Marxist authors. The central criticism shared by all these critics is that bank money would logically and economically precede state money (even though bank money may need the support of the state to be widely accepted, as some point out) so that it would make no sense to speak of leverage.

In support of this approach, it is often argued that entrepreneurs first plan an economic activity, then ask for bank loans to carry it out, and finally money is created endogenously by banks so that state money would play no role in this process. Some reinforce their arguments by pointing out that bank money has historically been independent of public authorities so that the same would be true today; and that institutional configurations such as those of the European Monetary Union, due to the impossibility of monetising public deficits, would demonstrate empirically that bank money precedes state money.

But the truth is that the MMT approach is more convincing to this writer: without the support of the state and the existence of its own promissory notes, the widespread acceptance of bank money would not be possible, since it is denominated in the state unit of account and is after all a commitment to deliver state promissory notes in the future. Before the existence of bank money, there must necessarily be state-regulated institutions that allow its origin and widespread acceptance. The state has full control over the banking system: just as it usually acts to achieve its survival, it could also act to achieve the opposite (either through a ban on leveraging with state IOUs or through the total nationalisation of the sector, to give just two examples). As for the historical argument, it does not seem easy to take a clear-cut position, but it would not be necessary either: as I argued in Chapter 1, whatever the role of bank money historically, what matters is what its role is today, since modern economies have very different institutions and behaviours from those of the past, so any historical factor should not necessarily be extrapolated to the present. And in the case of the Eurozone, I do not think it is worth analysing because it is a specific case in which the fiscal capacities of states have been voluntarily and politically restricted, so it cannot shed light on the essential and real nature of bank and state money.

On the other hand, the criticisms of the concept of leverage do not seem to me to be fair or appropriate: critics seem to wrongly equate "leverage" with constraints on bank money creation. In reality, it is perfectly compatible for banks to have ample room to create bank money through their lending with all those IOUs being leveraged into government IOUs.

I think most of the discrepancies can be explained by the different conceptions of central bank money: while critics see money that is set in motion by monetary policy as something essentially different from money that is set in motion by fiscal policy, for MMTers it is exactly the same. This brings us back to the debate in Chapter 4 on the relevance of theoretically consolidating the central bank and the treasury. I reiterate my position: consolidation makes sense if one wants to analyse the functioning of the economy as it might be ignoring certain institutional arrangements, not just as it is in reality at a particular time and place. The fact that in the Eurozone bank money precedes state money because of its current institutional design does not mean that it could not be otherwise with a less restrictive and complex design. Once such consolidation takes place, it seems reasonable to conceive that state money comes before bank money, and that bank money is highly dependent on state regulation and support.

I also believe that this debate could be more adequately and accurately addressed if critics were more mindful of the theoretical contributions of the "hierarchy of monies" by Minsky (1986), Foley (1987), or Bell (2001), as they often seem to ignore or underestimate them. It is much easier to understand the MMT view on the endogeneity of money if one conceives of bank money as an IOU that is referenced in government IOUs. This thought is shared by authors such as Smithin (2016): "it should also be said at the outset that a concept introduced some years ago by another member of the MMT school-namely Bell's (2001) notion of the 'hierarchy of money' might have been useful in reconciling some of these differences, but this idea was not much discussed" (Smithin, 2016, p. 65); and also by Nesiba, although he is not entirely convinced by the idea of the "hierarchy of money": "Bell (2001), in her discussion of money hierarchies, also provides background that can be used to inform this question [how state and bank money are related], but her arguments do not fully satisfy this reader" (Nesiba, 2013, p. 52).

On the other hand, the typical Marxist criticism that MMT has only an exogenous view of money and that therefore they should not arrogate to themselves an endogenous view is neither fair nor relevant, since it is perfectly possible to take both an endogenous and an exogenous view at the same time: the economic activity of the private sector, through its borrowing, causes the endogenous injection of bank money; but the public sector itself, through its fiscal deficit, can cause an exogenous injection of government IOUs (which are reflected in bank IOUs as long as they follow the circuits of the banking sector). Marxists would argue that all the money injected by the public sector exogenously would have no real backing in capitalist production (which is only fed by bank credit), so it would have no real value, but both MMT and I are far from such an approach, considering that fiscal policy can create as much or more value than capitalist economic activity itself, as we will discuss in more detail in the next chapter. It seems that some critics such as Cesaratto also see it in a similar way:

> Having said this, I would agree with the MMT argument that, in terms of economic policy, we should not forget the different status of the two sectors, private and public. While in the case of the private sector the process of endogenous money financing of spending is passive, that is, it depends on the vagaries of private spending decisions, state spending depends on the deliberate decisions of policymakers, in particular to satisfy the saving desire that at full employment is not met by private investment decisions.
>
> *(Cesaratto, 2016, pp. 64–65)*

Finally, it is worth mentioning an issue that, agreeing with Nesiba (2013), is not fully addressed by the MMTers: the limits that banks have in creating bank money through credit. I believe that a satisfactory and complete answer can be found mainly in the work of James Tobin (1963) and MacLeay et al. (2014). Following these works, we can identify five reasons that would explain the limits of banks when granting credit and that MMTers could well share (and perhaps do share, although, as far as I know, they have not explicitly taken a position on the matter).

First of all, banks cannot grant loans unilaterally; they need other economic actors to be willing to borrow. The banks can be absolutely eager to grant loans all the time, but if they can't find anyone interested in accepting them, they won't grant a single one. This is the first limit to the creation of bank money: the preferences of the private sector. Secondly, the competitive market in which banks operate causes them to compete with each other to attract customers, and the main way to do this is to make loans cheaper, which damages the profitability of the lending operation. Consequently, attracting new customers works against profitability so that there always comes a time when granting new loans is not worthwhile because it is not sufficiently profitable. Therein lies the second limit to bank money creation: the market forces that banks face. Thirdly, in order to grant a loan, it is not enough for an economic agent to want to obtain it, but that agent must have sufficient economic capacity to be able to repay it and also to pay the interest. Although banks can technically give as much credit as they want, it does not make sense for them to do so if they are going to make losses due to the insufficient solvency of their clients. Banks try to hedge against the risk of default by provisioning capital with government notes to absorb any losses that might be incurred, which hurts their profitability. The authorities also impose compulsory risk prevention measures that hamper the profitability of loans. As the number of loans granted increases, the higher the average default risk incurred by the bank, and thus the lower the profitability obtained. Again, there comes a point at which granting new loans is not worthwhile because it is not sufficiently profitable. Therein lies the third limit to bank money creation: the management of the risks associated with lending.

Fourthly, a bank's lending can lead to a loss of government IOUs as it extinguishes its own IOUs. And banks need to have enough government IOUs to meet their commitments. But despite this being achieved (selling assets, accessing the central bank window, taking new deposits, etc.) will come at a cost to the bank that will erode its economic profitability. Consequently, lending may become unprofitable if it entails a significant loss of government IOUs that has to be compensated by higher costs. Therein lies the fourth limit to bank money creation: the loss of IOUs as a result of transactions carried out by customers. Fifthly and finally, the monetary policy conducted by the authorities indirectly but decisively affects the demand for credit, namely through the manipulation of the interest rates set by the issuer of the IOUs. If these rates are high, the interest rate on loans granted by banks will also be high, which will discourage households and businesses from taking out loans. Therein lies the fifth limit to bank money creation: the reduction in the demand for credit as a result of monetary policy.

In short, banks, although they have no technical limits to create bank money by granting loans, would not be able to grant as many loans as they want because this would affect their profitability, which is their *raison d'être*. Moreover, by creating money through credit, they would need someone on the other side demanding credit, and this is what would explain why the amount of money created depends on the borrowing preferences of households and firms, which in turn depends on the economic cycle.

References

Bell Kelton, S. (2001). The role of the state and the hierarchy of money. *Cambridge Journal of Economic*, *25*(2), 149–163.

Bernanke, B. (2007, de junio 15). *The financial accelerator and the credit channel*. Conferencia en el congreso "The Credit Channel of Monetary Policy in the Twenty-first Century Conference", Federal Reserve Bank of Atlanta, Atlanta, Georgia. https://www.federalreserve.gov/newsevents/speech/bernanke20070615a.htm

Cesaratto, S. (2016). The state spends first: Logic, facts, fictions, open questions. *Journal of Post Keynesian Economics*, *39*(1), 44–71. https://doi.org/10.1080/01603477.2016.1147333

Culham, J., & King, J. E. (2013). Horizontalists and verticalists after 25 years. *Review of Keynesian Economics*, *1*(4), 391–405.

Ehnts, D. H. (2014). A simple macroeconomic model of a currency union with endogenous money and saving-investment imbalances. *International Journal of Pluralism and Economics Education (IJPEE)*, *5*(3), 279–297.

Etzrodt, C. (2018). Modern sovereign money—Part II: A synthesis of the Chicago plan, sovereign money, and the modern money theory. *Open Journal of Social Sciences*, *6*(9), 116–135. https://doi.org/10.4236/jss.2018.69008.

Febrero, E. (2009). Three difficulties with neo-chartalism. *Journal of Post Keynesian Economics*, *31*(3), 523–541. https://doi.org/10.2753/PKE0160-3477310308

Foley, D. (1987). Money in economic activity. In *The new Palgrave dictionary of economics*. Palgrave Macmillan. https://doi.org/10.1057/978-1-349-95121-5_808-1

Forstater, M., & Mosler, W. (2005). The natural rate of interest is zero. *Journal of Economic Issues*, *39*(2), 535–542. https://doi.org/10.1080/00213624.2005.11506832

Friedman, M. (1960). *A program for monetary stability*. Fordham University Press.

Fullwiler, S., Kelton, S., & Wray, L. R. (2012, January, 17–26). *Modern money theory: A response to critics*. Political Economy Research Institute. www.peri.umass.edu/fileadmin/pdf/working_papers/working_papers_251-300/WP279.pdf

Gnos, C., & Rochon, L. P. (2002). Money creation and the state: A critical assessment of chartalism. *International Journal of Political Economy*, *32*(3), 41–57.

Goodhart, C. A. E. (1984). *Monetary theory and practice: The UK experience*. Macmillan.

Graziani, A. (1990). The theory of the monetary circuit. *[Economies et sociétés] ("Série Monnaie et Production," 7)*, *24*(6), 7–36.

Holmes, A. (1969). *Operational constraints on the stabilization of money supply growth. Controlling monetary aggregates*. Federal Reserve Bank of Boston.

Innes, A. M. (2004 [1913]). What is money. In L. R. Wray (Ed.), *Credit and state theories of money* (pp. 14–49). Edward Elgar.

Knapp, G. F. (1924). *The state theory of money*. MacMillan & Company Limited.

Lapavitsas, C., & Aguila, N. (2020). Modern monetary theory on money, sovereignty, and policy: A Marxist critique with reference to the Eurozone and Greece. *Japanese Political Economy*, *46*(4), 300–326.

Lavoie, M. (1997). Loanable funds, endogenous money and Minsky's financial fragility hypothesis. In A. J. Cohen, H. Hagemann, & J. Smithin (Eds.), *Money, financial institutions and macroeconomics* (Recent Economic Thought Series, 53), pp. 67–82. Springer.

Lavoie, M. (1999). Understanding modern money: The key to full employment and price stability. *Eastern Economic Journal*, *25*(3), 370–372.

Lavoie, M. (2019). Modern monetary theory and post-Keynesian economics. *Real-World Economics Review*, *89*, 97–108.

Lerner, A. (1947). Money as a creature of the state. *American Economic Review*, *37*(2), 312–317.

Matthews, R. C. (1961). Liquidity preference and the multiplier. *Economica*, *28*(109), 37.

Mayhew. (2019). The sleights of hand of MMT. *Real-World Economics Review* *,89*, 129–137.

McLeay, M., Amar, R., & Ryland, T. (2014). Money in the modern economy: An introduction. *Bank of England Quarterly Bulletin*, *Q1*, 4–13.

Mehrling, P. (2000). Modern money: Fiat or credit? *Journal of Post Keynesian Economics*, *22*(3), 397–406.

Minsky, H. P. (1986). *Stabilizing an unstable economy*. Yale University Press.

Mitchell, W., Wray, L. R., & Watts, M. (2019). *Macroeconomics*. Red Globe Press.

Moore, B. J. (1988). *Horizontalists and verticalists: The macroeconomics of credit money*. Cambridge University Press.

Mosler, W. (1995). *Soft currency economics*. www.gate.net/~mosler/frame001.htm.

Mosler, W., & Forstater, M. (1999). General framework for the analysis of currencies and commodities. In P. Davidson & J. Kregel (Eds.), *Full employment and price stability in a global economy* (pp. 166–177). Edward Elgar.

Nersisyan, Y., & Wray, L. R. (2016). Modern Money Theory and the facts of experience. *Cambridge Journal of Economics*, *40*(5), 1297–1316.

Nesiba, R. F. (2013). Do institutionalists and post-keynesians share a common approach to Modern Monetary Theory (MMT)? *European Journal of Economics and Economic Policies: Intervention*, *10*(1), 44–60.

Nicholas, K. (1980 [1960]). *Essays on economic stability and growth*. Homes & Meier.

Palley, T. (2006). Dinero endógeno: Significado y alcance. In P. Piégay & L.-P. Rochon (Eds.), *Teorías monetarias poskeynesianas*, pp. 67–80. Akal.

Parguez, A., & Seccareccia, M. (2000). The credit theory of money: The monetary circuit approach. En J. Smithin (Ed.), *What is money?* (pp. 101–123). Routledge.

Pollin, R. (1991). Two theories of money supply endogeneity: Some empirical evidence. *Journal of Post Keynesian Economics*, *13*(3), 366–396.

Roberts, M. (2019). Modern monetary theory: A Marxist critique. *Class, Race and Corporate Power*, *7*(1), Article 1. https://doi.org/10.25148/CRCP.7.1.008316

Rochon, L.-P., & Rossi, S. (2004). *Administered interest rates and interbank settlements: Implications for theory and policy in the Canadian case* (Working Paper). Laurentian University and University of Fribourg.

Rochon, L. P., & Vernengo, M. (2003). State money and the real world: Or chartalism and its discontents. *Journal of Post Keynesian Economics*, *26*(1), 57–68.

Samuelson, P., Nordhaus, W. D., & Enrri, D. (2003). *Economía*. McGraw-Hill.

Schumpeter, J. A. S. (1912). *The theory of economic development*. Harvard University Press.

Smithin, J. (2016, September). Some puzzles about money, finance and the monetary circuit. *Cambridge Journal of Economics*, *40*(5), 1259–1274. https://doi.org/10.1093/cje/bew010

Tcherneva, P. (2016). *Money, power and monetary regimes* (Working Paper No. 861). Levy Economics Institute.

Tobin, J. (1963). *Commercial banks as creators of 'money'* (Cowles Foundation Discussion Paper No. 159).

Tobin, J., & Golub, S. (1998). *Money, credit, and capital*. Irwin McGraw-Hill.

Tymoigne, E. (2016). Government monetary and fiscal operations: Generalising the endogenous money approach. *Cambridge Journal of Economics*, *40*(5), 1317–1332.

Tymoigne, E., & Wray, L. R. (2013). *Modern money theory 101: A reply to critics* (Working Papers Series No. 778). Levy Economics Institute. https://ssrn.com/abstract=2348704

Winczewski, D. (2021). Neo-chartalist or Marxist vision of the modern money? Critical comparison. *International Critical Thought*, *11*(3), 408–426. https://doi.org/10.1080/21598282.2021.1966641

Wray, L. R. (1990). *Money and credit in capitalist economies: The endogenous money approach*. Edward Elgar.

Wray, L. R. (1992a). Commercial banks, the Central Bank, and endogenous money. *Journal of Post Keynesian Economics*, *14*(3), 297–310.

Wray, L. R. (1992b). Alternative theories of the rate of interest. *Cambridge Journal of Economics*, *16*(1), 69–89.

Wray, L. R. (1998). *Understanding modern money, the key to full employment and price stability*. Edward Elgar Publishing Ltd.

Wray, L. R. (2003). Seigniorage or sovereignty? In L.-P. Rochon & S. Rossi (Eds.), *Modern theories of money* (pp. 84–102). Edward Elgar.

Wray, L. R. (2004). Conclusion: The credit money and state money approaches. In L. R. Wray (Ed.), *Credit and state theories of money* (pp. 223–253). Edward Elgar.

Wray, L. R. (2012). *Modern money theory: A primer on macroeconomics for sovereign monetary systems*. Palgrave Macmillan.

Wray, L. R. (2015). *Minsky on banking: Early work on endogenous money and the prudent banker* (Working Paper no. 827). Levy Economics Institute of Bard College. https://ssrn.com/abstract=2547803

6

FUNCTIONAL FINANCE AND MODERN MONETARY THEORY'S VIEW OF THE INFLATION AND ITS CRITICISMS

Introduction

MMTers consider that everything discussed in the previous chapters corresponds to an objective description of modern monetary systems, in which there are no opinions or economic policy recommendations. In other words, all of the above would belong to the realm of positive economics: money would objectively be a creature of the state, the deficit would objectively be a simple accounting subtraction, bank money would objectively be a leveraging of government IOUs, and so on. MMTers would have limited themselves to describing what reality is like, not proposing changes to it: "MMT does not embody a prepackaged set of policies ready to be deployed across the global landscape. It is, first and foremost, a description of how a modern fiat currency works" (Kelton, 2020, p. 276).

In contrast, most of the rest of the remaining postulates in this book would fall within normative economics, as they would be suggestions or prescriptions for economic policy. And all of them would be aimed at using the capabilities of states with monetary sovereignty to achieve the highest possible welfare for their citizens, which would be achieved with full employment and price stability. That is why here we will talk about the real (non-financial) capabilities and limits that MMTers understand sovereign states to have to achieve this goal, which will lead us to talk about Functional Finance, unemployment, and inflation. And these aspects are precisely the most criticised, especially from the more orthodox schools of thought. In a final section, we will also discuss to what extent the international inflationary episode originating in 2021 is related to these policy prescriptions of the MMT, as many critics have claimed.

Functional Finance

Based on the Keynesian conception of monetary economies of production, the MMTers strongly emphasise that the production of goods and services is only useful if there is a flow of money to buy and sell them. It is of no use for a company to create products if it cannot sell them because nobody uses its money to buy them, since they would accumulate in its

DOI: 10.4324/9781003371809-7

warehouses without increasing the welfare of society. Hence the interest in the accounting equivalence between production and expenditure: every monetary unit produced must also be, by accounting identity, a monetary unit spent by someone. And for this monetary unit to be spent, it is obviously essential that there are economic agents with the capacity to spend. Here we find the link with everything we have dealt with up to now: in order to spend, money must be used (be it government or bank promissory notes).

The spending that gives an outlet for production can come from different economic agents, which can be grouped, for analytical reasons and for simplicity, into three: the domestic public sector, the domestic private sector (companies and households), and the foreign sector (public and foreign private sector). All three sectors spend to purchase part of domestic production, but typically in capitalist economies such spending is insufficient to purchase all of that production. Spending from the foreign sector will ensure that some domestic production is sold; spending by domestic firms and households will also buy a quantity of goods and services; and, finally, so will spending by the public sector. But, in our capitalist economies, many goods and services will typically go unsold. In Keynesian terms, effective demand is usually lower than the potential output of the economy. Keynes (1964), Davidson (1972), and Minsky (1986) all identified uncertainty as the main reason for this common state of the capitalist economy: households and firms, because they do not know what the future holds, do not spend all their income in order to have savings available to deal with any unforeseen future events. This unspent and saved income would explain the gap between effective demand and potential output.

And that would be a problem for firms that do not sell all their output, but also for the economy as a whole: if firms do not sell all they can produce, they will operate at lower output, run fewer machines, and hire fewer workers. In other words, not all available real resources, including labour, will be used. The result would be unemployment.

A simple solution to this problem of insufficient effective demand would be to raise spending. Then all products could be bought and the unemployed hired. But how to increase spending? Foreign sector spending depends on foreigners, and private sector spending depends on households and firms, so these are not variables that can be easily controlled. In contrast, the spending of a sovereign state is controllable, as it basically depends on the political will of its rulers. The authorities could increase public spending to directly cover this lack of spending, or to increase the spending capacity of firms and households so that they consume the unsold output. Alternatively, the authorities could also reduce taxes to increase the spending capacity of households and firms. However, there would be a limit to such a policy because, if aggregate spending were to grow above the economy's potential output, it would generate inflation: entrepreneurs, faced with demand exceeding their supply, would raise the prices of their products to make more money despite selling exactly the same thing. As Keynes said, a rise of effective demand "spends itself, partly in affecting output and partly in affecting price" and only if the elasticity of output approaches zero does a rise of effective demand cause "true inflation" (Keynes, 1964, p. 285). Consequently, the inferred policy recommendation is that spending should be increased sufficiently to end unemployment, but not so much as to generate inflation.

This is basically the chartalist Abba Lerner's first law of Functional Finance:

the first financial responsibility of the government (since nobody else can undertake that responsibility) is to keep the total rate of spending in the country on goods and services neither greater nor less than that rate which at the current prices would buy all the goods that it is possible to produce. If total spending is allowed to go above this there will be inflation, and if it is allowed to go below this there will be unemployment.

(Lerner, 1943, p. 39)

And this policy recommendation is adopted (at least in general terms as we shall see below) by MMTers:

whenever spending falls short of sustaining our output and employment, that is, when we do not have enough purchasing power to be able to buy what is for sale in those big stores we call the economy, the government can act to make sure that our output is sold either by lowering taxes or by increasing public spending.

(Mosler, 2014, p. 52)

They also take the view that aggregate spending in a situation of full employment causes inflationary pressures:

once full employment is reached, additional deficit spending will generate additional income that is likely to cause inflationary pressures – except in the unlikely case that all additional income represents desired net saving. Beyond full employment, then, any further reduction of taxes or increase of government spending (increasing deficit spending) is likely to reduce the value of money as prices are bid up.

(Wray, 1998, p. 84)

Of course, whether by increasing government spending or reducing taxes to fill the gap between demand and output and achieve full employment, the result is that the government deficit increases. And, although this is something that mainstream economic theory is usually concerned about, we have already seen (in Chapter 4) that this is not the case in Modern Monetary Theory. Not only because a sovereign state could maintain the public deficit indefinitely, but also because that level of deficit would reflect the total expenditure needed to buy all the goods and services produced without causing inflationary pressures, so there would be no negative consequences. In contrast to the dominant view of so-called Sound Finance, which limits public spending so that it does not exceed certain deficit and debt levels, Functional Finance proposes adjusting public spending and revenues as much as necessary – even if this results in a soaring public deficit – to achieve full employment, but without going beyond this to avoid inflation. It is about using fiscal policy in a functional way, with the aim of achieving a welfare objective, not making it conditional on meeting targets on indicators such as the public deficit (which would say nothing per se about the health of the economy). In Lerner's words: "Functional Finance rejects completely the traditional doctrines of 'Sound Finance' and the principle of trying to balance the budget over a solar year or any other arbitrary period" (Lerner, 1943, p. 41). Instead, he proposed the following:

The central idea is that government fiscal policy taxing, its borrowing and repayment of loans, its and its withdrawal of money, shall all be und only to the results of these actions on the eco established traditional doctrine about what is sound or unsound.

(Lerner, 1943, p. 39)

The MMTers fully endorse this approach:

> the sustainable goal for a government should be to maintain full employment and price stability and allow its fiscal balance to adjust accordingly to ensure aggregate demand is consistent with those goals. A sovereign, currency-issuing government can always meet those goals if it chooses.
>
> *(Mitchell et al., 2019, p. 91)*

Some authors linked to MMT have developed economic models that corroborate these central ideas of Functional Finance (Tanaka, 2022). The goal is to reach full employment, and if, once that point is reached (or close to it), inflationary pressures begin to emerge, then policymakers should intervene to prevent the problem from worsening:

> if the CBO [Congressional Budget Office] and other independent analysts concluded it would risk pushing inflation above some desired inflation rate, then lawmakers could begin to assemble a venue of options to identify the most effective ways to mitigate that risk.
>
> *(Kelton, 2020, p. 158)*

Accordingly, "inflation is the true limit to government spending not lack of financing" (Nersisyan & Wray, 2010, p. 20).

The MMT preference for reaching full employment through fiscal policy entails putting monetary policy on the back burner. Indeed, many MMTers suggest setting the benchmark interest rate at 0% and adjusting only government expenditures and revenues to the business cycle (Wray, 1998, p. 87, 2007, p. 22; Forstater & Mosler, 2005): "given these considerations, as well as the arguments advanced by Keynes, a monetary policy rule is preferred – set the overnight rate at zero, and keep it there. A properly programmed tin robot ought to do the trick" (Wray, 2007a, p. 22). Although other MMTers are not closed to the rate being somewhat higher: "with regard to the interest rate, it might make sense to leave it at zero to ensure that nobody earns risk-free rewards or to set it at 2% in order to support the inflation target of the same size" (Ehnts, 2022, p. 2). We will come back to this later.

As can be seen from the above quote from Lerner, not only did he propose raising the public deficit by as much as necessary to achieve maximum output and employment, but he also indicated that it was irrelevant how this increase in the public deficit was financed. In fact, Lerner believed that public bonds should be sold to the central bank or to private banks "on conditions which permit the banks to issue new credit money based on their additional holdings of government securities, [which] must be considered for our purposes as printing money" (Lerner, 1943, p. 41). In other words, like MMT, he considered that public deficit per se is equivalent to money creation, and that it was not necessary to issue public bonds unless its effects were desired: "the government should borrow money only if it is desirable have less money and more government effects of govern" (Lerner, 1943, p. 40).

Lerner was clear that it was spending that caused inflation, not the quantity or creation of money, hence he was indifferent as to whether the increase in government deficits was financed by money creation or by issuing government bonds:

> the creation of money has no effects on the economy as long as the printed money remains in the print shop. It is only when the money gets out into the economy that any effects come

about. Money which is newly created and kept locked up might as well never have been created.

(Lerner, 1951, p. 132)

Perhaps the clearest explanation of all he offered was the following:

All the decisions of any importance are made when it is decided to apply the fiscal instruments ... If any of the instruments involves the paying out of money ..., the effects are just the same whether the money paid out was previously resting in the treasury or whether it had to be printed because there was not enough available in the treasury to permit them to be carried out on the scale that was considered necessary to prevent deflation. The use of the instrument should never be hampered just because there may not be enough money stock in the treasury at the moment.

(Lerner, 1951, p. 133)

And all this despite the fact that Lerner was well aware of the rejection generated in the collective imagination by the simple idea of printing money:

the almost instinctive revulsion that we have to the idea of printing money, and the tendency to identify it with inflation, can be overcome if we calm ourselves and take note that this printing does not affect the amount of money spent.

(Lerner, 1943, p. 41)

Functional Finance inevitably recalls the work of John Maynard Keynes. Indeed, some excerpts from this British economist seem to allude directly to Functional Finance:

after meeting our daily needs by production and export, we shall find ourselves with a certain surplus of resources and of labour available for capital works of improvement. If there is insufficient outlet for this surplus, we have unemployment. If, on the other hand, there is an excess of demand, we have inflation.

(Keynes, 1978, p. 267)

But many point out that Abba Lerner's policy recommendation was more direct and bolder (Colander, 1984, p. 1574; Armstrong, 2019, p. 8). Lerner himself referred to Keynes' approach as a "less shocking" interpretation of his own theory (Lerner, 1943, p. 38). For his part, Keynes referred to Functional Finance as an idea, not a policy (Aspropomourgos, 2014). According to Armstrong (2019), Keynes' moderation was not due to a disagreement with the theoretical postulates of Functional Finance, but to the belief that it was politically more appropriate not to take them to the extreme:

Keynes's practical approach was very much in evidence in his approach to Functional Finance. He agreed with the underlying logic but felt it "went too far" in pushing his theory to a logical extreme and was unnecessary and potentially damaging to his postwar objectives. (...) He naturally preferred his own rather more politically astute approach of budget bifurcation as the means of encouraging the use of active fiscal policy to ensure full employment.

(Armstrong, 2019, p. 12)

Some other contemporary economists such as Alvin Hansen also favoured the use of public deficits to stimulate the economy, but as long as the ratio of public debt to national income remained at a tolerable level (Bell, 1999, p. 1). In contrast, this indicator did not concern Lerner, who believed that the level of public deficits should only be assessed in terms of their impact on employment and inflation. It may be striking that such an approach was so prevalent at the time; in fact, the liberal economist Milton Friedman himself also proposed something similar in a 1948 article, in which he basically argued that public deficits were necessary in times of economic recession in order to achieve full employment. Public deficits which, as he himself acknowledged, were equivalent to creating new money (Friedman, 1948). Some authors argue that during that time the postulates of Functional Finance were much more prevalent than they might seem today, as the war economy during the Second World War would make clear (Levey, 2021).

But it might be even more striking that Abba Lerner changed his mind a few decades later, replacing Functional Finance with a sound, budget-balanced, finance approach – not because government would run out of money, but because he worried about the inflationary impact. Moreover, he went even further than Keynes, as he did not even see the fiscal deficit being used even in recession – on the argument that monetary policy alone could steer the economy (Wray, 2018, p. 32). According to Randall Wray, Lerner abandoned the version of Functional Finance

> because those who lived through the accelerating inflation of the 1960s to the 1980s were traumatized by the experience. Lerner replaced Functional Finance with a combination of a certain kind of wage and price controls (marketed "permits" allowing wage or price hikes) plus Monetarism.
>
> *(Wray, 2018, p. 32)*

Abba Lerner was not the only one to abandon the simple and pure view of Functional Finance at that time; Hyman Minsky did so too, although in his case he was not as extreme as Lerner. Minsky advocated that public spending should not be general but targeted towards a specific goal, namely job creation to achieve full employment without inflation, and all this accompanied by wage improvements and reduced inequality (Wray, 2018, p. 33). This is precisely the refined view that MMTers adopt, hence they feel more indebted to Minsky than to Lerner (Wray, 2018, p. 1) – and which we will discuss in the next chapter.

These changes in views are surely due to the assimilation of many of the criticisms that pure Functional Finance received in those early years of its existence, many of which we will present below.

Sectoral balances

Closely related to Functional Finance is the MMT interpretation of the macroeconomic identity of sectoral balances derived from national accounts, as it is often used to contextualise the direction and degree of public balance in economies. It is important to note that Functional Finance does not recommend recording or raising the government deficit per se: it could be that an economy reaches full employment simply because of private and external spending, all coinciding with government surpluses. Thus,

> Functional Finance is rather a general approach within which a whole series of policies may be conducted (…) Thus Functional Finance does not advocate big deficits under any and all

circumstances, just as it does not view a balanced budget as inherently "good" in and of itself, independently of its impact on the economy.

(Forstater, 1999, p. 7)

It is therefore crucial to analyse public expenditure (and its balance) in conjunction with the other two types of expenditure: private and external. For this purpose, MMTers often resort to the identity of sectoral balances.

Based on national accounting, and grouping all economic agents into three sectors (public, private, and foreign), the following well-known accounting identity can be obtained:

$$NL_{private} + Nl_{public} + Nl_{foreign} = 0 \qquad (6.1)$$

where NL is the net lending balance of the corresponding sector. Consequently, the balances of the three sectors are offset, and their sum is equal to 0. Because of that, the level of the fiscal balance would always be reflected in the other two. For example, budgetary balance could only be obtained if the other balances were balanced or if the positive balance of one of the two was offset by the negative balance of the other. In the same way, a fiscal surplus could only be registered if at least one of the other two balances were in deficit. This approach has important implications: in order to achieve a balanced budget it would be necessary that (a) the national private sector spent more (or the same) than it receives; (b) the foreign sector spent more (or the same) than what it receives – that is, that it registered current account surplus or zero balance; or (c) a combination of a and b. Thus, only the economies with current account surpluses and/ or with private leverage could achieve public accounts surplus.

This analysis is used to criticise Sound Finance (and support Functional Finance), as it does not pay attention to the relationship between the public balance and the other sectoral balances, even though they are closely linked and their specific combination matters. The desired level of full employment and price stability may be achieved in one economy with, for example, a government deficit of 10% of GDP, but it may be achieved in another country with a government deficit of 1% of GDP, or even with a government surplus. Whether it happens at one level or the other will depend on the other two balances. This is why Sound Finance would be useless and biased, as it only focuses on one element of the equation without taking into account the other two. And those two other balances depend on many factors that are never taken into account by Sound Finance.

However, with the simple macroeconomic identity it is not possible to infer what these factors are, because it says absolutely nothing about the causality between the different balances: "unlike the macro accounting identity (which must be true), it is not possible to say with certainty what causes a particular sector's balance" (Wray, 2012a, p. 7). However, the MMTers believe it is possible to draw certain more or less reliable conclusions from the reading of sectoral balances, basically starting from the Keynesian premise that it is the expenditure (or deficit) of one economic agent that originates the income (or surplus) of another agent: "while we have identified an accounting relationship between the sectoral balances, we can also say something about the causal relationships between the flows of income and expenditure and the impact in stocks. (...) Aggregate spending creates aggregate income" (Mitchel et al., 2019, pp. 96–97). Inferring certain causalities between sectoral balances is precisely what Wynne Godley and her collaborators did in their day (Godley & Cripps, 1983; Godley & McCarthy, 1998; Godley, 1999; Godley & Wray, 2000) and as the Levy Institute does recently (Wray, 2012a, p. 7, 2012b; Papadimitrou et al., 2013, 2018). We are not interested here in dwelling on what kind of economic deductions and projections they made, but simply to point out a number of basic theoretical assumptions that they use and that serve to explain the ideas of MMTers.

There is a certain consensus in considering that the external balance depends to a greater or lesser extent on the productive, exporting, and importing structure of the economy in question, as well as on its own economic growth and that of its trading partners. For example, if an economy has a strong export sector, foreign spending will buy a lot of domestic products, which, together with private sector spending, may mean that it is not necessary to have much public spending to achieve maximum output and full employment. This is why such economies could have quite acceptable employment rates without the need for large public deficits, even if they have a public surplus. But the problem with this option is that not all economies can base their strategy on exports, because if one has a trade surplus it is because at least one has a deficit. World trade is a zero-sum game in which not all economies can win. Something that could happen if public spending were to be boosted to purchase all production.

As for the private balance, it would depend on the savings of households and firms, but above all on their indebtedness (creation of bank notes). It could happen that the spending of firms and households would soar thanks to this indebtedness and thus buy up a large part of national production, also making it unnecessary to have much public spending to reach maximum production and full employment. The problem with this particular phenomenon is that, if sustained over time, it could be unsustainable because firms and households would not be able to increase their indebtedness indefinitely (Minsky, 1986; Nikiforos & Zezza, 2017, p. 8), unlike a sovereign state, which could. That is why Modern Monetary Theory recommends that the public sector should increase public spending and deficits as much as necessary to achieve maximum output and full employment because it would be the only sector that could afford to do so.

All these theoretical assumptions lead MMTers to criticise the dominant view for welcoming the fact that the economy grows thanks to the foreign sector or the private sector (at the cost of debt), but questioning that it grows thanks to the public sector, despite the fact that in all three options there is aggregation of spending that is used to purchase existing production. What Modern Monetary Theory proposes is precisely the recourse to this third way, because it would be as valid as the others to increase production and employment, and in fact would be more sustainable than private borrowing. After all, as Randall Wray reminds us, from the perspective of the firm, it does not matter who buys the goods or services produced: the firm is equally satisfied whether it sells to domestic buyers, foreign buyers, or the public sector; what the firm wants is to sell in exchange for domestic currency to cover costs and make a profit (Wray, 2018). In the same vein, Bill Mitchell notes: "it may be that a budget surplus is necessary at some point in time – for example, if net exports are very strong and fiscal policy has to contract spending to take the inflationary pressures out of the economy" (Mitchell, 2009a). Conclusions that are not unique to MMT, as, for example, economist Michal Kalecki thought very similarly almost a century ago pointing out that the public deficit has a similar effect to that of an export surplus; it can be regarded as an artificial trade surplus (Kalecki, 1933).

Criticisms

Functional Finance

One of the most important and strongest criticisms that Functional Finance received very early on is that there is no guarantee that the new spending added to the economy through the public deficit will be used to buy the products of firms that can produce more, as economic agents might want to buy the products of firms that are already at full capacity because they are of better quality or better price, including foreign firms, in which case inflationary pressures and/or currency depreciations might occur before full employment is reached. A complementary criticism is that the employer faced with higher demand may not be able to find trained workers in his sector, even if there are still people unemployed. As Hyman Minsky already warned, "labor is not homogeneous and fluid" (Minsky, 1965, p. 188), so only by pure chance would aggregate demand be such as to generate enough jobs in the right places for all those who need them at wages high enough to support themselves and their dependents. This is what John Maynard Keynes also referred to in the following words: "the nearer we come to full employment, the greater the increase in total expenditure, the greater the increase in prices, and the smaller and smaller the increase in employment" (Keynes, 1964, p. 285). Lerner himself did not initially accept these criticisms, but eventually "recognised that prices might begin to rise before all resources were fully employed" (Bell, 1999, p. 3), as can be inferred from this qualification written in 1951: "[A]s long as it is possible for the supply of goods to increase along with the increase in spending, there will be no (permanent) increase in prices" (Lerner, 1951, p. 8).

These classical criticisms of Functional Finance often resonate today as well. For example, in the words of Thomas Palley:

> the economy consists of multiple sectors, and some hit the full employment barrier before others. Consequently, inflation starts bubbling up before there is aggregate full employment, and government lacks the capacity to target its demand injections sector by sector and market by market.
>
> *(Palley, 2020, p. 481)*

Another example:

> since excess aggregate demand causes inflationary pressures and government spending is part of aggregate demand, the government must identify idle areas of the economy to avoid inflation. However, once currency enters the economy, it escapes government control, making any goal of controlling aggregate demand unfeasible.
>
> *(Mueller & Vaz-Curado, 2019, p. 11)*

MMTers themselves have always been very mindful of this issue:

> the metaphor of a general "pump-priming" increase of aggregate demand, with across-the-board equal impacts on all sectors, is not useful for policy analysis. There are always winners and losers; there are always some industries that experience increased sales while others are left behind; there are some workers who face better job prospects while others remain unemployed.
>
> *(Wray, 2007, pp. 3–4)*

Thus, MMT does not adopt this simple and pure view of Functional Finance, but a more sophisticated one so that spending goes where there is the most economic slack, as we will explain in the next chapter.

A different critique of Functional Finance is made by the Austrian authors; they see idle productive capacity as a consequence of bad business decisions in the past, which increased that capacity beyond the real long-term needs of the economy, so that more public spending to fill the gap would only temporarily solve the problems:

> according to Mises' theory of the business cycle, the existence of "idle capacity" in the economy doesn't just fall out of the sky, but is instead the result of the malinvestments made during the preceding boom. So if we follow Kelton's advice and crank up the printing press in an attempt to put those unemployed resources back to work, it will simply set in motion another unsustainable boom/bust cycle.
>
> *(Murphy, 2020, p. 238)*

Another major criticism of Functional Finance concerns the possibility of stopping inflation in time once full employment has been achieved (or is close to it). Critics point out that MMTers underestimate the economic and political difficulties involved in reducing public deficits (by raising taxes or reducing spending) in order to stop aggregate demand-driven inflation. On the one hand, some critics such as Cochrane (2020) point out that it is not easy for policymakers to know when the productive capacity of different economic sectors is being fully utilised. On the other hand, some point out that reducing the public deficit would generate a lot of unrest as taxes would fall on those who "do most of the spending: poorer people and the middle class" (Triggs, 2021). Also referring to these policy difficulties, Summer and Horan (2019) ask:

> suppose that an MMT regime is implemented and inflation rises. The MMT prescription is to then raise taxes. Would Congress vote to increase taxes at a time when prices are already rising? Would the president also sign the legislation to increases taxes?
>
> *(Summer & Horan, 2019, p. 6)*

In a similar vein, Palley argues: "government does not just push a button so that taxes go up or spending goes down. There are vested interests working to stop their taxes being raised and stop favored spending programs being cut" (Palley, 2018).

For his part, Schotmann builds on the aforementioned critique of theoretical state and central bank consolidation to argue that the authorities would find it very difficult to stop inflation once it has already been generated: "what should happen if the proposed fiscal brake only works in theory, because MMT is based on a fictitious consolidation of the government and the central bank?" (Schlotmann, 2021, p. 26). Coats asks: "how would the government manipulate the sluggish adjustments in tax revenue to smooth over the monetary shocks of government spending and revenue mismatches?" (Coats, 2019, p. 573). Other authors, such as Skousen, add to the critique that even if inflation could be stopped, this would be at the cost of damaging economic growth: "can inflation be stopped once it starts? Studies show that once inflation gets started, it is almost impossible to stop without causing a recession" (Skousen, 2020, p. 17).

Finally, Newman points out that raising taxes would not even reduce inflation:

> in order to combat the higher inflation, MMT recommends raising taxes. However, higher taxes reduce the supply of savings and increase time preferences yet again. The higher taxes

will also most likely not even reduce inflation because politicians will use the additional revenue for more government spending.

(Newman, 2020, p. 8)

However, this critique is not consistent at all with the tenets of MMT since the taxes of a sovereign state would not finance any spending, but simply take money out of circulation.

MMTers have responded to this criticism by pointing to several elements. First and foremost, their sophisticated Functional Finance proposal, Job Guarantee – which will be discussed in the next chapter – would be originally designed to minimise inflation risks even at full employment. Thus, policymakers would have little need to worry about reducing inflation once full employment is reached, as in theory this would not occur: "inflationary pressures will already be dampened by the rise in taxes that occurs through the automatic stabilizers so a further increase of taxes (i.e. raising tax rates and/or imposing new taxes) may not be necessary" (Tymoigne & Wray, 2013, p. 46).

The MMTers emphasise that using taxes to control inflation after it has broken out is an inappropriate use of their expertise: "regardless of which policy tool is used in a particular context, demand management in general needs to lean much more heavily on the appearance of bottlenecks in specific industries instead of simply tracking changes in a general price index" (Fullwiler et al., 2019). Instead, what they propose is planning to prevent inflation from occurring in the first place: "we argue varying tax rates and other inflation offsets should be included in the budgeting process *from the outset*" (Fullwiler et al., 2019).

In any case, beyond all the criticisms of Job Guarantee that will be addressed in the next chapter, supporters of MMT have also introduced constructive criticism on this point. Murphy argues that if MMTers want to plan their policies in a way that avoids the emergence of inflation, they need to have a better understanding of the tax fraud that many taxpayers commit, as this makes it difficult to adjust the amount of aggregate spending to be non-inflationary: "if MMT is to succeed in the objective of collecting specified sums in tax to ensure the cancellation function of tax has macroeconomic integrity, then it is apparent that those tax gaps need to be estimated" (Murphy, 2019, p. 144).

The second element that MMTers have put forward to defend themselves against this type of criticism is that they do not just propose deficit reductions or tax increases to reduce inflation: "taxes are a critical part of a whole suite of potential demand offsets, which also includes things like tightening financial and credit regulations to reduce bank lending, market finance, speculation and fraud" (Fullwiler et al., 2019). But MMTers also contemplate more extreme measures such as price and wage controls or rationing: "if inflation is likely, we need to put in place anti-inflationary measures, such as well-targeted taxes, wage and price controls, rationing, and voluntary saving" (Nersisyan & Wray, 2019, p. 51)

Finally, there are authors who point to the policy limitations of applying Functional Finance from the outset, not only to reduce inflation once full employment is approaching; and this from both orthodox and heterodox positions. From an orthodox point of view, Jayadev and Mason argue that Functional Finance is, in essence, correct, but that the political incentives that governments have made it very difficult for them to apply it without falling into excesses that lead to inflation:

the problem, in this view, is not that financial constraints mean that governments cannot achieve the fiscal balance consistent with a zero output gap, but rather that in the absence of (real or imagined) financial constraints they would move toward larger deficits, regardless of demand conditions.

(Jayadev & Mason, 2018, p. 12)

Hence, they believe that mainstream economists prefer Sound Finance, not because they consider it technically better than Functional Finance, but because it limits the capabilities of rulers and reduces the risks of undesirable economic consequences: "this 'inflation bias' might be sufficient reason to prefer the conventional rule" (Jayadev & Mason, 2018, p. 12). As can be seen, this is not a criticism of Functional Finance, which is considered correct, but of the trust MMTers place in the rulers:

the different conclusions drawn by MMT and the mainstream and policy do not come from a different understanding of the economy, but from a different view of the capacities of policymakers, and in particular, of what kinds of policy errors are likely to be most costly.

(Jayadev & Mason, 2018, p. 2)

From a heterodox point of view, Colander argues that the state's fiscal lever faces many problems in achieving maximum spending using only public expenditures and revenues:

one can hold the position that Functional Finance provides important theoretical insights (a position I hold), but as an actual real-world policy is highly limited in its usefulness (a position I also hold). The reason is that Functional Finance, like the above described functional spending policy, has serious practical problems of implementation.

(Colander, 2019, p. 68)

For his part, Toporowski points out that a programme as radical as MMT would put the interests of big business and its allies at risk, so they would manoeuvre in many ways – including hiring economists – to make the public believe that such a programme would have harmful consequences for the economy:

even if there is no inflation, economists can be relied upon to provide models that will show inflation accelerating in the future (...) This simplistic thinking will add to the political difficulties of any expenditure programme undertaken by a radical government.

(Toporowski, 2019, p. 196)

Inflation because of creating money

So far we have presented critiques that relate the quantity of expenditure to the total productive capacity of the economy to identify the point at which inflation may originate. However, the most widespread views on the causes of inflation relate to the quantity of money created or in circulation to the economy's production, which substantially modifies the analysis, since the quantity of money is not the same as the quantity of expenditure. Let us recall Lerner's words:

the almost instinctive revulsion that we have to the idea of printing money, and the tendency to identify it with inflation, can be overcome if we calm ourselves and take note that this printing does not affect the amount of money spent.

(Lerner, 1943, p. 41)

Moreover, many analysts start from the premise that real output is coincident (or very close) to real productive capacity so that any increase in the quantity of money or spending would automatically boost inflation. This has been strongly criticised by MMT:

> in the textbook story, however, a fully employed economy is usually taken as the point of departure. Thus, it is usually assumed that the additional spending adds to a level of aggregate demand which is just sufficient to bring about full employment.
>
> *(Bell, 1999, p. 7)*

It is precisely the above that leads some authors to believe that inflation is merely a monetary phenomenon. Probably the best expression of this idea is monetarism, whose main exponent, Milton Friedman, in a talk he gave in India in 1963, stated that "inflation is always and everywhere a monetary phenomenon in the sense that it can only be produced by a faster increase in the quantity of money than in output". To the premise that the economy is always running at full capacity, this approach adds the consideration that the state is the only one that can put money into circulation, as Friedman made clear:

> inflation is produced in Washington because only Washington can create money. Consumers do not produce it, producers do not produce it, unions do not produce it, foreign sheiks do not produce it, oil importers do not produce it... What produces it is too much government spending and too much government money creation and nothing else.
>
> *(Libertypen, 2013)*

To support these claims it is often argued that empirical evidence would show a correlation between (government) money issuance and inflation (Mankiw, 2019, pp. 109–110) – even if some studies point out that such a correlation is only strong for countries with high inflation (Aguir et al., 2022, De Grauwe & Poland, 2005; Teles et al., 2015) – often citing as examples the hyperinflations[1] suffered by some Latin American countries (Summers, 2019; Ocampo, 2021; Triggs, 2021; Hogan, 2021; Drumetz & Pfister, 2021). In the words of Edwards: "in most of these episodes – Argentina, Bolivia, Brazil, Chile, Ecuador, Nicaragua, Peru, and Venezuela – policymakers used arguments similar to those made by MMTers to justify extensive use of money creation to finance very large increases in public expenditures" (Edwards, 2019, p. 532). But the hyperinflationary episodes in Europe in the mid-twentieth century, and Zimbabwe in 2008, are also often pointed to because of creating too much money: "printing money and monetizing debt–even when that debt was partly denominated in local currency–led to devastating inflation in Austria, Hungary, Poland, and Weimar Germany during the first half of the 20th century" (Hartley, 2020).

But this idea of linking the quantity of money created to inflation is not unique to monetarist views. For example, Paul Krugman also conceives of hyperinflation as the consequence of creating money: "when governments cannot raise taxes or borrow to pay for their spending, they sometimes resort to printing, trying to extract large amounts of seigniorage. This is the classic recipe for hyperinflation" (Krugman, 2010). And Marxist economists also link money creation – and not the amount of spending – with inflation or hyperinflation, no doubt because of their conception of money-commodity. An example:

> if the state chose to issue arbitrarily large quantities, there would be discord between the unit of account and the measure of value. The value of commodities would be unchanged

and measured as before, but it would be rendered into price through increasing volumes of fiat money. The result would be escalating inflation and disruption of circulation.

(Lapavitsas & Aguila, 2020, p. 8)

Another example:

the productivity of labor (real value) is not in the control of the state with all its dollar printing (…) If the government then goes on pumping money in when output cannot be raised further, inflation of commodity prices will follow and/or inflation in speculative financial assets.

(Roberts, 2019, p. 16)

This analysis leads them to consider that inflationary episodes such as those experienced in the 1970s and 1980s were due to "inconvertible central bank money" (Lapavitsas & Aguila, 2020, p. 11), not to supply or energy factors.

However, both MMTers and other heterodox analysts challenge these widespread ideas using three arguments. The first is to point out that such a correlation between money creation and inflation is not true in many cases (Fullwiler & Allen, 2007; Ryan-Collins, 2015; Carnevali & Deleide, 2023). Indeed, some MMTers go so far as to state that "there is no simple proportional relationship between increases in the money supply and increases in the general price level" (Mitchell et al., 2019). The MMTers argue that there are studies that would support this, such as Vague (2016), which concludes that out of 47 cases of rapid money growth analysed, none were associated with bursts of inflation. This would be so basically because of what was pointed out above: what matters is not the quantity of money but spending (and productive capacity). In the words of Tymoigne and Wray (2013): "inflation would result if the relation between government spending and taxing were wrong, not because the ratio of money supply (however measured) and GDP were wrong" (Tymoigne & Wray, 2013, p. 9). The divergence between money created and money spent would be explained by the private sector's desire to save; if this is high, there would be less spending and less scope for inflation, and conversely:

if the desired net saving of the domestic private sector is positive at full employment income, there is no inflationary pressures from a fiscal deficit.8 Similarly, if the budget deficit is too high relative to the desired net saving of the domestic private sector, there will be demand-led inflationary pressures around full employment.

(Tymoigne & Wray, 2013, p. 18)

The second argument is based on the fact that the correlation between quantity of money and inflation, even if revealed, does not imply causality, being precisely reversed in general terms: it is the fact that prices rise that would push up the quantity of money in circulation. The latter is precisely a corollary of the post-Keynesian endogenous money approach:

banks create money to finance the payment of wages, and the purchase of material inputs, among other things, leading to the conclusion that, in the general case, changes in the money supply follow changes in prices and nominal wages, and not vice versa.

(Febrero, 2009, p. 531)

Or, in the words of Bailly and Gnos: "the expansion of the money supply does not govern the evolution of the price level, but, on the contrary, depends on it" (Bailly & Gnos, 2006, p. 219). However, endogenetic post-Keynesians refer only to bank money, while MMTers extrapolate this to state money as well: state money also tends to increase through higher fiscal deficits because of strong price increases (mainly through aid, subsidies, and wage payments). And it is this correlation that would be interpreted inversely by the monetarist view: "this is not the simple Monetarist story in which government 'prints too much money' that causes high inflation, but rather a more complicated causal sequence in which high inflation helps to create deficits" (Wray, 2012a, p. 257). Indeed, Armstrong and Mosler study hyperinflation in Germany during the 1920s to conclude that massive money creation was a consequence of accelerating price increases and not the other way around:

> We identify the cause of the inflation as the German government paying continuously higher prices for its purchases, particularly those of the foreign currencies the Allies demanded for the payment of reparations, and we identify the rise in the quantity of money and the printing of increasing quantities of banknotes as a consequence of the hyperinflation, rather than its cause.
>
> *(Armstrong & Mosler, 2021, p. 1)*

A central argument they use refers to the fact that the German authorities commissioned new printing presses to cater for the enormous amount of money they needed to create, which would show that the initiative to create money did not come from the rulers: "more than thirty paper manufacturers worked at full capacity solely to provide paper for the Reichsbank notes. Yet even with this immense output the Reichsbank was unable to deliver enough banknotes to satisfy the demand" (Schacht, 1967, p. 68). The basic idea was that the First World War and the related sanctions had depressed the productive capacity of the German economy and that this was what had pushed prices up. Hyperinflation would not have been the consequence of creating money, but of having suffered a major supply shock.

MMTer Bill Mitchell also offers a detailed explanation of the causes of hyperinflation in Zimbabwe at the beginning of the twenty-first century, and, once again, these would have to do with a productive supply shock (derived from a major drought and political conflicts), and not with the excessive creation of money (Mitchell, 2009b).

Such supply shocks would be the main cause of all hyperinflationary processes, an idea that even seems to coincide with that of the Cato Institute researchers: "hyperinflation is an economic malady that arises under extreme conditions: war, political mismanagement, and the transition from a command to market-based economy" (Hanke & Krus, 2012, p. 11). Although the MMTers admit that this is not the only cause, however likely: "there are probably many paths to hyperinflation, but there are common problems: social and political upheaval; civil war; collapse of productive capacity (that could be due to war); weak government; and foreign debt denominated in external currency or gold" (Wray, 2012, p. 257).

In any case, what is clear is that money creation would not cause hyperinflation, if anything it would only make it worse:

> monetary factors may be important, but only as forces that propagate inflation, but do not cause it. What is of concern are the underlying forces which exert such pressure on the monetary authorities as to make expansion of the money supply almost inevitable.
>
> *(Grunwald, 1961, p. 460)*

As J. D. Alt points out:

> The issuing of too much hyper-inflationary money, however, is a reflexive, emergency government response to another underlying problem that caused the hyper-inflation to get started in the first place. To say that "printing money" causes hyper-inflation is like saying "flames" cause a fire. The underlying problem that has caused every historical (and contemporary) instance of hyper-inflation is the same: the significant and general collapse of a nation's production of goods and services.
>
> *(Alt, 2020)*

The third argument pointed out by MMT to question the monetarist idea is that it only focuses on money put into circulation by the state, completely ignoring bank money put into circulation through credit, which would reveal a clear ideological bias. Stephanie Kelton explains this bias as follows:

> when you go to a shop, the clerk doesn't know whether the money you are paying with comes from a bank loan or from government spending. Cash registers don't discriminate. The shop assistant is not going to increase prices because you are paying with money from government spending, and he is not going to stop increasing prices because you are paying with money from a bank loan.
>
> *(Gener, 2019)*

Monetary policy subordinated to fiscal policy

Much of the criticism levelled at Functional Finance – and MMT in general – has to do with the absolute prominence it confers on fiscal policy and the secondary or almost null role it reserves for monetary policy.

For example, Colander argues that Functional Finance is right to point out that there may be insufficient aggregate expenditure to provide an outlet for all potential output, but that it fails to propose that the only possible solution to fill this gap is through public deficits, since the same objective could be achieved with other types of policies, whether monetary or even direct or indirect regulation of external and private spending:

> the problem is that Functional Finance places the entire onus of adjusting spending on the government, when in Lerner's model it would be more efficient if the spending adjustment were distributed widely among all agents so that those with the lowest cost of adjusting their spending were incentivized to do the adjustment. (…) In theory, the same aggregate results could have been achieved without using fiscal policy at all.
>
> *(Colander, 2019, p. 67)*

Moreover, Colander also points out that Functional Finance is not concerned with the distributional character of fiscal policies, since nothing prevents reaching the aggregate maximum spending through tax cuts rather than spending increases: "Functional Finance abstracts from such distributional issues. (…) For example, Functional Finance is neutral on whether an expansion in aggregate spending is generated by increased government spending or by decreased taxes" (Colander, 2019, p. 68).

Paul Krugman (2019a) also criticises that Functional Finance gives absolute prominence to fiscal policy, leaving monetary policy in second place, as he considers that the latter can achieve the aggregate spending that allows full employment without resorting to fiscal policy: "as long as monetary policy is available, there is a range of possible deficits consistent with that goal [full employment]" (Krugman, 2019b). In a similar vein, Thomas Palley further emphasises that the effects of fiscal policy are intensified if monetary policy is left idle: "the greater the emphasis on fiscal looseness, the more the need to raise real interest rates to avoid excessive AD" (Palley, 2020, p. 481). Specifically, he argues that setting the interest rate at 0% could generate inflation and financial imbalances by stimulating spending through borrowing: "with the policy nominal interest rate set equal to zero, the real interest rate will be negative. That, in turn, will spur massive borrowing, particularly to finance asset purchases, unleashing more inflation and asset price bubbles" (Palley, 2015, p. 17). This criticism is shared by Drumets and Pfister (2021):

> MMT's prescription to keep nominal interest rates at a very low, near-zero level would also foster macroeconomic instability, with, during the upward phase of the cycle (until, according to MMT's doctrine, full employment is reached and taxes are increased), real rates falling and potentially causing higher inflation which would, in turn, lower real interest rates.
>
> *(Drumets & Pfister, 2021, p. 17)*

Mankiw (2020) takes a similar view:

> the expansion in the monetary base will increase bank lending and the money supply. Interest rates must then fall to induce people to hold the expanded money supply, again putting upward pressure on aggregate demand and inflation.
>
> *(Mankiw, 2020, p. 3)*

Moreover, Mankiw adds that the state money created ends up in the form of bank reserves that must be remunerated, which only further increases the amount of money created: "the ever-expanding monetary base will have further ramifications. Aggregate demand will increase due to a wealth effect, eventually spurring inflation" (Mankiw, 2020, p. 2).

Cochrane also believes that leaving interest rates at 0% causes inflation, but he uses a different reasoning; money that was previously used to buy government debt will then be used to invest in other assets or to buy goods and services:

> people value government debt and reserves as an asset, in a portfolio. If the government stops paying interest, people try to dump the debt in favor of assets that pay a return and to buy goods and services, driving up prices.
>
> *(Cochrane, 2020)*

Coats goes much further and points out that keeping the interest rate so low, specifically below the equilibrium rate, could lead to hyperinflation:

> if it persists in holding short-term interest rates below the equilibrium rate it will eventually fuel inflation, which will put upward pressure on nominal interest rates requiring ever increasing injections of base money until the value of the currency collapses (hyperinflation).
>
> *(Coats, 2019, p. 569)*

This analysis is also shared by Blanchard (Robb, 2019). Sumner and Horan's (2019) argument for criticising leaving monetary policy in second place is that, although fiscal policy does directly affect short-term fluctuations through higher productive capacity utilisation, it is monetary policy that affects underlying inflation: "short-term fluctuations in inflation are often correlated with changes in economic slack, but the underlying inflation process is caused by monetary policy, not economic overheating" (Sumner & Horan, 2019, p. 4).

MMTers have responded to this type of criticism by relying on the theoretical postulates of endogenous money: central bank monetary policy cannot do much to make households and firms borrow no matter how much interest rates fall since they will only do so when they need to, regardless of the price. That is why monetary policy could do little to stimulate aggregate spending through borrowing, since this would depend on the initiative of the private sector, not the monetary authorities:

> it does not follow, however, that cutting interest rates will work to induce enough spending to maintain full employment. You can't simply assume borrowers will always have the appetite for more private debt, even if you make it really cheap to borrow. Businesses borrow and invest when they're swamped with customers (or expect to be).
>
> *(Kelton, 2019)*

Papadimitriou and Wray reinforce this thesis with empirical evidence from the United States:

> the mantra for the past two decades is that the Fed controls inflation through control over inflation expectations. Yet, even with zero interest rate targets (ZIRP) and trillions of dollars of unconventional monetary policy, the Fed was unable to get inflation up to its 2 percent target.
>
> *(Papadimitriou & Wray, 2021, quoted in Nersisyan & Wray,*
> *2022, p. 2)*

Of course, this reasoning also works in reverse; MMTers do not believe that raising interest rates significantly drags down private borrowing and thus inflation (Fullwiler & Allen, 2007). Their argument is because "there is no empirical evidence to support the belief that raising interest rates fights inflation" (Wray, quoted in Hartley, 2020). Moreover, from MMT positions it is argued that raising interest rates can raise inflation for several reasons, among which are that paying more interest means increasing the amount of spending and that interest is a cost of production for firms that can be extrapolated to the price of their products. Mosler explains it as follows:

> To summarize, I see interest rate policy as both backwards and confused. First, the rate of inflation academically defined is an expression of the central bank's policy rates, so rate hikes directly increase that measure of inflation. Second, rate hikes constitute additional state deficit spending, which tends to also be an inflationary bias given currency institutional structure.
>
> *Mosler (2023)*

This idea is supported by some studies such as Bryan Fix:

> according to canon, higher interest rates slow the growth of the money supply, and thus reduce inflation. And yet, when we look at the evidence, there is no sign of this pattern.

Instead, higher interest rates are associated with both a *faster* expansion of the money supply, and *higher* rates of inflation.

(Fix, 2023)

With respect to the criticism that the near 0% interest rate may lead to financial instability, the MMTers point out that such a risk should be prevented through tighter banking regulations that make lending more difficult and less likely, not through rate increases: "taxes are a critical part of a whole suite of potential demand offsets, which also includes things like tightening financial and credit regulations to reduce bank lending, market finance, speculation and fraud" (Fullwiler et al., 2019). Therefore, the MMT concludes that "taxes and government expenditures are a more appropriate tool to regulate demand and inflation than central bank interest rates" (Leao, 2015, p. 21).

On the other hand, much of the criticism of Functional Finance moves into the (analytically speaking) swampy world of expectations. The very increase in public borrowing resulting from the implementation of Functional Finance would lead economic agents to believe that inflation would rise soon, and that belief alone would push up prices (Palley, 2020; Drumets & Pfister, 2021; Razmi, 2023). In the words of Edwars (2019): "MMT ignores (or minimizes) the role of expectations on interest rates. As is well established by empirical research, expected inflation is translated into higher interest rates through the so-called Fisher effect" (Edwards, 2019). As Kashama (2020) explains,

if private agents do not fully believe in the government's commitment to implement fiscal consolidation when inflation gets too high, rising inflation expectations can easily emerge if government spending programmes proliferate. When such expectations are sufficiently widespread, they can lead to a sudden and uncontrolled increase in actual inflation.

(Kashama, 2020, p. 6)

These ideas are closely linked to the belief in the need to maintain a monetary authority independent from government decisions, as it is argued that if there were doubts about this, economic agents would predict increases in inflation: "the evidence stemming from Latin America indicates that as soon as central bank independence is weakened, and the central bank begins to work for the government, inflation expectations take off, as does inflation proper" (Edwards, 2019). Hence, from orthodox positions, the theoretical consolidation between central bank and treasury by MMT is widely criticised as inflationary: "we argue that having an independent central bank tasked with an explicit inflation control mandate is essential for a well-functioning economy to anchor market perceptions about inflation" (Omran & Zelmen, 2021, p. 1). Some analyses go further and consider that this lack of independence could even lead to hyperinflation: "the central bank could then lose the ability to set monetary policy independently, possibly paving the way to hyperinflation and its devastating economic consequences" (Aguir et al., 2022, p. 22).

Another criticism is that Functional Finance invites rulers to spend too much and gain too much power, which "could cause increases in political power inequality relative to citizens not seen since the medieval era or before" (Hanley, 2021, p. 431). And other critics point out that full employment achieved through fiscal policy alone would require the economy to grow steadily, and since the economy is assumed to be in full employment, the growth of aggregate output must be entirely due to the growth of productivity, which can be realized by changing the composition of public spending in favor of productive expenditures.

(Sardoni, 2016)

Finally, there is also a proliferation of criticism that applying the Functional Finance thesis leads to currency depreciation and consequently also to higher inflation through imports of more expensive goods (Huber, 2015; Palley, 2015; Edwards, 2019, Rogoff, 2019; Kashama, 2020; Drumets & Pfister, 2021; Razmi, 2022; Dullien & Tober, 2022). In the words of Summers (2019), "but a policy of relying on central bank finance of government deficits, as suggested by modern monetary theorists, would likely result in a collapsing exchange rate" (Summers, 2019). The specific responses of MMTers to these criticisms will be presented in the next chapter as they are more relevant to the topic addressed there.

Political assessment and supply-side inflation

Despite all the above, the MMTers conclude that, even if the increase in public spending would cause inflation (once unemployment has been reached or even before), such a situation would be preferable to enjoying lower inflation rates but high unemployment rates:

> even if the CPI (or some other standard price index) did begin to rise before full employment had been reached, it is not at all clear that the "costs" associated with moderate price increases would outweigh the (social and economic) benefits of reduced unemployment.
>
> *(Bell, 1999, p. 7)*

The MMTers point here to an ideological question: the choice would be between a scenario with moderate unemployment and inflation, or full employment and higher inflation. Their supporters choose the second option, considering it fairer because it would benefit the neediest sections of the population, i.e. the unemployed, while they accuse many economists of favouring the first option, which would particularly favour the rentiers.

But not only do they argue that it would be preferable for the unemployed, but that it would not necessarily negatively affect the economy: "there are even studies that argue that moderate inflation is itself a net benefit rather than a net cost. (See: Schultze (1959); Minsky (1986); and Ackerlof, et al. (1996))" (Bell, 1999, p. 7). This view is in line with that of many other non-MMT analysts who indicate that inflation is often linked to economic growth, such as Ha-Joon Chang, who cites the South Korean and Brazilian economies as examples (Chang, 2008, pp. 149–150); but also Sarel (1996, pp. 199–215) for the International Monetary Fund, who estimates that, below 8%, inflation has little impact on growth – and that, in any case, the relationship is positive below that level, i.e. inflation helps rather than hinders economic growth; or even Robert Barro, who concludes in a study that moderate inflation (rates of 10–20%) has little negative effect on growth, and that, below 10%, inflation has no effect at all (Barro, 1996, p. 78).

In any case, MMTers point out that, although demand-driven inflation is theoretically possible, in practice it hardly occurs: "inflation generated by strong aggregate demand beyond full employment is rarely observed, apart from the immediate post-WWII period" (Tcherneva, 2023, p. 6). Instead, what explains most inflationary episodes would be supply-side factors: "when we suggest that a budget constraint be replaced by an inflation constraint, we are not suggesting that all inflation is caused by excess demand. Indeed, from our view, excess demand is rarely the cause of inflation" (Fullwiler et al., 2019). Among these factors, several stand out, such as energy prices: "a rising oil price can drive up the price level if the rising energy costs are passed on to consumers" (Ehnts, 2022). Some MMTers insist that energy is often the root cause and protagonist of almost all inflationary processes throughout history (Valadkhani & Mitchell, 2002).

Other important supply factors would be financial speculation on commodities, speculation on housing, and profit margin increases by firms:

> whether it's businesses raising profit margins or passing on costs, or it's Wall Street speculating on commodities or houses, there are a range of sources of inflation that aren't caused by the general state of demand and aren't best regulated by aggregate demand policies.
>
> *(Fullwiler et al., 2019)*

Another causal supply factor that MMT does not forget is wages, understanding them in the context of the conflict between employers and workers: "conflict theory situates the problem of inflation as being intrinsic to the power relations between workers and capital (class conflict), which are mediated by government within a capitalist system" (Mitchell et al., 2019, p. 255).

Precisely these factors have become much more analytically relevant with the inflationary episode of the pandemic era from 2021 onwards that we discuss below.

Pandemic-era inflation

The policies implemented in 2020 in the wake of the Covid-19 pandemic were seen by many economists as an important endorsement of the MMT thesis, as all states and central banks around the world pursued ultra-expansionary fiscal and monetary policies without concern for public deficit levels, interest rates on public debt, or the supposed inflationary pressures they could theoretically cause (Xing, 2020; Juniper, 2022; Chohan, 2020; Cruz et al 2020; Domazet, 2021). Although no state applied the specific policy recommended by the MMTers, Job Guarantee – which we will analyse in the next chapter – and, therefore, we cannot say that the recipes of the MMT were "applied" (Watkins, 2021)), at least there was a clearly heterodox way of proceeding that was in line with Functional Finance. After all, the public sector significantly increased its public spending to try to maintain aggregate spending at a time when the economy had collapsed due to the pandemic and health restrictions, which greatly increased public deficits and debts without, at least at the time, seeming to matter to the authorities (who, in fact, temporarily deactivated the fiscal rules of Sound Finance). Indeed, some authors began to use Modern Monetary Theory to argue for more and stronger public education financing (Backer, 2022), especially health financing – whose importance was highlighted during the pandemic (Hensher et al., 2021; Ehnts & Paetz, 2021; Pandit, 2022).

However, more than a year later, a global inflationary process slowly emerged, which reached its peak in 2022 and which served many economists to hold these expansionary policies responsible for the phenomenon and, therefore, to question the theoretical postulates of Functional Finance in particular and MMT in general. According to them, the extraordinary fiscal and monetary policies applied by the pandemic would have caused the inflationary episode, either through excessive money creation, high aggregate demand, and/or overheating of the labour market, all of which would prove that the postulates of MMT lead to inflation.

On the one hand, there are the authors who consider that expansionary monetary policy was mainly responsible for inflation (Gagliardone & Gertler, 2023). On the other hand, there are those authors who consider that expansionary fiscal policies drove inflation through overheating in the labour market and output exceeding the economy's potential, at least for the US case (Jordà et al., 2022; Blanchard, 2021; Edelberg & Sheiner, 2021; Ball et al., 2022; Cecchetti et al., 2023; Benigno & Eggertsson, 2023; Gagnon & Sarsenbayev, 2022). Among all these authors there are divergences in the importance they attach to the labour market and expansionary policies. For example, Reifschneider and Wilcox (2022) point out that the labour market could not have been to blame for the inflationary episode because the Philips curve is fairly flat and inflation expectations remained well anchored. Giovanni et al. (2023) estimate that recognising that inflationary effects in any country will be larger when aggregate demand is stimulated in a supply-constrained world, this demand would have contributed two-thirds of inflation. For their part, Bernanke and Blanchard consider that the inflation that started in 2021 was not exactly due to an overheated labour market, but to "shocks top prices given wages" due to "strong aggregate demand" and "constraints on sectoral supply" (Bernanke & Blanchard, 2023). In other words, although they focus more on the increase in aggregate demand than on the overheating of the labour market, they introduce supply-side problems caused by post-pandemic bottlenecks as a key element, as do Koch and Noureldin (2023) of the International Monetary Fund. Another cause of inflation is the shift in the composition of demand from services (mostly constrained by health measures) to durable goods, as it would have strained the productive capacity of the latter (Guerrieri et al., 2022; di Giovanni et al., 2023). Santacreu and LaBelle (2022) estimate that without the bottlenecks inflation would have been slightly lower, but they still blame the increase in aggregate demand for driving inflation. Finally, Shapiro (2022) finds that demand factors are responsible for about one-third of inflation, with the rest due to ambiguous factors.

But these interpretations, which focus mainly on demand factors to explain inflation, have been widely questioned by MMTers themselves (and also by many other – not necessarily heterodox – analysts): "aggregate demand has played a relatively minor role in generating inflation pressure" (Nersisyan & Wray, 2022, p. 3). In their view, the main cause would have been disruptions in the global supply chain as a consequence of the pandemic, as well as the enormous power of the companies that set international prices for energy products, as Pavlina Tcherneva explains:

> All evidence indicates that current price pressures are due to widespread global disruptions on the supply side: shutting down of factories, transportation routes, and ports; a slow resumption of production and working through backlogs in the supply chain; a shift in the structure of private demand away from services to goods, and price setting in the energy sector by OPEC. Price increases came from bottlenecks, logistical challenges, oil cartel production and pricing decisions, not from government spending beyond full employment.
>
> *(Tcherneva, 2023, p. 6)*

Now, some MMTers go so far as to admit that all the aid given to households and firms during the worst of the pandemic may have played some role in boosting inflation, but only very partially: "it may well be true that if the relief checks had never been sent, demand would be so low that dominant firms could not raise prices – so measured inflation would have been lower" (Nersisyan & Wray, 2022, p. 8). But, in any case, they qualify that most of the aid granted was not used to stimulate spending, but "to pay already overdue bills and to increase saving" (Nersisyan & Wray, 2022, p. 6). Be that as it may, they conclude that the main responsibility for inflation lies elsewhere, namely on "the supply side: supply chain disruptions, labor market disruptions, and corporations exercising pricing power" (Nersisyan & Wray, 2022, p. 3).

Of course, if anything, MMTers emphasise that inflation expectations played no role in the origin of inflation, despite the attention they often receive from orthodox economists: "it is remarkable that the current run-up of inflation was not caused by inflationary expectations – as actual rates have tripled while expectations remained subdued" (Nersisyan & Wray, 2022, p. 2). This is even acknowledged by authors from the International Monetary Fund itself: "the empirical analysis has also documented that UMP announcements during COVID-19 – including direct government financing by central banks in EMDEs similar to forms of MF – did not trigger an increase in inflation expectations" (Aguir et al., 2022, p. 22).

Although this inflationary phenomenon would have been caused by supply shocks resulting from the pandemic, MMTers also point out that the market power of many firms would have exacerbated the situation: "most prices are set by firms with the degree of pricing power dependent on the amount of competition that exists in the industry" (Nersisyan & Wray, 2022, p. 25). This thesis seems to be supported by the work of many other economists, who have identified increases in firm margins significantly above the increase in production costs (Terlep, 2021; Boesler et al., 2021; Bivens, 2022a; Doğüs, 2022; Stoller, 2021) and even central bank analysis (Weber & Wasner, 2023; Bivens, 2022b; Glover et al., 2023; Stiglitz & Regmi, 2022). As many MMTers point out, the possibility that corporate profits drive inflation is something that was recognised even by Adam Smith:

> High profits actually tend to raise the price of things much more than high wages. Our merchants and industrialists complain a lot about the harmful effects of high wages, because they raise prices and thus restrict the sale of their goods at home and abroad. They say nothing about the harmful effects of high profits. They are silent about the harmful consequences of their own profits. They only protest at the consequences of the profits of others.
>
> *(Smith, A. (1994) [1776], p. 95)*

Moreover, Abba Lerner himself also contemplated this phenomenon and came to call it "sellers-induced inflation" (Lerner, 1958).

However, not only the market power of the firms would have mattered, but also the context of generalised inflation itself, which would justify the firms' decision to increase prices without suffering a significant penalty from consumers:

> at the micro level, some firms exploited their market power (and media-stoked inflation worries) to raise prices, not only to cover rising costs, but also to pad profits, emboldened by the fact that customers had already begun to perceive price increases as "unavoidable".
>
> *(Tcherneva, 2023, p. 6)*

This thesis has been developed with remarkable success by Weber & Wasner (2023). According to these authors, industry-wide cost increases due to bottlenecks may generate an implicit agreement among firms to raise prices even if in normal situations there are high degrees of competition: "bottlenecks can create temporary monopoly power which can even render it safe to hike prices not only to protect but to increase profits" (Weber & Wasner, 2023, p. 186). In turn, public knowledge that costs have increased across the board serves firms to raise prices without suffering strong rejection by customers, who end up considering such a move justified: "publicly reported supply-chain bottlenecks and cost shocks can also serve to create legitimacy for price hikes and create acceptance on the part of consumers to pay higher prices, thus rendering demand less elastic" (Weber & Wasner, 2023, p. 186).

Since the MMTers' diagnosis of the causes of inflation is different from the conventional diagnosis, so are the solutions. MMTers contest that the vast majority of monetary authorities have chosen to raise interest rates to make financing more expensive and slow down economic activity, as well as to focus on wage growth to avoid possible wage-price spirals: "MMT rejects the conventional view that an economic slowdown, a reduction in wages, and unemployment are 'solutions' to inflationary pressures" (Tcherneva, 2023, p. 7). In fact, they very often point to the example of Japan to show that it is possible to maintain interest rates close to 0% and experience low inflation rates – even lower than in most economies – in addition to more expansionary fiscal policies than usual (Xing, 2020; Mitchell, 2023). In Bill Mitchell words: "Japan has lower inflation, no currency crisis and its citizens are better off as a result of the monetary-fiscal policy initiatives" (Mitchell, 2023).

Instead, what they propose is to take measures to alleviate bottlenecks: "the more appropriate solution would of course be to work to alleviate supply-side constraints. That, however, cannot really be achieved by monetary policy" (Nersisyan & Wray, 2022, p. 35). Indeed, many of these solutions would require increasing public spending and boosting economic activity, rather than weighing it down with restrictive monetary policy: "there are multiple ways to tackle a sustained increase in the price level, including investments that can alleviate bottlenecks or shortages on the supply side (which means more, not less, government spending)" (Tcherneva, 2023, p. 7). Other solutions that have been pointed to are price controls in key strategic sectors, such as energy or food (Nersisyan & Wray, 2022; Tcherneva, 2023; Weber & Wasner, 2023). And also, of course, the MMT's flagship policy: Job Guarantee (Tcherneva, 2023, p. 7), which will be discussed in the next chapter.

Criticism of sectoral balances

The MMT's interpretation of sectoral balances is not a central element of its theoretical framework, which is why it has received less attention and less criticism. We will highlight here only two of them. On the one hand, Sergio Cesaratto notes that he finds it a useful analytical tool, but that he is not entirely convinced by it being merely an ex-post picture:

> I have some reservations about the stock-flow consistent model – I am referring here to the simple three-sector balances – which I find quite useful to detect some patterns but which, as an ex-post accounting picture, tends to obscure the causal mechanisms revealed by the more traditional Keynesian (super)multiplier approach.
>
> *(Cesaratto, 2016, p. 66)*

Anne Mayhew criticises the MMTers for hiding behind the neutrality of accounting principles in order to reinforce a subjective interpretation that gives the public sector total prominence:

> Mitchell, Wray, and Watts are careful to say that the flow of funds approach is "based on accounting principles rather than being a behavioral (theoretical) framework for

understanding…" (p. 96). But throughout the text and in much of the other writing of MMT advocates, their sectoral flows analysis becomes, even if by default, the behavioral framework that is available. The reasonable conclusion is that Government will be the sector that will determine the level of national income, the level of employment, and how rapidly the overall price level will rise or fall. The private sector plays a secondary role in this analysis.

(Mayhew, 2019, p. 133)

However, this does not seem to be a fair criticism because precisely in the quoted excerpt from Mitchell, Wray, and Watts it is explained that the flow of funds approach is not a (theoretical) behavioural framework and that for this very reason they imprint their own theoretical considerations on it a posteriori in order to give it analytical utility and to find causalities. In other words, one thing would be the accounting principles of flows of funds which, in effect, do not allow us to identify causalities, and another would be the interpretation that the MMTers give it, using the Keynesian principles cited above to find causal links. It is not by chance that on the same page of the quoted extract these two parts are divided by a subtitle called "causal relationships". We copy the extended excerpt to get a full picture of the authors' views:

It should be emphasised that the flow of funds approach is based on accounting principles rather than being a behavioural (theoretical) framework for understanding why these flows occur. Nor do we gain any insights as to the adjustment processes that govern the change in net financial assets in each sector. That caveat is not to be taken as a criticism of the approach; but merely an observation of its restrictions. It also doesn't reduce the utility and insights that the approach provides. Often economists like to denigrate analyses that manipulate accounting identities as being too low brow. But any approach is valuable if it provides useful ways of thinking.

(Mitchell et al., 2019, p. 96)

Consequently, it does not seem true, as Mayhew (2019) seems to denounce, that MMTers confuse their subjective approach with the merely descriptive approach provided by a reading of accounting principles, as their attempt to explain the differences between the one and the other is palpable.

Conclusions

Abba Lerner's Functional Finance is one of the theoretical underpinnings of MMT. Unlike the postulates discussed in the previous chapters, this measure is a policy prescription, not simply a description of economic reality. It is basically that the state should increase its public spending by as much as is necessary for the aggregate expenditure of the economy to equal its potential output. If aggregate expenditure falls below that level, there would be unemployment; if it rises above that level, there would be inflation. How public spending is financed is irrelevant because the only thing that matters is that aggregate spending should be sufficient to provide an outlet for all output. Consequently, a state with monetary sovereignty, which does not need to worry about the sources of financing, could easily follow the recommendation of Functional Finance to reach full employment. However, this is not the concrete proposal of the MMT, which is aware of the limitations it faces, which is why they propose a major modification of Functional Finance (which we will analyse in the next chapter).

Among these limitations of Functional Finance is the fact that inflation would most likely start to originate even before full employment is reached, basically because not all added expenditure would be directed towards sectors where there is still economic slack to take advantage of unused productive capacity, but also because the workers needed for some sectors might not be available. This is undoubtedly the most important criticism and the one that pushed the MMTers to refine the proposal, but it is not the only one.

Another criticism is that Functional Finance puts all the responsibility for achieving the necessary aggregate spending on the fiscal lever since the same objective could be achieved using other tools, such as monetary policy, by favouring private borrowing. However, MMTers are totally opposed to this option because they consider that interest rate changes have little impact on the borrowing decisions of economic agents, who would be guided more by other factors such as expectations of corporate profits or consumption preferences. In fact, MMT usually recommends that interest rates should be set at around 0% so that fiscal policy is the only adjustment used by the state to achieve full employment. This has been strongly criticised by many analysts who believe that such a policy can lead to inflationary pressures and also to imbalances in the banking and financial sector. In my case, I welcome the MMTers' recommendation, not only because I believe that financial imbalances should be addressed by other types of policies (namely regulatory policies in the banking and financial sector) but also because it seems to me that keeping the interest rate at 0% is a fairer policy in redistributive terms, as it favours the neediest economic agents while not favouring (without reason) the least needy.

Another typical criticism is that raising the public deficit, especially if it is not financed by public bonds, leads to inflation (or even hyperinflation) long before full employment is reached. There are several arguments in support of this idea, but MMTers reject them all. On the one hand, there is the argument that creating more money without increasing output is inflationary. MMTers reply that it is spending that can raise inflation, not the quantity of money since the quantity of money does not have to be converted into spending. Moreover, modern economies normally operate with some economic slack, so there would be room to increase spending without causing inflationary pressures. Finally, MMTers point out the ideological bias of such criticism because they only focus on money injected by the state, but not by banks through the provision of credit. If the creation of state money were automatically inflationary, so would be the creation of bank money, and yet the critics never focus on that. On the other hand, there is the argument that the government deficit causes a crowding-out effect and an increase in interest rates, but MMTers contest this idea because in their view an increase in the government deficit would tend to reduce rates, not increase them. There is also the argument of inflation expectations and central bank independence: any doubts about the autonomy of the monetary authorities would lead to higher inflation expectations, and inflation expectations would lead to higher real price growth. However, this is speculative reasoning that is difficult to test and easily manipulated in order to reinforce certain arguments. On these last points, I am completely on the side of the MMTers.

Finally, many focus attention on the risk that increased aggregate spending would depreciate the currency through higher imports, and that this in turn would lead to imported inflation. This is something we will discuss in more detail in the next chapter.

In any case, many MMTers insist that, even if inflation originates before full employment is reached, they believe that some price increase and a level of employment close to the optimum is preferable to maintaining high unemployment rates in order to keep inflation very low. This would be a political and subjective decision that in one case would favour some and disadvantage others and in the other case practically the opposite: full employment with inflation would benefit the working class in general while it would disadvantage savers; certain unemployment rates with hardly any inflation would benefit savers while it would disadvantage the working class. MMTers are clearly in favour of the first option, as is this writer (with the exceptions and limitations I discuss in the next chapter).

However, this would only be the case for demand-side inflation, as it is not the only type of inflation that can arise. In fact, MMTers consider that demand-pull inflation is precisely the one that has been experienced the least throughout history. An example would be the inflationary episode that originated internationally in 2021, since according to many analysts (including MMTers) it would have been the consequence of international bottlenecks derived from the pandemic and the energy crisis derived from Russia's invasion of Ukraine in 2022, both of which are supply-side factors and not demand-side factors. In my case, based on the available empirical evidence, I cannot see it any other way.

Finally, closely related to Functional Finance is the MMTers' interpretation of sectoral balances, which is an analytical approach based on national accounting and the stock-flow model. This would make it easier to understand why the optimal level of public deficit to reach full employment is different across countries and periods, as it will depend on the current account position and private indebtedness (which in turn depends on a large number of factors such as export capacity or the business cycle itself). For example, an economy with a current account surplus and a high level of private indebtedness will already be contributing a lot of aggregate spending to the economy, so raising the public deficit will not be so necessary to achieve the desired goal. And the opposite: an economy with a current account deficit and little private borrowing will be contributing very little aggregate spending to the economy, making it crucial for the public deficit to fill the gap. In my view, this is an analytical tool that is as powerful as it is ignored, as I argue in Garzón (2021), although it is true that its usefulness and application takes us relatively far away from the main objective of Modern Monetary Theory.

Note

1 In his classic 1954 article, Phillip Cagan (1956) defined hyperinflation as a rate of price growth above 50% per month.

References

Aguir, I., Capelle, D., Dell'Ariccia, G., & Sandri, D. (2022). *Monetary finance: Do not touch, or handle with care?* IMF International Monetary Fund, Research Department DP/2022/001.

Akerlof, G., Dickens, W., & Perry, G. (1996, September–October, 11–17). Low inflation or no inflation: Should the federal reserve pursue complete price stability? *Challenge*.

Alt, J. D. (2020, March 26). Manhattan project to prevent hyper-inflation. *New Economic Perspectives*. http://neweconomicperspectives.org/2020/03/manhattan-project-to-prevent-hyper-inflation.html

Arjun, J., & Mason, J. W. (2018). Mainstream macroeconomics and modern monetary theory: What really divides them? John Jay College - CUNY. Department of Economics Working Paper 2018–8.

Armstrong, P., & Mosler, W. (2021). *Weimar republic hyperinflation through a modern monetary theory lens. Modern money studies.* https://gimms.org.uk/2020/11/14/weimar-republic-hyperinflation-through-a-modern-monetary-theory-lens/

Armstrong, P. (2019). Keynes's view of deficits and functional finance: A modern monetary theory perspective. *International Review of Applied Economics*, *33*(2), 241–253. https://doi.org/10.1080/02692171.2018.1475139

Aspromourgos, T. (2014). *Keynes, Lerner and the question of public debt.* https://varoufakis.files
.wordpress.com/2014/01/ta-on-debt-paper-1.pdf

Backer, D. (2022). *Modern monetary theory and education (February 11).* https://ssrn.com/abstract
=4032757 or http://dx.doi.org/10.2139/ssrn.4032757

Bailly, J.-L., & Gnos, C. (2006). Definición e integración del dinero: La aportación de la tesis de la
endogeneidad. In P. Piegay & L. P. Tochon (Eds.), *Teorías monetarias poskeynesianas* (pp. 219–230).
Akal.

Ball, L., Leigh, D., & Mishra, P. (2022, September). *Understanding U.S. inflation during the COVID era.*
Presented at the Brookings Papers on Economic Activity fall conference, Washington DC.

Barro, R. (1996). Inflation and growth. Review of Federal Reserve Bank of St. Louis, 78(3), 153–169.

Bell, S. (1999). *Functional finance: What, why, and how?* Levy Economic Institute Working Paper No. 287.

Benigno, P., & Eggertsson, G. (2023, April). *It's Baaack: The surge in inflation in the 2020s and the
return of the non-linear Phillips curve.* NBER Working Paper 31197.

Bernanke, B., & Blanchard, O. (2023). *What caused the U.S. pandemic-era inflation?* Hutchins
Center Working Paper 86. https://www.brookings.edu/research/what-caused-the-u-s-pandemic-era
-inflation/

Bivens, J. (2022a, April 21). *Corporate profits have contributed disproportionately to inflation. How
should policymakers respond?* Economic Policy Institute. https://www.epi.org/blog/corporate-profits
-have-contributed-disproportionately-to-inflation-how-should-policymakers-respond/

Bivens, J. (2022b). *Wage growth has been dampening inflation all along—And has slowed even more
recently.* Economic Policy Institute. https://www.epi.org/blog/wagegrowth-has-been-dampening
-inflation-all-along-and-has-slowed-even-more-recently/

Blanchard, O. (2021, February, 18). *In defense of concerns over the $1.9 trillion relief plan.* Peterson
Institute for International Economics.

Boesler, M., Deaux, J., & Dimitrieva, K. (2021, November 30). Fattest profits since 1950s debunk wage-
inflation story of CEOs. *Bloomberg.*

Cagan, P. (1956). The monetary dynamics of hyperinflation. In M. Friedman (Ed.), *Studies in the quantity
theory of money* (pp. xx–xx). University of Chicago Press.

Carnevali, E., & Deleidi, M. (2023). The trade-off between inflation and unemployment in an 'MMT
world': An open-economy perspective. *European Journal of Economics and Economic Policies,
20*(1), 90–124. https://doi.org/10.4337/ejeep.2022.0080

Cecchetti, S., Feroli, M., Hooper, P., Mishkin, F., & Schoenholtz, K. (2023, February 24). DP18068
Managing Disinflations. CEPR Discussion Paper No. 18068. CEPR Press, Paris & London. https://
cepr.org/publications/dp18068.

Cesaratto, S. (2016). The state spends first: Logic, facts, fictions, open questions. *Journal of Post
Keynesian Economics, 39*(1), 44–71. https://doi.org/10.1080/01603477.2016.1147333

Chang, H.-J. (2008). *Bad Samaritans: The myth of free trade and the secret history of capitalism.*
Bloomsbury.

Chohan, U. W. (2020). *Modern Monetary Theory (MMT): A general introduction.* CASS Working Papers
on Economics & National Affairs, Working Paper ID: EC017UC (2020). https://ssrn.com/abstract
=3569416 or http://dx.doi.org/10.2139/ssrn.3569416

Coats, W. (2016, December 4). Not with a bang, but a whimper: MMT for conservatives. *The
Minskys.* https://www.theminskys.org/warren-coats-blog/not-with-a-bang-but-a-whimper-mmt-for
-conservatives

Coats, W. (2019). Modern monetary theory: A critique. *Cato Journal, 39*(3), 563–576.

Cochrane. (2020, June 5). 'The deficit myth' review: Years of magical thinking. *Wall Street Journal.*
https://www.wsj.com/articles/the-deficit-myth-review-years-of-magical-thinking-11591396579. Last
access 15 August 2023

Colander, D. (1984). Was Keynes a Keynesian or a Lernerian? *Journal of Economic Literature, 22*(4),
1572–1575.

Colander, D. (2019). Are modern monetary theory's lies "plausible lies"? *Real-World Economics Review
89,* 62–71.

Cruz, E., Parejo, F., Garzón, E., & Rangel, J. (2020). Es el momento de la política fiscal: Repensar los estabilizadores automáticos contra la pandemia. *Revista de Economía Mundial*, *56*, 1–22.

Davidson, P. (1972). *Money and the real world*. Macmillan.

De Grauwe, P., & Polan, M. (2005). Is inflation always and everywhere a monetary phenomenon? *Scandinavian Journal of Economics*, *107*(2), 239–259.

Dögus, I. (2022). *Market power and inflation. Monetary policy institute blog*. Retrieved August 15, 2023, from https://medium.com/@monetarypolicyinstitute/market-power-and-inflation -ea917ac86f67

Domazet, T. (2021). Modern monetary theory and COVID-19 crisis. In N. Vidaković & I. Lovrinović (Eds.), *Macroeconomic responses to the COVID-19 pandemic*. Palgrave Macmillan. https://doi.org/10 .1007/978-3-030-75444-0_11

Drumetz, F., & Pfister, C. (2021). De quoi la MMT est-elle le nom? *Revue Française d'Économie*, *XXXVI*, 3–46. https://doi.org/10.3917/rfe.214.0003

Dullien, S., & Tober, S. (2022). A monetary Keynesian view of modern monetary theory. *European Journal of Economics and Economic Policies*, *19*(2), 227–237.

Edelberg, W., & Sheiner, L. (2021). *The macroeconomic implications of Biden's $1.9 trillion fiscal package*. Brookings Institution. Retrieved August 15, 2023, from https://www.brookings.edu/wp -content/uploads/2021/01/BidenTA_FINAL.pdf

Edwards, S. (2019). Modern monetary theory: Cautionary tales from Latin America. *Cato Journal*, *39*(3). https://doi.org/10.36009/CJ.39.3.3

Ehnst, D. (2022). Modern monetary theory: The right compass for decision-making. *Intereconomics*, *57*(2), 128–134. https://doi.org/10.1007/s10272-022-1041-x

Ehnst, D., & Paetz, M. (2021). Wie finanzieren wir die Corona-Schulden?: Versuch einer richtigen" Antwort auf eine falsche" Frage aus Sicht der modern monetary theory [How do we finance the Corona debt? Attempting a "right" answer to the "wrong" question from the perspective of modern monetary theory]. *Wirtschaftsdienst*, *101*(3), 200–206. German. https://doi.org/10.1007/s10273-021 -2874-9. Epub 2021 Mar 17. PMID: 33746304; PMCID: PMC7964462

Febrero, E. (2009). Three difficulties with neo-chartalism. *Journal of Post Keynesian Economics*, *31*(3), 523–541. https://doi.org/10.2753/PKE0160-3477310308

Fix, B. (2023). *Do high interest rates reduce inflation? A test of monetary faith. Economics from the top down*. Retrieved August 15, 2023, from https://economicsfromthetopdown.com/2023/02/04/do-high -interest-rates-reduce-inflation-a-test-of-monetary-faith/

Forstater, M. (1999). Functional finance and full employment: Lessons from Lerner for today. *Journal of Economic Issues*, *33*(2), 475–482. http://www.jstor.org/stable/4227461

Forstater, M., & Mosler, W. (2005). The natural rate of interest is zero. *Journal of Economic Issues*, *39*(2), 535–542.

Friedman, M. (1970). *The counter-revolution in monetary theory*. Institute of Economic Affairs Occasional Paper, No. 33.

Fullwiler, S., & Allen, G. (2007). Can the fed target inflation? Toward an institutionalist approach. *Journal of Economic Issues*, *XLI*, 485–494. https://doi.org/10.1080/00213624.2007.11507037

Fullwiler, S., Allen, G., & Grey, R. (2019, March 1). An MMT response on what causes inflation. *Financial Times*. https://www.ft.com/content/539618f8-b88c-3125-8031-cf46ca197c64

Gagliardone, L., & Gertler, M. (2023). *Oil prices, monetary policy and inflation surges*. [Manuscript], New York University Press.

Gagnon, J., & Sarsenbayev, M. (2022). *25 years of excess unemployment in advanced economies: Lessons for monetary policy* (Working Paper 22–17). Peterson Institute for International Economics, October.

Garzón, E.. (2021). *Vínculo entre saldo fiscal y endeudamiento privado. Propuesta analítica y estudio empírico*. [PhD Thesis] Autónoma University of Madrid, Madrid.

Gener. (2019). *Entrevista a Stephanie Kelton sobre su libro "El mito del déficit"*. Retrieved August 15, 2023, from https://www.eldiario.es/economia/stephanie-kelton-gobierno-contribucion-financiera _128_1360422.html

Giovanni, J. D., Kalemli-Özcan, S., Silva, A., & Yıldırım, M. A. (2023). *Supply chains, trade, and inflation. VoxEu.* Retrieved August 15, 2023, from https://cepr.org/voxeu/columns/supply-chains-trade-and-inflation

Glover, A., Mustre-del-Río, J., & von Ende-Becker, A. (2023). How much have record corporate profits contributed to recent inflation? *The Federal Reserve Bank of Kansas City Economic Review.* https://doi.org/10.18651/ER/v108n1GloverMustredelRiovonEndeBecker

Godley, W. (1999). Seven unsustainable processes: Medium-term prospects and policies for the United States and the world. Economics Strategic Analysis Archive 99-10, Levy Economics Institute.

Godley, W., & Cripps, F. (1983). *Macroeconomics,* Oxford University Press, Oxford.

Godley, W., & McCarthy, G. (1998). Fiscal policy will matter. *Challenge, 41*(1), 38–54.

Godley, W., & Wray, L. R. (2000). Is goldilocks doomed? *Journal of Economic Issues, 34*(1), 201–206.

Grunwald, J. (1961, julio-septiembre). La escuela 'estructuralista', estabilización de precios y desarrollo económico; el caso chileno. *El Trimestre Económico.*

Guerrieri, V., Lorenzoni, G., Straub, L., & Werning, I. (2022). Macroeconomic implications of Covid-19: Can negative supply shocks cause demand shortages? *American Economic Review, 112*(5), 1437–1474.

Hanke, S., & Krus, N. (2012). *World hyperinflations.* Cato Institute Working Paper.

Hanley, B. P. (2021). Is modern monetary theory's prescription to spend without reference to tax receipts an invitation to tyranny? *Acta Oeconomica, 71*(3), 431–450.

Hartley, J. (2020, Summer). The weakness of modern monetary theory. *National Affairs, 56.* Retrieved August 15, from https://www.nationalaffairs.com/publications/detail/the-weakness-of-modern-monetary-theory

Hensher, M., Robson, S., Kelton, S., Hail, S., & McCall, L. (2021). *Modern monetary theory and healthcare in Australia.* Institute for health Transformation, Deakin University. Position Paper.

Hogan, T. L. (2021). *Review of Stephanie Kelton's the deficit myth.* AIER Sound Money Project Working Paper No. 2021-05. https://ssrn.com/abstract=3767562 or http://dx.doi.org/10.2139/ssrn.3767562

Huber, J. (2014). Modern money theory and new currency theory: A comparative discussion-part I. *International Journal of Pluralism and Economics Education, 5*(4), 346–364.

Huber, J. (2015). *Modern money theory: A primer on macroeconomics for sovereign monetary systems.* Palgrave Macmillan.

Jordà, Ò. et al 2022. Why is U.S. inflation higher than in other countries? Federal Reserve Bank of San Francisco. Economic Letters. March 28. https://www.frbsf.org/economic-research/publications/economic-letter/2022/march/why-is-us-inflation-higher-than-in-other-countries/

Juniper, J. (2022). An MMT perspective on how Agenda 30 could be implemented in Australia. In T. Chaiechi & J. Wood (Eds.), *Community empowerment, sustainable cities, and transformative economies.* Springer. https://doi.org/10.1007/978-981-16-5260-8_3

Kalecki, M. (1933). The determinants of profits. In M. Kalecki (Ed.), *Selected essays on the dynamics of the capitalist economy, 1933–1970* (pp. xx–xx). Cambridge University Press.

Kashama, M. K. (2020). An assessment of modern monetary theory. NBB Economic Review ¡ September 2020. Retrieved August 15, 2023, from https://www.nbb.be/doc/ts/publications/economicreview/2020/ecorevii2020_h6.pdf

Kelton, S. (2019). *Paul Krugman asked me about modern monetary theory. Here are 4 answers. Blog de Stephanie Kelton.* https://stephaniekelton.com/paul-krugman-asked-me-about-modern-monetary-theory-here-are-4-answers/

Kelton, S. (2020). *El mito del déficit: La teoría monetaria moderna y el nacimiento de la economía de la gente.* Pengüin Random House.

Keynes, J. M. (1930). *The treatise on money: The pure theory of money* (Vol. I). Macmillan.

Keynes, J. M. (1964 [1936]). *The general theory of employment, interest, and money.* Harcourt-Brace and World.

Keynes, J. M. (1978). Activities 1940–1946: Shaping the post-war world: Employment and commodities. In E. Johnson & D. Moggridge (Eds.), *The collected writings of John Maynard Keynes* (Vol. XXVII). Macmillan.

Koch, C., & Noureldin, D. (2023, March, 21–23). How we missed the recent inflation surge. *Finance and Development. International Monetary Fund*, 21–23.

Krugman, P. (2010, March 18). Stagflation versus hyperinflation. *The New York Times.* https://krugman.blogs.nytimes.com/2010/03/18/stagflation-versus-hyperinflation

Krugman, P. (2019a, February 12). What's wrong with functional finance? (Wonkish). *The New York Times.* https://www.nytimes.com/2019/02/12/opinion/whats-wrong-with-functional-finance-wonkish.html

Krugman, P. (2019b, 25 de febrero). Running on MMT (Wonkish). *The New York Times.* https://www.nytimes.com/2019/02/25/opinion/running-on-mmt-wonkish.html

Lapavitsas, C., & Aguila, N. (2020). Modern monetary theory on money, sovereignty, and policy: A Marxist critique with reference to the Eurozone and Greece. *The Japanese Political Economy, 46*(4), 300–326.

Leão, P. (2015). *Is a very high public debt a problem?* Levy Economic Institute, Working Paper No. 843.

Lerner, A. (1943). Functional finance and the federal debt. *Social Research, 10*, 38–51.

Lerner, A. (1951). *The economics of employment.* McGraw Hill.

Lerner, A. P. (1958). Inflationary depression and the regulation of administered prices. In Holt, Rinehart and Winston (Eds), *The relationship of prices to economic stability and growth: Compendium of papers submitted by panelists appearing before the Joint Economic Committee* (pp. 257–268). Government Printing Office.

Levey, S. (2021). Modern money and the war treasury. *Journal of Economic Issues, 55*(4), 1034–1065. https://doi.org/10.1080/00213624.2021.1994780

Libertypen. (2013). *Milton Friedman - Only government creates inflation* [Video]. Youtube. https://www.youtube.com/watch?v=F94jGTWNWsA

Mankiw, N. G. (2019). *Macroeconomics* (10th ed.). Worth Publishers.

Mankiw, N. G. (2020). A skeptic's guide to modern monetary theory. *AEA Papers and Proceedings, 110*, 141–144.

Mayhew. (2019). The sleights of hand of MMT. *Real-World Economics Review 89*, 129–137.

Minsky, H. P. (1965). The role of employment policy. In M. S. Gordon (Ed.), *Poverty in America* (pp. 175–200). Chandler.

Minsky, H. P. (1986). *Stabilizing and unstable economy.* Yale University Press.

Mitchell, B. (2009a). *Functional finance and modern monetary theory. Bill Mitchell – Modern monetary theory.* http://bilbo.economicoutlook.net/blog/?p=5762

Mitchell, B. (2009b). *Zimbabwe for hyperventilators. Bill Mitchell – Modern monetary theory.* http://bilbo.economicoutlook.net/blog/?p=3773

Mitchell, B. (2023, May 4). *Japan has lower inflation, no currency crisis and its citizens are better off as a result of the monetary-fiscal policy initiatives. William Mitchell modern monetary theory blog.* https://billmitchell.org/blog/?p=60811

Mitchell, W., Wray, L. R., & Watts, M. (2019). *Macroeconomics.* Red Globe Press.

Mosler, W. (2014). *Los siete fraudes inocentes capitales de la política económica.* ATTAC España.

Mosler, W. (2023). A framework for the analysis of the price level and inflation. In L. R. Wray, Phil Armstrong, Sara Holland, Claire Jackson-Prior, Prue Plumridge and Neil Wilson (Eds), *Modern monetary theory* (pp. 87–93). Edward Elgar Publishing.

Mueller, A. P., & Vaz-Curado, S. F. L. (2019). Modern Monetary Theory (MMT): An evaluation of its premises and its political consequences. *Mises Journal, 7*(2). https://www.revistamises.org.br/misesjournal/article/view/1211

Murphy, R. (2019). Tax and modern monetary theory. *Real-World Economic Review, 89*(89), 138–147.

Murphy, R. (2020). Book review: 'The deficit myth: Modern monetary theory and the birth of the People's economy'. *Quarterly Journal of Austrian Economics, 23*(2), 232–251.

Nersisyan, Y., & Wray, L. R. (2010). *Does excessive sovereign debt really hurt growth? A critique of this Time Is Different, by Reinhart and Rogoff.* Working Paper No. 603, Levy Economics Institute of Bard College.

Nersisyan, Y., & Wray, L. R. (2019). *How to pay for the green new deal* (SSRN Scholarly Paper ID3398983). Social Science Research Network. https://papers.ssrn.com/abstract=3398983

Nersisyan, Y., & Wray, L. R. (2022). *What's causing accelerating inflation: Pandemic or policy response?* Levy Economic Institute, Working Paper No. 1003.

Newman, P. (2020). Modern monetary theory: An Austrian interpretation of recrudescent Keynesianism. *Atlantic Economic Journal, 48*(1), 23–31.

Nikiforos, M., & Zezza, G. (2017). Stock-flow consistent macroeconomic models: A survey. *Journal of Economic Surveys, 31*(5), 1–36.

Ocampo, E. (2021). MMT: Modern monetary theory or magical monetary thinking? *Revista de Instituciones, Ideas y Mercados, 72*, 34–83.

Omran, F., & Zelmer, M. (2021, March 11). Deficits do matter: A review of modern monetary theory. *C.D. Howe Institute Commentary 593*. https://ssrn.com/abstract=4094414 or http://dx.doi.org/10.2139/ssrn.4094414

Palley, T. (2018). *Modern Money Theory (MMT) vs. structural Keynesianism. Thomas Palley – Economics for democratic and open societies.* https://thomaspalley.com/?p=1145

Palley, T. (2020). What's wrong with Modern Money Theory: Macro and political economic restraints on deficit-financed fiscal policy. *Review of Keynesian Economics, 8*(4), 472–493.

Palley, T. I. (2015). Money, fiscal policy, and interest rates: A critique of modern monetary theory. *Review of Political Economy, 27*(1), 1–23.

Pandit, J. J. (2022). Modern monetary theory for the post-pandemic NHS: Why budget deficits do not matter. *British Journal of Healthcare Management, 28*(1), 37–46.

Papadimitrou, D. B., Nikiforos, M., & Zezza, G. (2013, July). *The Greek economic crisis and the experience of austerity: A strategic analysis.* Levy Economics Institute of Bard College Strategic Analysis.

Papadimitrou, D. B., Nikiforos, M., & Zezza, G. (2018, November). *Can Greece grow faster?* Levy Economics Institute of Bard College Strategic Analysis.

Papadimitriou, D. B., & Wray, L. R. (2021). *Still flying blind after all these years: The Federal Reserve's continuing experiments with unobservables.* Levy Economics Institute of Bard College, Public Policy Brief No. 156.

Razmi, A. (2023). MMT and policy assignment in an open economy context: Simplicity is useful, oversimplification not so much. *Metroeconomica, 74*(2), 328–350.

Reifschneider, D., & Wilcox, D. (2022). *The case for a cautiously optimistic outlook for US inflation* (Policy Brief 22–23). Peterson Institute for International Economics.

Robb, G. (2019, June 11). What modern monetary theory gets 'plain wrong,' according to former IMF chief economist. *Market Watch.* https://www.marketwatch.com/story/what-modern-monetary-theory-gets-plain-wrong---former-imf-chief-economist-2019-06-11/

Roberts, M. (2019). Modern monetary theory: A Marxist critique. *Class, Race and Corporate Power, 7*(1), 1.

Rogoff, K. (2019, 4 March). Modern monetary nonsense. *Project Syndicate.* https://www.project-syndicate.org/commentary/federal-reserve-modern-monetary-theory-dangers-by-kenneth-rogoff-2019-03?barrier=accesspaylog

Ryan-Collins, J. (2015). *Is monetary financing inflationary? A case study of the Canadian economy, 1935–75* (Working Papers No. 848). Levy Economics Institute of Bard College.

Santacreu, A. M., & LaBelle, J. (2022). *Global supply chain disruptions and inflation during the COVID-19 pandemic.* Federal Reserve Bank of St Louis Review.

Sardoni, C. (2016). A note on the sustainability of full employment in the presence of budget deficits. *Review of Political Economy, 28*(1), 79–89.

Sarel, M. (1996). Non linear effects of inflation on economic growth. *IMF Staff Papers, 43*(1), 199–215.

Schacht, H. (1967). *The magic of money.* Purnell and Sons.

Schlotmann, O. (2021). Is now the Time for modern monetary theory or permanent monetary finance? Credit and capital markets. *Kredit und Kapital, 54*(1), 17–36.

Schultze, C. L. (1959). *Recent inflation in the United States.* Joint Economic Committee.

Shapiro, A. H. (2022). How much do supply and demand drive inflation? *FRBSF Economic Letter*, *15*, 1–6.

Skousen, M. (2020). There's much ruin in a nation: An analysis of modern monetary theory. *Atlantic Economic Journal*, *48*(1), 11–21.

Smith, A. (1994 [1776]). *La riqueza de las naciones*. Alianza Editorial.

Stiglitz, J. E., & Regmi, I. (2022, December). *The causes of and responses to today's inflation*. Roosevelt Institute. https://rooseveltinstitute.org/publications/the-causes-of-and-responses-to-todays-inflation/

Stoller, M. (2021, December 29). Corporate profits drive 60 percent of inflation increases. *BIG by Matt Stoller Blog*.

Summers, L. (2019, March 4). The left's embrace of modern monetary theory is a recipe for disaster. *Washington Post*. https://www.washingtonpost.com/opinions/the-lefts-embrace-of-modern-monetary-theory-is-a-recipe-for-disaster/2019/03/04/6ad88eec-3ea4-11e9-9361-301ffb5bd5e6_story.html

Sumner, S., & Horan, P. (2019). *How reliable is modern monetary theory as a guide to policy?* Mercatus Policy Brief Series. https://ssrn.com/abstract=4221193

Tanaka, Y. (2022). Debt to GDP ratio from the perspective of functional finance theory and MMT. *International Journal of Computational and Applied Mathematics & Computer Science*, *2*, 44–50.

Tcherneva, P. R. (2023). *Three lessons from government spending and the post-pandemic recovery* (Working Paper No. 01). Open Society University Network Economic Democracy Initiative.

Teles, P., Uhlig, H., & Valle e Azevedo, J. (2015). Is quantity theory still alive? *Economic Journal*, *126*, 442–464.

Terlep, S. (2021, October 24). U.S. corporate giants bet shoppers will keep paying higher prices. *Wall Street Journal*.

Toporowski, J. (2019). The political economy of modern money theory, from Brecht to Gaitskell. *Real-World Economics Review 89*, 194–202.

Triggs, A. (2021). Modern Monetary Theory: A solution in search of a problem. *The Canberra Times*. https://www.canberratimes.com.au/story/6902695/a-solution-in-search-of-a-problem/

Tymoigne, E., & Wray, L. R. (2013). *Modern money theory 101: A reply to critics* (Working Papers Series No. 778). Levy Economics Institute. https://ssrn.com/abstract=2348704

Vague, R. (2016, December 2). *Rapid money supply growth does not cause inflation*. Institute for New Economic Thinking. https://www.ineteconomics.org/perspectives/blog/rapid-money-supply-growth-does-not-cause-inflation

Valadkhani, A., & Mitchell, W. F. (2002). Assessing the impact of changes in petroleum prices on inflation and household expenditures in Australia. *The Australian Economic Review*, *35*(2), 122–132.

Watkins, J. P. (2021). The policy response to COVID-19: The implementation of modern monetary theory. *Journal of Economic Issues*, *55*(2), 484–491. https://doi.org/10.1080/00213624.2021.1909350

Weber, I., & Wasner, E. (2023). Sellers' inflation, profits and conflict: Why can large firms hike prices in an emergency? *Review of Keynesian Economics*, *11*(2), 183–213.

Wray, L. R. (1998). *Understanding modern money, the key to full employment and price stability*. Edward Elgar Publishing Ltd.

Wray, L. R. (2007). *The employer of last resort programme: Could it work for developing countries?* Economic and Labour Market Papers. International Labour Office.

Wray, L. R. (2012a). *Modern money theory: A primer on macroeconomics for sovereign monetary systems*. Palgrave Macmillan.

Wray, L. R. (2012b). *Imbalances? What imbalances? A dissenting view* [Working Paper No. 704]. Levy Economics Institute of Bard College.

Wray, L. R. (2018). *Functional finance: A comparison of the evolution of the positions of Hyman Minsky and Abba Lerner* [Working Paper No. 900]. Levy Economics Institute and Bard College.

Xing, Y. (2020). Japan's practice of modern monetary theory amid the pandemic recession. *East Asian Policy*, *12*(4), 47–56.

7
JOB GUARANTEE

The path to full employment of Modern
Monetary Theory and its critics

Job Guarantee

Job Guarantee is the main economic policy recommended by the MMT to achieve full employment without inflation. This proposal is a refined modification of the Functional Finance approach that addresses the limitations of the latter. It was proposed long ago by economists such as Hyman Minsky but has been developed and detailed by the authors of the MMT. As we shall see, it connects very well with all the theoretical postulates analysed so far and which, according to the MMT, were only intended to describe economic reality as it is: "the prescriptive side of MMT takes us to the other side of the mirror, to a discussion of what fiscal and monetary policy might look like in a world inspired by modern monetary theory itself" (Kelton, 2020, p. 279). Job Guarantee would be that principal policy prescription that derives from such inspiration and has been analysed in various academic works since the 1990s (Mitchell, 1994; Mosler, 1997; Forstater, 1998; Wray, 1997 Mitchell & Muysken, 2008; Murray & Forstater, 2013; Tcherneva, 2020; Garzón & Guamán, 2015).

According to the concept of Functional Finance, a sufficient increase in public spending allows the economy's aggregate expenditure to provide an outlet for all output, thereby utilising all idle resources, including the labour force. However, it suffers from two major obstacles (at least from a heterodox point of view).

The first obstacle was already mentioned in the previous chapter: there is no way to ensure that the new aggregate expenditure is directed only to the sectors that need it, and there is no way to ensure that the workers needed by those sectors are exactly those who are unemployed and available for work. This has been a classic criticism of Keynesian policies of fiscal expansion, concluding therefore that their application leads to inflation before full employment is achieved. As early as 1926 Irving Fisher devised a graphical curve that would illustrate that if you are close to full employment, low inflation is not possible (Fisher, 1926). This curve was popularised by William Philips (1958), hence the name Philips Curve. Years later, in 1975, Franco Modigliani and Lucas Papademos, using similar reasoning, proposed the *Non-Accelerating Rate of Unemployment* (or Nairu), which would be the rate of unemployment

DOI: 10.4324/9781003371809-8

that could not be reduced without causing inflation (Modigiliani & Papademos, 1975). This idea is often used by many policymakers and academics to justify that in modern economies there is always a certain level of unemployment and has been heavily criticised by both heterodox economists in general and MMTers in particular (Mitchell, 1998; Mitchell & Mosler, 2002; Mitchell & Muysken, 2008). The criticisms focus on the fact that there is no natural rate of unemployment, that its nature is fragile, multiple, and cyclically sensitive as an equilibrium, and that it is not supported by empirical evidence: "the evidence would suggest that the NAIRU-NRU concepts do not provide a robust foundation upon which useful theory can be built" (Mitchell, 1987, p. 116).

The second obstacle is that in a situation of near full employment, workers would lose their fear of becoming unemployed, so they would become emboldened and demand wage increases from their employers, who would be forced to succumb to such demands in the face of the impossibility of disciplining them with the threat of dismissal. Consequently, in addition to raising wages, they might also raise prices in order not to lose profit margins, which could lead to second-round inflationary pressures. In turn, such a further increase in prices could reactivate the cycle described above and thus trigger a prolonged period of inflation over time (a so-called wage-price spiral). This is probably best explained by Michal Kalecki, who said:

> under a regime of permanent full employment, the "sack" would cease to play its role as a disciplinary measure. The social position of the boss would be undermined, and the self-assurance and class-consciousness of the working class would grow. Strikes for wage increases and improvements in conditions of work would create political tension.
>
> *(Kalecki, 1943, p. 335)*

This is basically the classical idea of Karl Marx when he spoke of the industrial reserve army, the pool of unemployed that is of interest to the employers and that would be an indispensable condition for the proper functioning of the capitalist economy: "an industrial reserve army – a permanent army of unemployed – is necessary for the proper functioning of the capitalist system of production and the necessary accumulation of capital" (Marx, 1867, p. 91). So, although mainstream economic theories argue that a certain level of unemployment is necessary to avoid inflation, other theories consider that this other reason seems to explain better why there is political opposition to full employment: because the existence of a certain level of unemployment suits the employers.

To get around all these drawbacks, Modern Monetary Theory proposes a new recipe: Job Guarantee. Instead of trying to achieve full employment indirectly through maximum production, with the risk of price increases in some sectors, it is to achieve full employment directly. It would not be a matter of trying to get employers – hoping to make more profit in the face of higher demand – to hire all the unemployed, but to reach full employment by hiring the unemployed directly. This would lead to full employment, which would be the important goal, even if it would not lead to maximum production, which would not be the important goal (and might even be harmful in environmental terms). It would mean abandoning the typical Keynesian policy of stimulating aggregate demand by flooding the entire economy with spending – which is what would normally generate inflationary pressures – and injecting spending only where it is most needed: into the pockets of the unemployed. MMTers have characterised this policy as *targeted demand* rather than *aggregate demand* (Tcherneva, 2012, 2014):

the new approach fundamentally reorients policy away from the conventional aggregate demand approach toward a targeted demand approach with a superior automatic stabilizer that aims to narrow, not an ambiguous demand gap for output, but a very clearly defined demand gap for labor, in a manner that produces measurable socioeconomic outcomes.

(Tcherneva, 2014, p. 50)

This is basically what Hyman Minsky proposed in 1965, naming the measure Employment of Last Resort (ELR) (Minsky, 1965; Bell & Wray, 2004; Wray, 2008). This name is inspired by the role of central banks, which are known as lenders of last resort because they lend money to banks when they cannot obtain it otherwise. The Employer of Last Resort would be the state, which would guarantee a living wage job to people when they need it. As Hyman Minsky himself explained, spending should go directly to the unemployed, rather than to the leading sectors of the economy, in the hope of benefiting lagging sectors and poor households. For this reason, he argued that an employment programme of last resort should accept workers as they are and provide them with jobs that match their skills (Minsky, 1965, 1968, 1986). In his own words:

> Work should be made available for all able and willing to work at the national minimum wage. This is a wage support law, analogous to the price supports for agricultural products. … To qualify for employment at these terms, all that would be required would be to register at the local U.S.E.S. (US Employment Service). Part time and seasonal work should be available at these terms. … National government agencies, as well as local and state agencies would be eligible to obtain this labor. They would bid for labor by submitting their projects, and a local "evaluation" board would determine priorities among projects. … The basic approach is straight forward – accept the poor as they are and tailor make jobs to fit their capabilities. After this is done, programs to improve the capabilities of low income workers are in order.
>
> *(Minsky, 1965, pp. 299–300)*

This is something that a state with monetary sovereignty could do without any financial constraint. Since such a state can buy whatever is for sale in the unit of account it creates, and since the unemployed want to work in exchange for a wage expressed in that unit of account, the state could hire everyone without any constraint. This would ensure that no one would be unemployed and at the same time no firm would be flooded with expenditure, thus solving the first drawback mentioned above: bottlenecks would no longer be generated in certain sectors.

To solve the second drawback mentioned above – inflationary tensions on the wage side as a consequence of the empowerment of workers through full employment –, Job Guarantee uses two ways. The first is to provide Job Guarante workers with a fixed wage that is non-negotiable upwards and downwards, but which ensures a decent living. This is to ensure that full employment does not push other workers to demand wage increases because, although there is no longer the threat of unemployment, there is still a less attractive alternative to working in the conventional private or public sector, which is to receive the wage offered by Job Guarantee, which is the lowest in the labour market. Thus, the mechanism of employer discipline that makes it difficult to raise wages still exists, only in this situation the undesirable alternative to losing one's job is not unemployment but Job Guarantee. This would be a substantial improvement for the unemployed and workers (from being paid nothing to a minimum wage) which at the same time would not encourage employers to raise prices in order not to lose profit margins. As Pavlina Tcherneva summarises it, Job Guarantee achieves "a pool of employed individuals for the purpose rather than a reserve army of the unemployed" (Tcherneva, 2018, p. 7). MMTers thus expect such a wage to be non-inflationary: "by fixing the wage paid under this ELR program at a level that does not disrupt existing labor markets – that is, a wage level close to the existing minimum wage-substantive price stability can be expected" (Mosler, 1997, p. 168).

At the same time, the wage set in Job Guarantee would become the de facto minimum wage for the whole economy, because no one would work anywhere for less, since he or she would always have the possibility to work for Job Guarantee for the minimum wage that has been set. This would give some bargaining power to workers at the lower end of the labour market: any private sector worker with working conditions below those of Job Guarantee would be able to demand an improvement to that level from his or her employer under threat of leaving the job. And since employers would need the work to be done and no one would be willing to do it for less pay, they would be forced to increase it. But only up to that level and no higher because the wage of the Guaranteed Job is fixed. The aim is to establish a real minimum wage: it would be much more powerful than the minimum wage in labour legislation, which is often not enforced. As Pavlina Tcherneva explains,

> Job Guarantee would help to establish a real minimum wage for the economy as a whole. As noted, jobs with wages below the poverty line would face competition from the public living wage alternative and companies would be pressured to meet these standards when hiring.
>
> *(Tcherneva, 2020, p. 45)*

In this way, the MMTers believe that the second drawback would be overcome: full employment would be achieved without the threat of wage inflation.

The second way to avoid stimulating inflation is to link the value of the currency to something real, namely working hours. MMTers argue that the state guaranteeing jobs at a fixed wage helps to stabilise the value of the currency and reduce inflationary pressures. The guaranteed wage would be paid in monetary units per hour worked, so that every hour, minute, or second of time would have its value in monetary units. Money would have a real equivalent, and this measure could be used as a reference to establish the price of other products. This is called the labour standard, paralleling the old gold standard. Just as during the gold standard the state was obliged to exchange an amount of its currency for an amount of gold, thus linking its value to that precious metal, here the state would be obliged to exchange an amount of its currency for a given amount of labour. Job Guarantee would be a way of anchoring the value of the currency, thus preventing inflation. As Wray explains:

> While the government can, in principle, set the price of anything and everything that it wants to buy, it is probably preferable and certainly sufficient ... for the government to fix only one important price. The market would then establish all other prices relative to that price. In the past governments fixed the price of gold or some other precious metal. In the modern economy it is far preferable to stabilize the price of labour. This is done by creating and maintaining a "buffer stock" of labour ..., with the price of that labour fixed by government.
>
> *(Wray, 1998, p. 3)*

Tcherneva also emphasises this point:

> as the examples of gold and grain show, an employment equalisation reserve would stabilise the price of an essential resource for the economy (labour), a necessary input for the production of all other commodities, and thus stabilise all other prices as well.
>
> *(Tcherneva, 2020, p. 40)*

In conclusion, taking into account these elements that overcome the above-mentioned drawbacks, the MMTers claim that full employment can be achieved without inflation: "the primary policy conclusion that comes out of this analysis is, perhaps, shocking, but it can be stated simply: it is possible to have truly full employment without causing inflation" (Wray, 1998, p. 8).

There is a third obstacle of Functional Finance that has not yet been pointed out: that the requirement to reach full employment is through maximum production, which has its ecological impact in terms of natural resource use and pollutant discharge. Consequently, the unemployment problem would be solved only at the cost of aggravating the environmental problem.

To solve this third drawback, some MMTers propose that the activities to be carried out by workers should be oriented towards environmental care and also towards the care of people, which are the least intensive in natural resources. For example, reuse, repair, and recycling of products, electrification of certain highly polluting activities, energy rehabilitation of many buildings, reforestation, care of fauna, flora, and ecosystems, combating the loss of biodiversity, care of children and dependent adults, etc. In fact, the authors of Modern Monetary Theory have recently advocated the inclusion of Job Guarantee in a programme oriented towards environmental care that has usually been called the "Green New Deal" (Forstater, 2003, 2005, 2006; Hail, 2017; Nersisyan & Wray, 2019; Fullwiler et al., 2019; Baker & Murphy, 2020; Galvin & Healy, 2020; Tcherneva, 2020; Garzón & Cruz, 2021; Yajima, 2021; Bracarense & Bracarense, 2022; William & Taylor, 2022; Olk et al., 2022).

But beyond the supposed overcoming of the above drawbacks, MMTers argue that Job Guarantee has other advantages that typical Keynesian policies do not.

One of them is that Job Guarantee would be highly stabilising for the economic cycle. This means that it would boost the economy in times of recession, and cool it down in times of growth. When there is an economic crisis or recession, employers lay off many of their workers and these workers no longer receive their wages, so they spend less and generate less sales for the firms. In contrast, with Job Guarantee, these people could continue to work and receive a salary, even if it was at the minimum wage level, so they could continue to spend at a certain level and to a certain degree boost the economy. On the other hand, when there is economic growth, employers need more workers, and they could hire them from the pool of Job Guarantee workers by offering them a higher wage than would be charged in Job Guarantee, which is the minimum wage. In this way, the state would stop spending so much and therefore not add so much to the total expenditure in the economy. As Bill Mitchell and Martin Watts explain it: "the BSE proposal would automatically increase government employment and spending as jobs were lost in the private sector, and decrease government jobs and spending as the private sector expanded" (Mitchell & Watts, 1997, pp. 441–442). One of the advantages of this automatic stabilisation would be that job creation and destruction would be very rapid and independent of policy decisions:

it is not necessary to wait on policy makers to reach decisions and act. Policy need not wait on legislation by Congress, or upon decisions by courts. Stabilization will not depend on which party is in power. Nor does it rest on the frequently weak and unreliable effects of interest rates and monetary policy.

(Nell, 2003, p. 7)

That the state guarantees a job to everyone who is willing and able to work does not mean that the type of employment is that of a civil servant or other conventional public figure. Job Guarantee would create a new type of employment, which would not be in the private sector, but not in the public sector either, characterised by a fixed salary, and which would always be available to everyone. There would be no entrance exams or public competition, but simply the citizen would have the right to be guaranteed a job by the state: "the programme is voluntary and exclusive. It is open to anyone who is of legal working age and wants to work, regardless of their labour market status, race, sex, colour or creed" (Tcherneva, 2020, p. 66). This would make it possible for people who find it more difficult to study and train to work.

Some MMTers propose that the activities to be carried out should not be decided by the government of the day, but by civil society. Anyone could go to their local council to give their opinion and vote on which activities would be carried out thanks to the Job Guarantee, as it is argued that it is the residents who know best what activities are most necessary and useful. Perhaps they detect that there are needs for childcare, or needs in the health centre or hospital, or in the school, or in the care of the forests near the locality, etc. As Fadhel Kaboub explains:

ELR also has the potential to ensure grassroots participation at the local decision making level, thus enhancing democratic processes. Furthermore, it allows the community to value non-market economic activities, such as elderly care, child rearing, and unpaid household work. Such a strategy could be a vehicle for encouraging communal and nonexploitative production processes that utilize technologies that do not displace labor and do not degrade ecosystems.

(Kaboub, 2008, p. 227)

Moreover, these jobs could be embedded in an existing organisation, if it is non-profit. The advantage noted is that these organisations already have some infrastructure, knowledge, and experience, and are likely to have problems finding additional labour because they cannot afford to pay salaries. In this case, if civil society decides that the activity is necessary and useful, new jobs would be approved, the management of the activities would correspond to the organisation and the only thing the state would do would be to pay the salary (and control that there are no irregularities) (Garzón & Guamán, 2015; Tcherneva, 2018). As Fadhel Kaboub also explains:

a central feature of the ELR program is that it is completely decentralized in its design and implementation. Local community groups and NGOs will survey the needs of the community and will hire workers to provide such services. Naturally, the ELR workers will only produce services that are not supplied (or are undersupplied) by the private sector, thus avoiding competition with the private sector. The only centralized feature of the program is the source of its funding, which is the federal government.

(Kaboub, 2008, p. 224)

In any case, many MMTers often make recommendations about the social activities that would be preferable to be covered through Job Guarantee, as for example Bill et al. (2016) do with employment programmes for people with psychiatric disability. Other authors have proposed that the Job Guarantee should take into account the dynamics of labour productivity and be oriented towards innovation activities: "[We] propose an extension of the ELR programme, arguing that it can be used for the application of innovations by the state" (Colacchio & Davanzati, 2020, p. 1). Another example is provided by Nell (2003): "ELR could be designed to provide workers for venture capital projects, promoting innovation" (Nell, 2003, p. 18).

MMTers emphasise that being a Job Guarantee worker has a huge advantage over being unemployed. Not only because that person would receive a wage and in unemployment would not, but because by working he/she would learn new knowledge, acquire new skills, gain experience, meet other people, feel useful by contributing to society, etc.: "teach and prepare for other job opportunities through training, accreditation, education and other comprehensive services on the job itself" (Tcherneva, 2020, p. 48). Indeed, it is pointed out that receiving an income is often not the most valuable part of working. To reinforce this thesis, the MMTers use the experience of Argentina after the 2001 crisis, when 2 million jobs in community services were created in less than 5 months, following a logic similar to that of Job Guarantee. When their beneficiaries were asked if they were satisfied with their work and why, receiving an income was the fifth most chosen answer. The first one was that they could do something, the second one that they worked in a good environment, the third one that they helped the community, and the fourth one that they learned something (Tcherneva & Wray, 2005; Kostzer, 2008, 2023; Tcherneva, 2013). Moreover, all this professional development could then serve the Job Guarantee workers to be hired by a firm, to which he/she could already prove that he/she works properly (not as it would happen when unemployed because firms usually shy away from them as they do not know if they will be good workers); or it could even serve him/her to set up his/her own activity or business.

The cost and financing of a Guaranteed Job would not be a problem for a state issuing the money, but the MMTers stress that, even if we are talking about a state without the capacity to issue its own, the implementation of this policy should not be paralysed (Wray, 2013; Garzón & Guamán, 2015; Cruz et al., 2020); in Wray's words: "even if it is believed that governments are already operating against very tight fiscal constraints, ELR can be implemented by reordering priorities" (Wray, 2007, pp. 20–21). The argument is that although creating jobs for everyone who wants to work may be quite expensive, it would be much more expensive to keep all those inactive people unemployed. In strictly monetary terms, it should be understood that public administrations spend a lot of money on unemployment benefits and subsidies, on training programmes for the unemployed, on aid and social benefits for families without resources … and all this expenditure would not be necessary if everyone had a job and a salary. In addition, there is a huge amount of public spending that goes to alleviate many problems that arise from unemployment, such as psychological care for people who have been unemployed for a long time, social work to combat social exclusion, and even spending on security and justice forces to control crime partly due to poverty and social exclusion, etc.: "the costs of unemployment are staggering. These include the permanent loss of output of goods and services, but also the social costs resulting from increased crime, illness, and other social problems" (Forstater, 1999, p. 2). If there were full employment, there would be less poverty, less inequality, less exclusion, and greater social peace, so that much of this public expenditure would diminish in the medium and long terms. As Abba Lerner said, "the economic gains from full employment are enormous" (Lerner, 1951, pp. 31–32).

That is why it is argued that monetary gains are not the only important thing, since it would be much more expensive in economic, social, and ecological terms to keep people idle and unproductive instead of them working on all kinds of socially and environmentally beneficial tasks. Mathew Forstater is as blunt as that:

> There is no policy with as many potential benefits as full employment with a living wage. This is because of the tremendous social and economic costs of unemployment. Studies have shown that unemployment is directly related to physical illness and mental health. Individuals blame themselves, leading to depression. Financial insecurity creates stress and anxiety. Studies have even shown a link between unemployment and suicide. Unemployment increases crime rates, especially in income-generating crimes.
>
> *(Forstater, 2017)*

There are several studies that aim to estimate the budgetary costs of implementing a Job Guarantee for different countries and to study its implementation: the United States (Fullwiler, 2005, 2012; Kaboub, 2013); Australia (Burgess & Mitchell, 1998; Cowling & Mitchell, 2007); Eurozone (Mosler & Silipo, 2017; Watts et al., 2017; Cruz et al., 2021), Germany (Landwerh, 2020), Italy (Levrero, 2019; Colacchio & Davanzati, 2020); Greece (Antonopoulos et al., 2014), Spain (Garzón & Guamán, 2015; Garzón & Cruz, 2021), Mexico (Sovilla, 2018; Sovilla et al., 2021), Saudi Arabia (Kaboub, 2017), and Tunisia (Kaboub, 2007, 2012).

In short, Job Guarantee is a formula that would make it possible to perfect Abba Lerner's Functional Finance to overcome its difficulties and thus achieve full employment without inflation. Moreover, it would not only lead to job creation but also contribute to improving the working conditions of the lower end of the labour market by establishing a de facto minimum wage. Finally, it would not only provide an income for the unemployed but also offer them the opportunity to feel more useful and to develop professionally, while at the same time engaging in activities that are beneficial for society and the environment. MMTers are confident that Job Guarantee would be a win-win situation for everyone, and that its implementation cost (both economically and socially) would be significantly lower than keeping people unemployed.

Criticisms

The Job Guarantee proposal has been criticised from many different approaches and according to many different criteria. Here we will review the criticisms that we consider to be the most important of all, making it clear that they must necessarily be abstract since the policy has never been put into practice, so the only possible analysis is through imagination and speculation. Moreover, these difficulties are compounded by the fact that it is a proposal whose concrete materialisation depends on its particular design (not all MMTers propose exactly the same details) and its concrete coupling in the different institutions (labour and administrative, but also cultural and idiosyncratic) of the country in question.

A typical criticism of the Job Guarantee relies on the NAIRU to basically point out that it would be impossible to reach full employment before inflation. For example, Triggs (2021) states that "if the unemployment rate falls below NAIRU, the unemployment rate that does not accelerate inflation (…), inflation rises, damaging investment, reducing consumption and causing unemployment to return to this natural rate". Another example: "it could be argued that the ELR would lead to accelerating inflation, since unemployment would fall well below the NAIRU level" (Sawyer, 2003, p. 27). However, we have already highlighted that MMTers contest this analytical tool as useless for explaining reality (Mitchell, 1987, 1998; Mitchell & Mosler, 2002; Mitchell & Muysken, 2008; Mitchell & Wray 2004), and furthermore, in a world with Job Guarantee, this NAIRU would become a NAIBER (Non-Accelerating-Inflation Buffer Employment Rate), which would be much lower than the former thanks to its design features (basically, there would still be a reserve army, but of workers instead of unemployed), which would allow full employment to be achieved without inflation. As Bill Mitchell and Warren Mosler argue:

> clearly, if we introduce a JG scheme, the initial level of JG employment will deliver a higher demand level than inherited under the NAIRU economy. Logically, in a NAIRU-world this should be inflationary. But the JG policy introduces "loose full employment" for the reasons noted above. In this sense, the inflation restraint exerted via the NAIBER is likely to be more effective than using a NAIRU strategy.
>
> *(Mitchell & Mosler, 2002, p. 250)*

As the MMTers comment, the design of the Job Guarantee would be crucial for this NAIBER to be low enough to reach full employment without inflation: "the NAIBER is actually below the NAIRU in the sense that (non-ELR) employment can be higher before the inflation barrier is reached. A poorly designed ELR (say, where ELR wages were indexed to inflation, while unemployment compensation was not) could result in a NAIBER above the NAIRU. But this would not reflect our proposal" (Mitchell & Wray, 2005, p. 238).

Some authors are not convinced that setting a fixed, minimum wage for the Job Guarantee would solve supply-side inflation problems. Moreover, some believe that such a measure could be inflationary by raising many private sector wages as well: "the fact that the PSE sets the effective minimum wage floor for the entire economy may have inflationary consequences and cause job losses in other parts of the economy" (Drumets & Pfister, 2021, p. 19). What other analysts argue is that private sector employees, no longer facing the threat of unemployment, would become empowered and demand higher wages, which could cause employers to raise prices in order not to lose profit margins:

> since the policy objective is to create a pool of workers, the result is upward pressure on wages when the private sector increases its demand for labour. (…) the private sector demands work and turns to government-employed workers, who demand higher wages to switch jobs.
>
> *(Mueller & Vaz-Curado, 2019, p. 6)*

Marc Lavoie is also concerned about supply-side inflation:

> but in a world of high employment utilization, even before the ELR buffer stock shrinks, the wage rate and the mean private wage rate could expand. To claim that ELR programs will also provide price stability probably claims too much.
>
> *(Lavoie, 1999, p. 372)*

Although he immediately qualifies that this should not necessarily be negative if full employment is achieved: "this being said, since inflation haters have never demonstrated that moderate inflation has negative economic consequences, the fear of price inflation should not deter deci-sion makers from trying to achieve full employment" (Lavoie, 1999, p. 372). Seccareccia (2004) points out that, in order to avoid such inflationary risks, great care should be taken with the wage level of the Job Guarantee, as too high a level could generate important imbalances: "the higher becomes the ELR wage (in figure 4), and the more destabilizing would be the implemen-tation of such a program on the wage structure over time" (Secareccia, 2004, p. 34). In any case, he also does not believe that in the short run a Job Guarantee wage increase would have signifi-cant effects on other wages, and therefore prices: "following an ELR wage increase, one would not expect across-the-board wage spillover effects in all sectors that would be accompanied by a proportional increase in prices, at least not in the short run" (Seccareccia, 2004, p. 30).

Tony Aspromourgos stresses that the only way in which the minimum wage in the Job Guarantee would not prove inflationary is if such an employment programme turned out to be the worst possible option in the entire labour market, only preferable to being unemployed, so that wage discipline pressure would continue to be in force: "at some point this could work, as long as buffer employment is so awful a prospect that the threat or fear of entering it can discipline wider wage claims" (Aspromourgos, 2000, p. 153). However, he considers that such a scenario would conflict with other supposed virtues of Job Guarantee, such as, for example, achieving improved working conditions in the private sector:

> this points to a certain tension, if not contradiction, in the several meanings that Wray ascribes to BSE. In particular, on the one hand the buffer is supposed capable of setting the pace for wider working conditions (e.g. with respect to health insurance in the US case); and on the other, it is supposed to be a wage inflation deterrent.
>
> *(Aspromourgos, 2000, p. 153)*

This is something that has also been pointed out by Mario Seccareccia, since the purpose of avoiding inflationary pressures on the wage side could imply that one is simply replacing the current system of unemployed people on benefits with a system of Job Guarantee workers on low wages:

> one could simply be recreating an ELR system that mirrors the current system. That is, we would simply have changed the status of the involuntary unemployed to that of an ELR worker, but the role of the individual would be substantially the same: to avoid wage inflation.
>
> *(Seccareccia, 2004)*

Seccareccia points out that this scenario could be reached because, as much as it is not the goal of MMTers, "there is nothing that would prevent government authorities to set the ELR level below a 'living wage'" (Seccareccia, 2004, p. 34).

On the other hand, Kriesler and Alevi rely on another reason to argue that the Job Guarantee is more inflationary than the current system:

> in the advent of inflation, without the scheme, people dropping from employment to unem-ployment reduce inflationary pressure both by reducing demand and by reducing the mili-tancy of the labour force (à la the reserve army). With the buffer scheme, people will drop from employment to buffer employment.
>
> *(Kriesler & Alevi, 2001, p. 9)*

From this they deduce that this would come at a cost in terms of more private sector layoffs: "the contraction in the private sector needs to be much more severe to have the same impact on inflation" (Kriesler & Alevi, 2001, p. 9). However, this in particular is partially countered by MMTers indicating that not all newly unemployed will immediately move to the Job Guarantee programme: "many of those losing jobs will prefer to undertake full-time search rather than accepting temporary ELR work" (Wray, 1998, p. 127). In other words, "the relatively low pay will act as a disincentive for many job losers" (Mitchell & Wray, 2005, p. 239).

To the other criticisms noted above, MMTers have responded using a variety of arguments. The first is that employing Job Guarantee workers is no more inflationary than leaving them unemployed because they remain on the bottom rung of the labour market, with no bargaining power, with the only important difference being that they would be receiving more income and getting much more benefit from working:

> The JG program is explicitly a "rightly distributed" spending program in which government spending is directed precisely to those who want to work. This places no direct pressure on wages and prices because the workers in the program were part of the "surplus" or "redundant" labor force and are still available for private employers (at a small mark-up over the JG program wage – the minimum wage). For that reason, employing workers in the JG program is no more inflationary than leaving them unemployed.
>
> *(Tymoigne & Wray, 2013, p. 46)*

Moreover, they insist that, in a hypothetical inflationary process caused by full employment, "business is more likely to resist wage demands from its existing workforce if it has the option of hiring ELR workers" (Mitchell & Wray, 2005, p. 237).

The second argument used is that the existence of a pool of Job Guarantee workers (with higher skills than the unemployed) available to employers would reduce inflationary pressures by reducing hiring costs: "the JG should lower recruiting and hiring costs as employers would have an employed pool of workers demonstrating readiness and willingness to work, which should reduce inflation pressures" (Tymoigne & Wray, 2013, pp. 46–47).

A third argument is that the Job Guarantee would be much more beneficial to the working class than the current system because inflation is currently fought by generating unemployment and hurting the most needy, whereas under a Job Guarantee programme inflation would have to be fought with other types of policies, such as tax increases on the wealthy: "we are surprised that our critics appear to prefer to use unemployment and poverty to fight inflation, which forces the least able to bear more of the costs" (Tymoigne & Wray, 2013, p. 47).

Another recurrent criticism is that, because in times of economic expansion employers would hire Job Guarantee workers at higher wages, many activities that were presumably useful and necessary would cease to be performed. This is what Malcolm Sawyer points out with regard to eldercare work: "when aggregate demand is low, care of the elderly would be provided to generate ELR jobs; when aggregate demand is high, such care would not be provided since ELR jobs would not be required" (Sawyer, 2003, p. 17). To solve this problem, Mitchell and Wray propose that there should be two types of jobs in the Job Guarantee sphere: a core one that performs the most necessary activities, and a perimeter one that performs the expendable activities:

> the buffer stock should be split into two components: 1. A stable core component that represents the "average" buffer stock over the typical business cycle determined by structural

issues and macroeconomic policy settings. 2. A transitory component that fluctuates around the core as private demand ebbs and flows.

(Mitchell & Wray, 2005, p. 239)

Tcherneva summarises this idea as follows: "permanent or essential public services must always be adequately staffed" (Tcherneva, 2020, p. 86).

On the other hand, there are those who believe that the stabilising mechanism of Job Guarantee would only work to prevent deflation (as in a time of economic recession many unemployed would go to work and receive an income), but not inflation:

the job guarantee called for by MMT does have the merit of being an automatic stabilizer. However, it is likely to be more effective in preventing deflation than inflation, since even in the most favorable case it merely allows the labor market reserve to be integrated more smoothly into the economic process, that is, the labor supply that can be activated immediately is larger.

(Dullien & Tober, 2022, p. 233)

Some other criticisms have to do with the logistics required to implement Job Guarantee. On the one hand, it is questioned whether the characteristics of a Job Guarantee job fit the most valued and needed economic activities:

the proponents of ELR have listed many worthwhile jobs which could be undertaken within ELR (as indicated in the next section), though we question whether such jobs would fit the criteria of an ELR job (readily available, paying "basic wage", unskilled and requiring little capital equipment).

(Sawyer, 2003, p. 15)

It is argued that many of these activities, especially capital activities, require training and skills that are not compatible with minimum wages: "much of the work on capital projects is skilled work for which wages are usually significantly above the minimum wage" (Sawyer, 2003, p. 16). On the other hand, some consider that the logistical complexity of implementing Job Guarantee prevents it from successfully achieving its objective:

the success of such a programme rests on a number of conditions (Buiter & Mann, 2019) that may not be all met. In particular, the authorities must manage a permanent inventory of productive, meaningful jobs and job openings, ready to be filled at short notice in the public sector.

(Drumets & Pfister, 2021, p. 19)

To this the MMTers have responded by agreeing that the Job Guarantee poses a significant logistical challenge, but that it will always be socially preferable to keeping people unemployed, and that, in any case, logistical difficulties can be addressed and minimised:

the program could be phased in to reduce logistical problems. After the phase-in, administrators would prioritize work allocations from a broad array of community-enhancing activities. (…) So long as marginal benefits are above zero, it is socially beneficial to put unused resources to work.

(Mitchell & Wray, 2005, pp. 239–240)

For her part, Tcherneva points out that there are already logistically very complex policies that have enormous social and economic benefits, such as the public education system:

to say that its implementation would be an impossibly difficult task is anything but self-evident. In fact, history suggests the opposite (…) While it is to no one's advantage to deny that there will be administrative difficulties specific to the programme, it does not appear that they will be any greater than those of other policies.

(Tcherneva, 2020, p. 80)

Some critics point out that the MMTers underestimate the cost of implementing a Job Guarantee to achieve full employment. On the one hand, it is argued that the calculations made to know the budgetary cost only take into account the wage cost, but not the other production costs such as materials or logistics:

Wray, for example, derives his estimates by multiplying the ELR wage by the number of workers involved, thus assuming that there are no further costs involved such as material costs, costs of capital equipment and costs of supervisory labor. These costs are likely to be substantial and raise the cost estimates significantly (perhaps of the order of doubling them).

(Sawyer, 2003, p. 12)

This has been countered by Mitchell and Wray arguing that, while this is true, it is offset by the savings achieved by Job Guarantee in other areas:

Sawyer rightly argued that ELR workers will need some capital and office/management support. Hence, total ELR spending will be higher than the sum of wages and benefits spent on ELR workers. However, implementation of ELR also allows some savings to be made (outlays which support unemployment programs would be shifted to the employment program).

(Mitchell & Wray, 2005, p. 236)

On the other hand, it is often pointed out that such calculations only take into account the number of unemployed according to conventional unemployment indicators, and so do not take into account either people who are underemployed (working part-time but want to work more hours), people who are discouraged (not looking for work for some reason but might want to work), or people who might want to move from the private to the public sector:

a further cause of underestimation of costs arises in so far as recorded unemployment under-estimates overall unemployment, and the prospects of ELR jobs would draw people into the labor force. Hence the number of jobs to be created would exceed the current measured level of unemployment.

(Sawyer, 2003, p. 13)

This line of reasoning has led some critics to believe that "a job guarantee plan entails a higher government debt to GDP ratio compared with conventional spending" even although entails a lower government debt level in absolute value (Sawyer & Pasarella, 2021, p. 384).

The same reasoning that the Job Guarantee will draw many workers from the private sector is used by other critics to claim that the policy would affect the private sector very negatively: with a notably high wage, "workers would be siphoned out of productive, private sector employment and into the government realm, providing dubious service at best at the direction of political officials" (Murphy, 2020, p. 249). It is pointed out that this risk would be greater the better the working conditions compared to those in the private sector: "the PSE may have other drawbacks, such as the displacement of private sector production if workers prefer better-paid or less intensive PSE jobs" (Drumets & Pfister, 2021, p. 19). This is why, among other things, authors such as Mario Seccareccia insist that the wage in the Job Guarantee must be appropriate: "it ensues that the choice of the ELR wage would be of significance in bringing the economy closer to potential output since any variation in the ELR wage could trigger changes in the labour force participation rate" (Seccareccia, 2004, p. 16).

Another criticism concerns the time period in which Job Guarantee would be implemented, stressing that it would not be enough to pay a wage, but that many other steps would have to be taken that would require more time than is usually indicated by MMTers: "job creation under the ELR approach still requires administration, provision of capital equipment and materials etc., leading to some delays in the provision of such jobs" (Sawyer, 2003, p. 15).

A concern shared by many critics is that Job Guarantee could be used to replace or devalue typical conventional public sector jobs. If someone is to be hired at minimum wage to perform an activity very similar to that already performed by a higher paid public employee, there could be significant discrimination and/or wage reductions in conventional public employment. In the words of Malcom Sawyer: "some of the jobs provided by ELR schemes are substitutes for 'mainline' public sector employment, and as such threaten to undercut the wages of some public sector workers" (Sawyer, 2003, p. 19). Marc Lavoie is also concerned about this risk:

> another important issue is whether governments (in particular state or local governments, which do not pay the cost of the program) would reduce their low-skill labor force and hire cheaper ELR applicants. The ELR program would then increase employment but have a detrimental effect on average salaries.
>
> *(Lavoie, 1999, p. 372)*

Another analyst who has expressed concern is Mario Seccareccia:

> in a period of fiscal austerity in the public sector, what would prevent a local government concerned with the size and cost of its own employed labour force from shedding some of its workers with relatively higher wages and trade union protection and replacing them with low wage ELR workers?
>
> *(Seccareccia, 2004, p. 33)*

MMTers have responded to this by pointing to several elements. On the one hand, Wray argues that an important condition when designing the tasks to be performed by Job Guarantee workers is that they do not duplicate activities that are already being performed:

Job Guarantee workers would be engaged in socially useful activities, but it is important that the activities of Job Guarantee do not compete with those of the private sector and that the public sector is not allowed to replace public employees with Job Guarantee workers.

(Wray, 2012)

On the other hand, James Juniper, Timothy Sharpe and Martin Watts respond to this criticism as follows:

under a more enlightened public sector administration in which cost cutting and cost shifting were not viewed as a badge of honor by senior management and politicians, ELR jobs and standard public sector jobs would be distinguished. Also public sector expansion at market wages and the establishment of an ELR are not mutually incompatible.

(Juniper et al., 2014, p. 301)

Finally, Tcherneva argues that this criticism is quite poor:

this criticism implies that establishing a public alternative – any public alternative – degrades the already existing rights of people who may not need access to such an alternative (...) Public alternatives do not trigger a race to the bottom, but rather raise and secure floors.

(Tcherneva, 2020, p. 84)

Other authors, on the other hand, see the Job Guarantee as a kind of unemployment benefit system since the activities performed by the workers would add little economic value: "public sector employment in activities that add little economic value or maintenance of skills at a guaranteed wage would simply be equivalent to unemployment benefits in disguise" (Drumets & Pfister, 2021, p. 19). To these, the MMTers respond by pointing out that Job Guarantee has to be evaluated by social efficiency, not by market efficiency: "even neoclassical theory recognizes the difference between private and social values. There are countless activities that have near zero value in the private market place but could have positive social value" (Mitchell & Wray, 2005, p. 241). Tcherneva summarises this idea as follows: "employing someone is no less productive than keeping them unemployed. In fact, given the detrimental effects of unemployment on individual and household welfare, one could argue that the productivity of the unemployed is in fact negative" (Tcherneva, 2020, p. 81).

Some critics believe that this substitution risk would disappear if public employment were created directly instead of Job Guarantee workers: "why not go directly to expanding employment in the public sector proper?" (Aspromourgos, 2000, p. 151), although the problem, according to them, is that it would in any case be inflationary.

Another typical criticism has to do with the currency depreciation that could occur due to the added aggregate demand implied by the Job Guarantee. The increase in the purchasing power of Job Guarantee workers could translate into higher imports (of greater intensity as the shortcomings in the productive structure of the economy in question become more important), which would tend to depreciate the currency and generate inflationary pressures through this channel: "full employment policies may generate an external trade deficit before the target is reached (...). The exponents of MMT are only partially aware of this" (Cesaratto, 2020). According to some authors, this is one of the key critical points of MMT in general and of Job Guarantee in particular: "the impact of 'full employment' fiscal policies on the current-account position of a country seems to be one of the major critical points of the prescriptions elaborated within this theoretical framework" (Carnevali & Deleide, 2023, p. 90).

Using a different argumentation, authors such as Kriesler and Halevi warn that such currency depreciation could originate from capital flight by capitalists, who would consciously use such a weapon to boycott the implementation of the Job Guarantee as putting their interests at risk:

> if capitalists perceive such schemes as threats to their profits or economic power – which is extremely likely considering the increased government expenditure and reduced levels of unemployment with which they are associated – then we would expect them to react. At the very least, if one country adopted such policies in isolation, capital flight would be a global way of disciplining the offending government.
>
> *(Kriesler & Halevi, 2001, p. 10)*

MMTers defend themselves against this type of criticism on three grounds. The first is that such a depreciation need not necessarily occur, because the import effect could be offset, for example, by increased inflows of foreign capital in search of higher returns in a growing economy with full employment (thanks to the Job Guarantee) (Wray, 2007; Kaboub, 2012, 2017).

The second point is that, even in a worst-case scenario, such a depreciation need not be intense or eternal. At some point the value of the currency would stabilise, favouring exports over a stable development strategy that would not be sustained by commodity prices or the risk-seeking of international investors. However, the initial sacrifice to break international dependence would require a battery of trade, industrial, monetary, and fiscal policies that would minimise as much as possible the lack of foreign exchange to import those inputs required for domestic production, always without boycotting the operability of a Job Guarantee (Wray, 2007; Tcherneva & Wray, 2005; Kaboub, 2012, 2017; Murray & Forstater, 2013).

The third element is that since these programmes operate as a mechanism that dilutes the ills associated with unemployment, their costs will also be diluted. Thus, there is a trade-off between the rents generated by these programmes and those that previously went to fight the ills associated with unemployment, promoting a more productive release of resources and resource mobilisation, which could reduce currency depreciation pressures (Wray, 2007; Nersisyan & Wray, 2019).

In any case, some MMTers point out that the effect on currency depreciation could be limited by setting much of the remuneration in kind, as was partially done with some job creation programmes during the US New Deal (Rose, 2009). In other words, a percentage of wages would be paid in the form of basic goods and services provided domestically: food, clothing, furniture, etc.:

> poverty still can be reduced if the ELR total compensation package includes extra-market provision of necessities. This could include domestically-produced food, clothing, shelter, and basic services (healthcare, childcare, eldercare, education, transportation). Because these would be provided "in kind", ELR workers would be less able to use monetary income to substitute imports for domestic production.
>
> *(Wray, 2007, p. 37)*

Finally, as with inflation risk, the MMTers point out that it may be socially and ethically preferable to suffer some depreciation (and consequent inflation) if full employment is achieved:

> should policymakers accept some inflation and currency depreciation in order to eliminate unemployment and poverty? There are strong ethical arguments against using poverty and unemployment as the primary policy tools to achieve price and exchange rate stability-especially given that costs of poverty and unemployment are not shared equally across the population. And even if price and currency stability are highly desired, it is doubtful that a case can be made for their status as a human right on par with the right to work.
>
> *(Wray, 2007, p. 3)*

Conclusions

The main economic policy proposal of MMT is Job Guarantee, which is a refined development of Abba Lerner's Functional Finance and is inspired by Hyman Minsky's Employer of Last Resort. Its aim is to achieve full employment without inflation, and the means to achieve this is to guarantee employment directly from the state to anyone willing and able to work, paying a fixed minimum wage that acts as a floor and anchor for wages and prices. In this way, the "reserve army of unemployed" would become a "reserve army of Job Guarantee workers", significantly improving their economic and social situation, but at the same time maintaining the threat of being in the worst possible situation in the labour market if they are made redundant, thus avoiding upward wage pressures. It is argued that this way of increasing aggregate demand is less inflationary than typical Keynesian policies of aggregate demand expansion, since in this case the increase in demand is targeted where there is less income – the unemployed population – and not in a generalised and indiscriminate way. Its implementation would not be a financial problem for states with full monetary sovereignty, since they can buy whatever is for sale in the currency they control, and labour is one of those options. In any case, MMTers argue that the economic cost of employing all the unemployed is greater than keeping them out of work, since unemployment – especially long-term unemployment – entails very significant social costs that ultimately lead to economic costs (unemployment benefits, subsidies, health services, fighting crime, etc.).

This policy prescription has been criticised on many fronts and on various grounds, all of which are necessarily speculative since Job Guarantee has never been applied in any country, making an analysis based on empirical evidence impossible.

Surely the most important criticism, which I share, is that it is optimistic about achieving full employment without inflation. But, in my case, it would not be so much on the supply side since, unlike many critics, I do believe that maintaining a fixed minimum wage can act as an anchor against wage pressures in the labour market (at least, as long as such a wage level is low enough to keep the fear of losing private sector employment at work and not to alter labour market participation too much, although it should also be high enough to ensure a decent living and to distance itself significantly from the option of unemployment).

My concern has more to do with inflationary pressures on the demand side. After all, the increase in aggregate demand that the application of the Job Guarantee would entail (higher the higher the unemployment rate) could put stress on certain economic sectors and generate bottlenecks that would translate into price increases. Moreover, this increase in aggregate demand could be channelled towards the purchase of foreign products (the more so the more dependent the economy is on foreign trade), which would tend to depreciate the currency and could lead to imported inflation. Therefore, the higher the unemployment rate and the more dependent the economy is on the external sector, the greater the likelihood that the Job Guarantee could cause inflation on the demand side: perhaps an economy with low unemployment and a strong productive structure could apply the Job Guarantee without suffering inflation, but the same would not seem to be true of an economy with high unemployment and/or a weak productive structure. Moreover, to all this, we must add the considerations on the international position of the national currency in the hierarchy of currencies that we made in Chapter 3: an economy with a currency in demand at the international level will have more possibilities of applying a Job Guarantee without suffering depreciation and inflation than an economy with a currency that is weakly demanded at the world level.

In any case, I share the MMTers' value judgement on the available policy options and prefer the implementation of the Job Guarantee even if it leads to some increase in inflation, rather than maintaining large pockets of unemployment with moderate inflation. However, I also believe that in certain economies (especially the less developed ones) the application of the Job Guarantee should be done with great care so that such inflationary pressures do not spiral out of control and end up generating more economic and social damage than certain levels of unemployment currently do. In this respect, it would seem important to implement the policy progressively over time and also by granting Job Guarantee workers a wage that is partly in kind so as not to generate so much monetary imbalance.

The implementation of a Job Guarantee is undoubtedly a tremendous logistical and administrative challenge (the higher the unemployment rate) and, while this should not be an excuse to stop implementing it, it should alert managers to the many design and implementation risks that could be incurred and which could ultimately derail the policy. For this very reason, the design and planning of the Job Guarantee needs to be well thought out from the outset to minimise the risks and potential pitfalls that such a complex and ambitious policy inevitably entails. The more shortcomings are identified a posteriori and the more corrections are needed, the less likely it will be that the Job Guarantee will end up being valued and accepted by the population (which, on the other hand, is a prerequisite for it to achieve its objective).

References

Antonopoulos, R., Adam, S., Kim, K., Masterson, T., & Papadimitriou, D. B. (2014). *After austerity: Measuring the impact of a job guarantee policy for Greece*. Levy Economics Institute of Bard College Public Policy Brief No. 138.

Aspromourgos, T. (2000). Is an employer-of-last-resort policy sustainable? A review article. *Review of Political Economy, 12*(2), 141–155.

Baker, A., & Murphy, R. (2020). Modern monetary theory and the changing role of tax in society. *Social Policy & Society, 19*(3), 454–469.

Bell, S., & Wray, R. (2004). *The war on poverty after 40 years: A Minskyan assessment*. Levy Economic Institute Public Policy Brief No. 78.

Bill, A., Cowling, S., Mitchell, W., & Quirk, V. (2016). Employment programs for people with psychiatric disability: The case for change. *Australian Journal of Social Issues, 41*(2), 209–220.

Bracarense, N., & Costa, P. A. B. (2022). Green jobs: Sustainable path for environmental conservation and socio-economic stability and inclusion. *Review of Political Economy*. https://doi.org/10.1080/09538259.2022.2041311

Bruno, S. (2018). Increasing the minimum wage with the state as employer of last resort: A "predistribution" proposal for Mexico. *International Journal of Political Economy*, *47*(3–4), 330–351. https://doi.org/10.1080/08911916.2018.1517463

Buiter, W., & Mann, C. L. (2019). Modern Monetary Theory (MMT) - What's right is not new, what's new is not right, and what's left is too simplistic. *Citi GPS Insights*. https://www.citivelocity.com/citigps/modern-monetary-theory-mmt/

Burgess, J., & Mitchell, W. F. (1998). Unemployment, human rights and a full employment policy in Australia. *Australian Journal of Human Rights*, *4*(2), 76–94. https://doi.org/10.1080/1323238X.1998.11911001

Carnevali, E., & Deleidi, M. (2023). The trade-off between inflation and unemployment in an 'MMT world': An open-economy perspective. *European Journal of Economics and Economic Policies*, *20*(1), 90–124.

Cesaratto, S. (2020). Money and the external constraint. In *Heterodox challenges in economics*. Springer. https://doi.org/10.1007/978-3-030-54448-5_5

Colacchio, G., & Forges Davanzati, G. (2020). Modern money theory: A critical assessment and a proposal for the state as innovator of first resort. *Review of Political Economy*, *32*(1), 77–98. https://doi.org/10.1080/09538259.2020.1741893

Cowling, S., & Mitchell, W. (2007). Taking the low road: Minimum wage determination under work choices. *Journal of Industrial Relations 49*(5), 741–756.

Cruz, E., Parejo, F., Garzón, E., & Rangel, J. (2020). Es el momento de la política fiscal: Repensar los estabilizadores automáticos contra la pandemia. *Revista de Economía Mundial*, *56*, 1–22.

Cruz-Hidalgo, E., Ehnts, D. H., & Tcherneva, P. R. (2021). Completing the euro: The euro treasury and the job guarantee. *Revista De Economía Crítica*, *1*(27), 100–111. https://revistaeconomiacritica.org/index.php/rec/article/view/217

Drumetz, F., & Pfister, C. (2021). De quoi la MMT est-elle le nom? *Revue française d'économie*, *XXXVI*, 3–46. https://doi.org/10.3917/rfe.214.0003

Dullien, S., & Tober, S. (2022). A monetary Keynesian view of modern monetary theory. *European Journal of Economics and Economic Policies*, *19*(2), 227–237.

Fisher, I. (1926). A statistical relation between unemployment and price changes. *International Labour Review*, *13*, 785–792.

Forstater, M. (1998). Flexible full employment: Structural implications of discretionary public sector employment. *Journal of Economic Issues*, *32*(2), 557–563. https://doi.org/10.1080/00213624.1998.11506064

Forstater, M. (1999). Functional finance and full employment: Lessons from Lerner for today? Levy Economic Institute Working Paper No. 272.

Forstater, M. (2003). Public employment and environmental sustainability. *Journal of Post Keynesian Economics*, *25*(3), 385–406. https://doi.org/10.1080/01603477.2003.11051364

Forstater, M. (2005). Reply to Malcolm Sawyer. *Journal of Economic Issues*, *39*(1), 245–255. https://doi.org/10.1080/00213624.2005.11506789

Forstater, M. (2006). Green jobs: Public service employment and environmental sustainability. *Challenge*, *49*(4), 58–72. https://doi.org/10.2753/CHA0577-5132490405

Forstater, M. (2017). *Trabajo-Dinero-Deuda (Vlog No. 105): Sentido Común Económico – auténtico Pleno Empleo* [Video]. Global Institute for Sustainable Prosperity. https://www.youtube.com/watch?v=OUQROJxI1F4

Fullwiler, S. (2012). The costs and benefits of a job guarantee: Estimates from a multicountry econometric model. In M. Murray & M. Forstater (Eds.), *The job guarantee. Toward true full employment* (pp. 73–94). https://ssrn.com/abstract=2194960

Fullwiler, S., Grey, R., & Tankus, N. (2019, March, 1). An MMT response on what causes inflation. *Financial Times*. https://www.ft.com/content/539618f8-b88c-3125-8031-cf46ca197c64

Fullwiler, S. T. (2005). The job guarantee and economic stability. Creating a Culture of Full Employment: Incorporating the 7th Path to Full Employment Conference and 12th National Conference on Unemployment University of Newcastle, Centre of Full Employment and Equity.

Galvin, R., & Healy, N. (2020). The green new deal in the United States: What it is and how to pay for it. *Energy Research & Social Science, 67*, 1–9.

Garzón, A., & Guamán, A. (2015). *El Trabajo Garantizado: una propuesta necesaria frente al desempleo y la precarización*. Akal.

Garzón, E., & Cruz, E. (2021). Trabajo garantizado verde y morado: el principal componente de un Green New Deal. *Revista Inclusiones, 8*(especial abril-junio), 74–97.

Hail, S. (2017). *Economics for sustainable prosperity*. Palgrave Macmillan.

Juniper, J., Sharpe, T. P., & Watts, M. J. (2014). Modern monetary theory: Contributions and critics. *Journal of Post Keynesian Economics, 37*(2), 281–307.

Kaboub, F. (2007). *ELR-led economic development: A Plan for Tunisia (May 14)*. Levy Economics Institute Working Paper No. 499. https://ssrn.com/abstract=986310 or http://dx.doi.org/10.2139/ssrn.986310

Kaboub, F. (2008). Elements of a radical counter-movement to neoliberalism: Employment-led development. *Review of Radical Political Economics, 40*(3), 220–227.

Kaboub, F. (2012). From neoliberalism to social justice: The feasibility of full employment in Tunisia. *Review of Radical Political Economics, 44*(3), 305–312.

Kaboub, F. (2013b). The fiscal cliff mythology and the full employment alternative: An affordable and productive Plan. *Review of Radical Political Economics, 45*(3), 305–314.

Kaboub, F. (2017). Financial sovereignty and the possibility of full employment in Saudi Arabia. In M. Murray & M. Forstater (Eds.), *The job guarantee and modern money theory. Binzagr institute for sustainable prosperity*. Palgrave Macmillan.

Kalecki, M. (1943). Political aspects of full employment. *Political Quarterly, 14*(4), 322–330.

Kelton, S. (2020). *El mito del déficit: La teoría monetaria moderna y el nacimiento de la economía de la gente*. Penguin Random House.

Kostzer, D. (2008). *Argentina: A case study on the Plan Jefes y Jefas de Hogar Desocupados, or the employment road to economic recovery*. Levy Economics Institute Working Paper No. 534.

Kostzer, D. (2023). Checklist of an employment guarantee programme: The Plan Jefes de Hogar from Argentina revisited 20 years later. In L. R. Wray, Phil Armstrong, Sara Holland, Claire Jackson-Prior, Prue Plumridge, & Neil Wilson (Eds), *Modern monetary theory* (pp. 226–252). Edward Elgar Publishing.

Kriesler, P., & Halevi, J. (2001). *Political aspects of "buffer stock" employment*. Centre for Applied Economic Research Working Paper No. 2001/02.

Landwehr, J. J. (2020). *The case for a job guarantee policy in Germany: A political-economic analysis of the potential benefits and obstacles*. Berlin Institute for International Political Economy Working Paper No. 150/2020.

Lavoie, M. (1999). Understanding modern money: The key to full employment and price stability. *Eastern Economic Journal, 25*(3), 370–372.

Lerner, A. (1951). *The economics of employment*. McGraw Hill.

Levrero, E. S. (2019). On the criticisms of and obstacles to the employer of last resort policy proposal. *International Journal of Political Economy, 48*(1), 41–59.

Marx, K. (1867). El capital: crítica de la economía política. *Siglo, XXI*.

Minsky, H. (1965). The role of employment policy. In M. S. Gordon (Ed.), Poverty in America. pp. 175–200, Chandler Publishing Company.

Minsky, H. P. (1968). Effects of shifts of aggregate demand upon income distribution. *American Journal of Agricultural Economics, 50*(2), 328–339.

Minsky, H. (1986). *Stabilizing an unstable economy*. Yale University Press.

Mitchell, B., & Watts, M. (1997). The path to full employment. *The Australian Economic Review, 30*(4), 436–443.

Mitchell, B., & Wray, R. (2004). *In defense of employer of last resort: A response to Malcom Sawyer*. Centre of Full Employment and Equity Working Paper No. 04-03.

Mitchell, W. F. (1987). The NAIRU, structural imbalance and the macroequilibrium unemployment rate. *Australian Economic Papers, 26*(48), 101–118.

Mitchell, W. F. (1994). Restoring full employment. *Australian Economic Review, 27*(1), 24–30.

Mitchell, W. F. (1998). The buffer stock employment model and the NAIRU: The path to full employment. *Journal of Economic Issues, 32*(2), 547–555.

Mitchell, W. F., & Mosler, W. (2002). Fiscal policy and the job guarantee. *Australian Journal of Labour Economics, 5*(2), 243–259.

Mitchell, W. F., & Muysken, J. (2008). *Full employment abandoned.* Edward Elgar,

Mitchell, W. F., & Wray, R. (2005). In defense of employer of last resort: A response to Malcolm Sawyer. *Journal of Economic Issues, 39*(1), 235–244.

Modigliani, F., & Papademos, L. (1975). Targets for monetary policy in the coming year. *Brookings Papers in Economic Activity, 1*(1), 141–163.

Mosler, W. (1997). Full employment and price stability. *Journal of Post Keynesian Economics, 20*(2), 167–182.

Mosler, W., & Silipo, D. B. (2017). Maximizing price stability in a monetary economy. *Journal of Policy Modeling, 39*(2), 272–289.

Mueller, A. P., & Vaz-Curado, S. F. L. (2019). Modern Monetary Theory (MMT): An evaluation of its premises and its political consequences. *Mises Journal, 7*(2), 1–22.

Murphy, A. (2020, June 22). Book review: "The deficit myth: modern monetary theory and the birth of the People's economy". *LSE.* https://blogs.lse.ac.uk/lsereviewofbooks/2020/06/22/book-review -the-deficit-myth-modern-monetary-theory-and-the-birth-of-the-peoples-economy-by-stephanie -kelton/

Murray, M., & Forstater, M. (Eds.). (2013). *The job guarantee. Toward true full employment.* Palgrave Macmillan.

Nell, E. J. (2003). Short-run macroeconomic stabilization by an employer of last resort. In E. J. Nell & M. Forstater (Eds.), *Reinventing functional finance.* Chapter 17, pp. 319–327.

Nersisyan, N., & Wray, L. R. (2019). *How to pay for the green new deal.* Levy Economics Institute Working Papers No. 931.

Olk, C., Schneider, C., & Hickel, J. (2022). *How to pay for saving the world: Modern monetary theory for a degrowth transition.* https://ssrn.com/abstract=4172005 or http://dx.doi.org/10.2139/ssrn.4172005

Phillips, A. W. (1958). The relation between unemployment and the rate of change of money wage rates in the United Kingdom, 1861–1957. *Economica, 25*(100), 283–299.

Rose, N. E. (2009). *Put to work: The WPA and public employment in the great depression.* Monthly Review Press.

Sawyer, M. (2003). Employer of last resort: Could it deliver full employment and price stability? *Journal of Economic Issues, 37*(4), 881–907.

Sawyer, M., & Passarella, M. V. (2021). A comprehensive comparison of fiscal and monetary policies: A comparative dynamics approach. *Structural Change and Economic Dynamics, 59*, 384–404.

Seccareccia, M. (2004). What type of full employment? A critical evaluation of government as employer of last resort policy proposal. *Investigacion Economica, 63*(247), 15–43.

Sovilla, B. (2018). Increasing the minimum wage with the state as employer of last resort: A "predistribution" proposal for Mexico. *International Journal of Political Economy, 47*(3–4), 330–351.

Sovilla, B., Morales Sánchez, E., & Gómez Méndez, K. G. (2021). Trabajo garantizado y política salarial para reducir la pobreza en México. *El Trimestre Económico, 88*(349), 5–37.

Tcherneva, P. (2012). Permanent on-the-spot job creation—The missing Keynes plan for full employment and economic transformation. *Review of Social Economy, 70*(1), 57–80.

Tcherneva, P. (2014). Reorienting fiscal policy: A bottom-up approach. *Journal of Post Keynesian Economics, 37*(1), 43–66.

Tcherneva, P. (2018). *The job guarantee: Design, jobs, and implementation.* Levy Economic Institute of Bard College Working Paper No. 902.

Tcherneva, P. (2020). *En favor del Trabajo Garantizado.* Lola Books.

Tcherneva, P. R. (2013). Beyond full employment: What Argentina's Plan Jefes can teach us about the employer of last resort. In *Employment Guarantee Schemes. Job Creation and Policy in Michael Murray and Mathew Forstater. Developing Countries and Emerging Markets.* Palgrave Macmillan.

Tcherneva, T., & Wray, R. (2005). Employer of last resort: A case study of Argentina's Jefes program. Levy Economic Institute Working Paper No. 41.

Triggs, A. (2021, August 31). Modern monetary theory: A solution in search of a problem. *National Affairs*. https://insidestory.org.au/modern-monetary-theory-a-solution-in-search-of-a-problem/

Tymoigne, E., & Wray, L. R. (2013). *Modern money theory 101: A reply to critics.* Levy Economics Institute Working Papers Series No. 778.

Watts, M. J., Sharpe, T. P., & Juniper, J. (2017). The job guarantee and Eurozone stabilisation. In M. Murray & M. Forstater (Eds.), *The job guarantee and modern money theory*, pp. 89–115. Binzagr Institute for Sustainable Prosperity.

William, S. J., & Taylor, R. (2022). *Sustainability and the new economics synthesising ecological economics and modern monetary theory.* Springer.

Wray, L. R. (1997). *Government as employer of last resort: Full employment without inflation.* Levy Economics Institute Working Paper No. 213.

Wray, L. R. (1998). *Understanding modern money, the key to full employment and price stability.* Edward Elgar Publishing Ltd.

Wray, L. R. (2007). The employer of last resort programme: could it work for developing countries? Economic and Labour Market Papers International Labour Office Geneva August 2007/5.

Wray, L. R. (2008). Financial markets meltdown: What can we learn from Minsky? Public Policy Brief No. 94. Levy Economics Institute of Bard College.

Wray, L. R. (2012). *Modern money theory: A primer on macroeconomics for sovereign monetary systems.* Palgrave Macmillan.

Wray, L. R. (2013). The euro crisis and the job guarantee: A proposal for Ireland. In M. Murray & M. Forstater (Eds.), *The job guarantee. Toward true full employment* (pp. 161–177), Palgrave Macmillan.

Yajima, G. T. (2021). *The employer of last resort scheme and the energy transition: A stock-flow consistent analysis* [Working Papers Series]. Levy Economics Institute.

FINAL CONCLUSIONS

Modern Monetary Theory (MMT) is a heterodox approach to economic theory that draws on post-Keynesian, Chartalist, and Minskyan approaches, focusing on monetary issues, fiscal policy, and full employment. It originated in the 1990s, but its popularity soared with the economic and financial crisis of 2008 and especially from 2019 onwards thanks to its emergence on the front line of US politics. The Covid-19 pandemic that began in 2020 led to even more talk of MMT, first from its advocates – who were putting it in value at a time when states were spending public money without limits – and later from its detractors – who saw MMT as responsible for the inflationary phase that began in 2021. This growing popularity has led to an explosion in the number of critical analyses of MMT, and this book has simply tried to collect most of them in order to get the fullest possible picture and draw informed and solid conclusions about the strengths and weaknesses of this new economic approach.

It is important to note that not everything in MMT is subject to debate; there are some achievements of MMT that are widely recognised. Firstly, MMT has become popular in the academy and beyond, and this is an indisputable merit because it has been a long time since a heterodox approach has achieved anything like this. The very fact that it has made its way into the public debate is an achievement in itself, and one that is undoubtedly helping to redirect economic discussion towards more heterodox and useful coordinates for economic analysis. Secondly, another undoubted achievement of MMT is that it effectively helps to overturn many orthodox economic postulates that have proved to be erroneous and useless (despite their hegemony in faculties and schools of economics). While it is true that the raw material to combat these orthodox postulates has existed in academia for some time, it is also true that if it were not for MMT these approaches would probably remain in a hidden place, little known to the majority of analysts and the general population. Thirdly and finally, the emergence of MMT has provoked a flood of criticisms, many of which (not all) have strengthened and enriched economic analysis on monetary, fiscal, and employment issues in general, either to validate the MMT thesis, to discard it, or to qualify it. It is precisely this issue that motivated the writing of this book.

DOI: 10.4324/9781003371809-9

All the criticisms analysed have been classified into seven chapters that deal with seven fundamental TMM themes. The first three chapters deal precisely with the aspects in which this economic approach has the most weaknesses according to the present analysis: the origin and nature of money and the concept of monetary sovereignty.

Regarding the origin of money, the TMM relies on archaeological, anthropological, and numismatic studies to question the metallist and evolutionary thesis of money and to reinforce the money-credit thesis and the chartalist thesis. It is undeniable that the MMT view is solidly supported by empirical evidence and that it provides important contributions in this field, but it is no less true that it is insufficient to completely discard the evolutionary view of money as many critics point out. To take just one example, the chartalist view faces many difficulties when trying to explain why so many different societies chose precious metals as a means of payment for so long. And, like this question, there are others that fit better with the evolutionary view of money. My conclusion is that both views help to explain the origin of money, only they refer to different spheres: the chartalist approach would help to explain the origin of money in the territory controlled by each of the human societies, while the evolutionary approach would help to explain the origin of money in the geographical and economic sphere that is tangential to each of those territories, a space over which no society has sovereign control, basically the space of international trade. Consequently, it would not be a matter of invalidating the evolutionary vision as the MMT does by considering it incompatible with the chartalist one, but of circumscribing the two visions to different economic spheres that constantly interact with each other.

In any case, this historical debate may be irrelevant to the MMT's view of today's economy and its policy proposals. After all, money may have had an origin in the past that has nothing to do with its nature today. Consequently, even if the MMT's view of the origin of money were not accepted, this would not be enough to discredit the rest of its postulates.

On the specific question of the nature of money, MMT fully embraces the chartalist view, which sees money as a creation of the state whose value and acceptability are based on its taxing power. This approach is theoretically and empirically sound, but it is not free of problems. On the one hand, it is clear that there are other very important factors in explaining the acceptability of money that are not taken into account by chartalism, such as the number and scope of money contracts as a whole, the social positioning of any debt, the banks' own lending operations, and the power and influence – in general terms, not just taxation – of the state in question. On the other hand, taxing in one currency might not result in that currency being widely accepted by the public, since the public might also use a different one that gives it greater stability and confidence. In fact, the latter would not necessarily challenge the chartalist thesis, since such state currencies are not usually displaced by private currencies, but by other state currencies issued by states with greater international monetary power and influence. But the issue is much more complex than the MMT presents: taxes explain part of the story, but not the whole story.

And the latter connects us to the MMT concept of monetary sovereignty, which is quite useful for analysing the different economic situations of states from a perspective that is unusual in academia, but which is manifestly incomplete and can be much improved. To begin with, full monetary sovereignty approaches are not equally applicable to all economies around the world, especially developing economies. While I believe that advocates of MMT are right to point out that any economy could enjoy full monetary sovereignty (own currency, flexible exchange rate, and own currency debt) and thus mobilise all the real resources at its disposal (whether many or few), I also believe that they minimise the economic problems that many of them would face if they tried to do so. In particular, I have not found much mention of the problem of imported inflation by supporters of MMT. Even if we agree with them that currency depreciation cannot last forever and that it might even benefit the poorest and hurt the richest, the real problem is that during this time the rise in import prices can raise the prices of domestic products significantly, dealing a heavy blow to economic activity and the population as a whole. However, this problem is hardly considered by supporters of the MMT, and when they do address it, they minimise its importance. And it is not merely a question of a lack of real resources, it is a specifically monetary issue that could make things very difficult for the economy concerned beyond its material wealth: even with full employment, if inflation is out of control, the situation may be worse for the whole population, not just for the wealthiest. But, in any case, I agree with MMTers that this is a political and ideological question: it depends on whether one wants to give more weight to full employment or to price stability. Still, in my view, the best possible solution to this complex problem should come from a pooled approach by developed economies, as some MMT advocates have proposed, not from developing economies individually.

I also believe that part of this incomplete analysis of monetary sovereignty is due to a strictly economic definition of monetary sovereignty, when in fact, as many critics point out, monetary sovereignty is not only an economic concept but also a political one. Proponents of MMT speak of monetary sovereignty as a gradient of situations in which only the institutional details (currency issuance, exchange rate, and debt issuance) matter, but they forget that the position of each of these states on the geopolitical chessboard is fundamental. And this omission prevents them from providing convincing explanations for some situations, such as the fact that the US currency is the most widely used in the world, or that there are states that, even though they have full monetary sovereignty, do not manage to have their currency used in their own territory and that part of the transactions are carried out in foreign currencies (usually the US dollar). However, all these cases can be better explained by incorporating the political issue: the US dollar is hegemonic because its State is the world's number one economic, military, cultural, and technological power; and there are countries in which economic agents use currencies other than those issued by their State because their political power is weakened or in question.

Nor do I think that this implies a challenge to the concept of monetary sovereignty used by MMT; rather, I see the incorporation of the political question as enriching the analysis without overthrowing the concept. After all, the institutional details of the monetary sphere raised by MMT are crucial for analysing countries' fiscal room, and that is a very valuable contribution. The only thing is that the concept of monetary sovereignty falls short of accurately explaining the reality. But the incorporation of the political question into the analysis need not be understood as an element alien to the postulates of MMT but can be understood precisely as a derivative of the very analysis that links money with the concept of political sovereignty. Money is a tool of state power and, as such, is linked to the degree of power exercised by the state. In other words, the value of a state's currency will depend on the degree of political sovereignty it achieves, and not only on the degree of taxation it manages to impose. This qualifies the central postulate of chartalism whereby the value of money depends on taxation; in this case, it would depend on the degree of political sovereignty or power exercised by the state, which is a concept that encompasses taxation but goes well beyond it.

So far we have presented the main weaknesses of the MMT that we have identified throughout the book. Now it is the turn of its main strengths, which are to be found in the remaining chapters dealing with public accounts, bank money, inflation, and the Job Guarantee.

The concepts of public deficit and public debt used by MMT are far superior to those used by the orthodoxy and are little criticised by the heterodoxy. Public spending is understood as equivalent to money creation and tax collection is equivalent to its destruction, so that the public deficit would be an expost indicator that simply shows the amount of money injected into the economy, hence it does not even make sense to talk about its financing. The only sticking point for heterodox critics has to do with the theoretical consolidation between the Treasury and the central bank, as they consider this to be a simplification that is not true to reality. In their view, not only is the treasury a very different institution from the central bank, but each country has very different institutional arrangements that make it impossible for the MMT simplification to fit all of them adequately. Moreover, some criticise that MMT is confusing the institutional design they would like to have with the institutional design that prevails in real economies. The rejection of such consolidation leads critics to question whether government deficit is equivalent to money creation and whether government expenditure is chronologically prior to government revenue, as MMT argues. For their part, MMTers justify the theoretical simplification by claiming that the institutional and operational separation between central bank and treasury is artificial, voluntary, and ideologically motivated, which only serves to hide the fact that sovereign states have full financing capacity. Moreover, according to them, in all economies treasuries are obliged to coordinate their activities with their central bank, hence consolidation makes sense because it simplifies the analysis without changing the results.

From the point of view of this writer, it is very difficult to state categorically, as the MMT does, that the theoretical consolidation between central bank and state does not distort the practical analysis in all countries of the world, since there is a wide variety of institutional arrangements and it would be necessary to know them all in detail. In any case, this does not seem to me to be a relevant issue. Instead, the important question would be whether such a consolidation is feasible in any country and whether it is much more reasonable and appropriate than the clearly ideological separation between the two institutions. And my answer is clearly affirmative; the theoretical consolidation of the treasury and the central bank seems to me appropriate and powerful because it allows us to talk about a scenario that, although it does not currently exist in any country, can be achieved provided there is political will. Focusing the analysis on an institutional arrangement that is artificial and circumstantial, however real it may be in many countries, only obscures the analysis and prevents us from understanding the potential of sovereign states. In other words, while it may not make sense under the current institutional arrangement in a particular country to say that public spending comes before public revenue, or that public deficits are equivalent to creating money, that does not mean that this could not be the case if the institutional design were simply slightly modified. And, since the ultimate aim of MMT is to recommend economic policies that will lead to full employment with price stability (and not so much to describe reality as it is), it seems to me that such a theoretical consolidation is appropriate and relevant.

Another area where MMT has important strengths is in the conception of bank money. MMTers adopt the post-Keynesian view of the endogeneity of money, but incorporate nuances and elements to adapt it to their own chartalist view, thus drawing a holistic view of state money and bank money. In this way, bank money would be an IOU (I owe you) that banks create autonomously when they grant credit, hence its origin and quantity depend endogenously on economic activity. Up to this point, this view coincides with the post-Keynesian one. The novelty is that for the MMTers these IOUs are quantified in the unit of account of the state and are commitments to deliver state IOUs in the future, hence they are considered as a leveraging of state money. Bank promissory notes would be widely used because they are convertible into state IOUs (the only ones that serve to settle tax debts, which is what would give them value) and because the state manoeuvres so that this conversion is always – or almost always – possible due to its interest in maintaining the health of the banking system. In short, banks have the autonomy to increase the amount of money used in the economy, but their own operations and survival ultimately depend on the state.

The central criticism shared by critics is that bank money would logically and economically precede state money (even though bank money may need state support to be widely accepted, as some point out), so it would make no sense to speak of leverage. In support of this approach, it is often argued that entrepreneurs first plan an economic activity, then ask for bank loans to carry it out, and finally money is created endogenously by banks so that state money would play no role in this process. Some people reinforce their arguments by pointing out that bank money has historically been independent of public authorities, so the same would be true today.

But the MMT approach is more convincing to this writer: without the support of the state and the existence of its own IOUs, the widespread acceptance of bank money would not be possible, because bank money is denominated in the state's unit of account and is after all a commitment to deliver state IOUs in the future. Before the existence of bank money, there must necessarily be state-regulated institutions that allow its origin and widespread acceptance. The state has full control over the banking system: just as it usually acts to achieve its survival, it could also act to achieve the opposite (either through a ban on leveraging with state IOUs or through the total nationalisation of the sector, to give just two examples). As for the historical argument, it does not seem easy to take a clear-cut position, but it would not be necessary either: whatever the historical role of bank money was, what matters is what its role is today, since modern economies have very different institutions and behaviours from those of the past, so any historical factor should not necessarily be extrapolated to the present.

On the other hand, the criticisms of the concept of leverage do not seem to me to be fair or appropriate: critics seem to wrongly equate "leverage" with constraints on bank money creation. In reality, it is perfectly compatible for banks to have ample room to create bank money through their lending with all those IOUs being leveraged into government IOUs.

I think most of the disagreement can be explained by the different conception of central bank money: while critics see money that is set in motion by monetary policy as something essentially different from money that is set in motion by fiscal policy, for MMTers it is exactly the same thing. This brings us back to the debate on whether it is appropriate to theoretically consolidate the central bank and the treasury. I reiterate my position: consolidation makes sense if one wants to analyse the functioning of the economy as it might be ignoring certain institutional arrangements, not just as it is in reality at a particular time and place. For example, the fact that in the Eurozone bank money precedes state money because of its current institutional design does not mean that it could not be otherwise with a less restrictive and complex design. Once such consolidation takes place, it seems reasonable to conceive that state money comes before bank money, and that bank money is highly dependent on state regulation and support.

I also believe that this debate could be more adequately and accurately addressed if critics were more mindful of the theoretical contributions of the "hierarchy of monies", as they often seem to ignore or underestimate them. It is much easier to understand the MMT view on the endogeneity of money if one conceives of bank money as an IOU that is referenced in government IOUs.

On the other hand, the typical Marxist criticism that MMT has only an exogenous view of money and therefore should not arrogate to itself an endogenous view is neither fair nor relevant, since it is perfectly possible to take both an endogenous and an exogenous view at the same time: the economic activity of the private sector, through its borrowing, leads to the endogenous injection of bank money; but the public sector itself, through its fiscal deficit, can lead to an exogenous injection of government notes (which are reflected in bank notes as long as they follow the circuits of the banking sector).

There is also an issue that is not fully addressed by the MMTers: the limits to banks' ability to create bank money through credit. I believe that a satisfactory and complete answer can be found mainly in the work of James Tobin and MacLeay. Following these works, we can identify several reasons that would explain the limits of banks when granting credits and that MMTers could well share (and perhaps do share, although, as far as I know, they have not explicitly taken a position on the matter).

With respect to Functional Finance, which is basically that the state should increase its public spending as much as necessary to make the aggregate spending of the economy equal its potential output – thus achieving full employment –, it is important to clarify that MMT does not adopt it directly but draws on it to propose a very specific and supposedly superior policy known as the Job Guarantee. Therefore, criticisms aimed at questioning Functional Finance are not fully extrapolable to criticisms aimed at the MMT. MMTers are fully aware of the limitations facing the idea proposed by Abba Lerner, especially the most important one: that inflation is likely to start originating even before full employment is reached, basically because not all added spending would be directed towards sectors where there is still economic slack to take advantage of unused productive capacity, but also because the workers needed for some sectors might not be available.

A major criticism often levelled at MMT is that it places all the responsibility for achieving the necessary aggregate spending on the fiscal lever since the same objective could supposedly be achieved using other tools, such as monetary policy, by favouring private borrowing. However, MMTers are totally opposed to this option because they consider that interest rate changes have little impact on the borrowing decisions of economic agents, who would be guided more by other factors such as expectations of corporate profits or consumption preferences. In fact, MMTers usually recommend that interest rates should be set at around 0% so that fiscal policy is the only adjustment used by the state to achieve full employment. This has been strongly criticised by many analysts who believe that such a policy can lead to inflationary pressures and also to imbalances in the banking and financial sector. In my case, I welcome the MMTers' recommendation, not only because I believe that financial imbalances should be addressed by other types of policies (namely regulatory policies in the banking and financial sector) but also because I believe that keeping the interest rate at 0% is a fairer policy in redistributive terms, as it favours the most needy economic agents while not favouring (without reason) the least needy.

Another typical criticism is that raising the public deficit, especially if it is not financed by public bonds, leads to inflation (or even hyperinflation) long before full employment is reached. There are several arguments in support of this idea, but MMTers reject them all. On the one hand, there is the argument that creating more money without increasing output is inflationary. MMTers reply that it is spending that can raise inflation, not the quantity of money since the quantity of money does not have to be converted into spending. Moreover, modern economies normally operate with some economic slack, so there would be room to increase spending without causing inflationary pressures. Finally, MMTers point out the ideological bias of such criticisms because the critics only focus on money injected by the state, but not by banks through the provision of credit. If the creation of state money were automatically inflationary, so would the creation of bank money, and yet the critics never focus on that. On the other hand, there is the argument that the government deficit causes a crowding-out effect and an increase in interest rates, but MMTers contest this idea because in their view an increase in the government deficit would tend to reduce rates, not increase them. There is also the argument of inflation expectations and central bank independence: any doubts about the autonomy of the monetary authorities would lead to higher inflation expectations, and inflation expectations would lead to higher real price growth. However, this is speculative reasoning that is difficult to test and easily manipulated in order to reinforce certain arguments. On these last points I am completely on the side of the MMTers.

In any case, many MMTers insist that, even if inflation originates before full employment is reached, they find it preferable to have a certain price increase and a level of employment close to the optimum than to maintain high unemployment rates in order to keep inflation very low. This would be a political and subjective decision that in one case would favour some and disadvantage others and in the other case practically the opposite: full employment with inflation would benefit the working class in general while it would disadvantage savers; certain unemployment rates with hardly any inflation would benefit savers while it would disadvantage the working class. MMTers are clearly in favour of the first option, as is this writer (with some exceptions and limitations).

In any case, this would only be the case for demand-side inflation, as it is not the only type of inflation that can arise. In fact, MMTers consider that demand-pull inflation is precisely the one that has been experienced the least throughout history. For example, the inflationary episode that originated internationally in 2021, according to many analysts (including MMTers), it would have been the consequence of international bottlenecks derived from the pandemic and the energy crisis derived from Russia's invasion of Ukraine, both of which are supply-side factors and not demand-side factors. In my case, based on the available empirical evidence, I cannot see it any other way.

Finally, there is the critique of the Job Guarantee, which is the main economic policy proposal of the MMT. Its aim is to achieve full employment without inflation, and the means to achieve this is to guarantee a job directly from the state to anyone who wants and is able to work, paying a fixed minimum wage that acts as a floor and anchor for wages and prices. This policy prescription has been criticised on many fronts and on the basis of various arguments, all of which are necessarily speculative since Job Guarantee has never been applied in any country, making it impossible to make an analysis based on empirical evidence.

Probably the most important criticism, which I share, is that it is optimistic about achieving full employment without inflation. But, in my view, it would not be so much on the supply side since, unlike many critics; I do believe that maintaining a fixed minimum wage can act as an anchor against wage pressures in the labour market (at least, provided that this wage level is low enough to keep the fear of job loss in the private sector at work and not to alter labour market participation too much, although it should also be high enough to ensure a decent life and to distance itself significantly from the option of unemployment).

My concern has more to do with inflationary pressures on the demand side. After all, the increase in aggregate demand that the application of the Job Guarantee would entail (higher the higher the unemployment rate) could strain certain economic sectors and generate bottlenecks that would translate into price increases. Moreover, this increase in aggregate demand could be channelled towards the purchase of foreign products (the more dependent the economy is on foreign countries), which would tend to depreciate the currency and could lead to imported inflation. Therefore, the higher the unemployment rate and the more dependent the economy is on the external sector, the greater the probability that the Job Guarantee could cause inflation on the demand side: perhaps an economy with low unemployment and a strong productive structure could apply the Job Guarantee without suffering inflation, but this would not seem to be the case in an economy with high unemployment and/or a weak productive structure. Moreover, to all this must be added considerations about the international position of the national currency in the hierarchy of currencies: an economy with a currency in demand internationally will be more likely to apply a Job Guarantee without suffering depreciations and inflation than an economy with a currency that is in weak demand worldwide.

In any case, I share the MMTers' value judgement on the policy options available and I prefer the Job Guarantee to be applied even if it leads to some increase in inflation rather than maintaining large pockets of unemployment with moderate inflation. However, I also believe that in certain economies (especially less developed ones) the application of the Job Guarantee should be done very carefully so that such inflationary pressures do not spiral out of control and end up generating more economic and social damage than certain levels of unemployment currently do. In this respect, it would seem important to implement the measure progressively over time and also by giving Job Guarantee workers a wage that is partly in kind so as not to generate so much monetary imbalance.

The implementation of a Job Guarantee is undoubtedly a tremendous logistical and administrative challenge (the higher the unemployment rate) and, while this should not be an excuse to stop implementing it, it should alert managers to the many design and implementation risks that could be incurred and which could ultimately derail the policy. For this very reason, the design and planning of the Job Guarantee needs to be well thought through from the outset to minimise the risks and potential pitfalls that such a complex and ambitious policy inevitably entails. The more shortcomings are identified a posteriori and the more corrections are needed, the less likely it is that the Job Guarantee will be appreciated and accepted by the population (which is, on the other hand, a prerequisite for its success).

In short, after an exhaustive analysis of the MMT and the criticisms it receives, I conclude that this new theoretical framework has very important contributions and strengths, but that it is not free of problems and limitations that are often minimised and ignored by its precursors. MMTers have already achieved a lot, and will probably achieve more in the future, but it will be crucial for them to be aware of their weaknesses and not just their strengths.

INDEX